BURRARD INLET

A HISTORY

BURRARD INLET

A HISTORY

Doreen Armitage

HARBOUR PUBLISHING

Published by **Harbour Publishing**
P.O. Box 219, Madeira Park, BC Canada V0N 2H0
www.harbourpublishing.com

Cover design, page design and composition by Martin Nichols
Front cover photo by Ken Rogers/AAA Imagemakers.com, back cover photo by Marv Pelkey, author photo by Janis Jean
Printed and bound in Canada

Key to photograph sources: British Columbia Archives; BHS: Burnaby Historical Society; CVA: City of Vancouver Archives; DA: Doreen Armitage photograph; GSC: Geological Survey of Canada; JH: Jim Hayes photograph; HF: Hugh Fraser photograph; MBMW: McKenzie Barge and Marine Ways Collection; MP: Marv Pelkey photograph; MC: Mike Cotton Collection; NVMA: North Vancouver Museum and Archives; RC: Rose Casano Collection; VMM: Vancouver Maritime Museum; VPL: Vancouver Public Library; WVMA: West Vancouver Museum and Archives; ZL: Zellah Leyland Collection.

THE CANADA COUNCIL | LE CONSEIL DES ARTS
FOR THE ARTS | DU CANADA
SINCE 1957 | DEPUIS 1957

Harbour Publishing acknowledges the financial support of the Government of Canada through the Book Publishing Industry Development Program (BPIDP) and the Canada Council for the Arts, and the Province of British Columbia through the British Columbia Arts Council, for its publishing activities.

National Library of Canada Cataloguing in Publication Data

Armitage, Doreen, 1931–
    Burrard Inlet

    Includes bibliographical references and index.
    ISBN 1-55017-272-7

    1. Burrard Inlet (B.C.)—History.   I. Title.
FC3845.B87A75 2001   971.1'33   C2001-910910-5
F1089.B87A75 2001

To Lynn and Lauren
. . . with love

CONTENTS

ACKNOWLEDGEMENTS

I extend my deep appreciation to the following people who have contributed to this book:

Patricia Banning-Lover, of WBT Wild Bird Trust; Graham Clark, of Coast Ferries/Harbour Tours; Jeff Crawford, Neptune Bulk Terminals; Ray Goode, B.C. Coast Pilots Ltd.; Hugh Johnston, West Vancouver; Leonard McCann and Rachel Grant, Vancouver Maritime Museum; Bob Muckle, Capilano College; Marv Pelkey for his great photos; William G. Robinson, past president, Royal Philatelic Society of Canada; Jim Roddick, Geological Survey of Canada; Alvin Sholund, Port Moody and Ioco; Ross Stevens, SeaBus; Joe Stott, Burrard Inlet Environmental Action Program; and Bruce Ward, for his advice on early explorations of the inlet.

For the wonderful stories they shared with me, I thank Captain Cyril Andrews, the *Green Hill Park*; Heinz Berger, West Vancouver; Harvey Burt, Indian Arm and the squatters; Aiden Butterfield, Point Grey; Mike Cotton, Belcarra; Howie Keast, gas barge explosion; Zellah Leyland, Indian Arm; Malcolm McLaren, Allied Shipbuilding; Don McMahon, sounds of the inlet; Bob McKenzie and Margaret Jorgenson, McKenzie Barge and Marine Ways; Eileen Scott, Lions Gate Bridge; Les Rimes, memories of the inlet; and David Stone, Underwater Archaeological Society of BC.

For their willing assistance with my research, thanks to the staffs at the BC Archives, Burnaby Archives and Historical Society, the City of Vancouver Archives, the National Archives of Canada, the North Vancouver Archives, the Port Moody Station Museum, the Vancouver Public Library and the West Vancouver Archives.

For their continuing support and encouragement I'm grateful to my friends; you know who you are.

And I thank Bill, my ever-lovin' husband and research assistant extraordinaire.

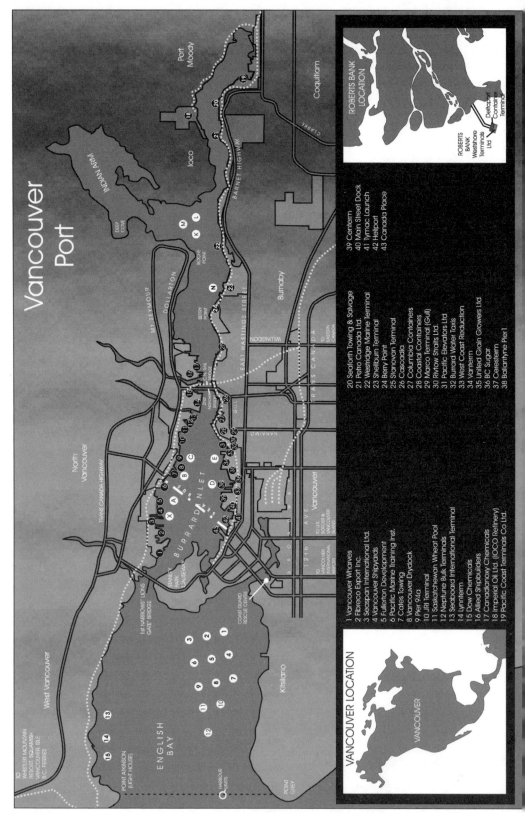

Vancouver Port

VANCOUVER LOCATION

ROBERTS BANK LOCATION

Deltaport Container Terminal
ROBERTS BANK Westshore Terminals Ltd.

1 Vancouver Wharves
2 Fibreco Export Inc.
3 Seaspan International Ltd.
4 Vancouver Shipyards
5 Fullerton Development
6 Pacific Marine Training Inst.
7 Cates Towing
8 Vancouver Drydock
9 Pier 94a
10 JRI Terminal
11 Saskatchewan Wheat Pool
12 Neptune Bulk Terminals
13 Seaboard International Terminal
14 Lynnterm
15 Dow Chemicals
16 Allied Shipbuilders
17 Canadianoxy Chemicals
18 Imperial Oil Ltd. (IOCO Refinery)
19 Pacific Coast Terminals Co Ltd.

20 Seaforth Towing & Salvage
21 Petro Canada Ltd.
22 Westridge Marine Terminal
23 Shellburn Terminal
24 Berry Point
25 Stanovan Terminal
26 Cascadia
27 Columbia Containers
28 Coastal Containers
29 Marco Terminal (Gull)
30 Rivtow Straits Ltd.
31 Pacific Elevators Ltd.
32 Burrard Water Taxis
33 West Coast Reduction
34 Vanterm
35 United Grain Growers Ltd
36 BC Sugar
37 Cerestern
38 Ballantyne Pier 1

39 Centerm
40 Main Street Dock
41 Tymac Launch
42 Heliport
43 Canada Place

Burrard Inlet and the Port of Vancouver 2001. *Courtesy Chamber of Shipping of British Columbia*

INTRODUCTION

Burrard Inlet is a body of salt water lying between Greater Vancouver and its North Shore communities. The inlet's western boundary, where it meets the Strait of Georgia, follows a line from Point Atkinson south to the western tip of Point Grey. Its 114.7 square kilometres of water area lap 152.6 kilometres of shoreline. The inlet sweeps from West Vancouver to North Vancouver, up Indian Arm, around to Port Moody, on past Burnaby to Vancouver and Stanley Park, False Creek, English Bay and the beaches of Spanish Bank (not "Banks," as Vancouverites call the sandy spit). The mouth of English Bay actually lies between Spanish Bank and Stanley Park 4.8 kilometres to the northeast, although people refer informally to the entire outer harbour as English Bay.

The shore of the inlet has a variety of uses today: in West Vancouver it's mainly residential and parkland; in North Vancouver there are many waterfront industries, with some residences and parkland to the east; the long, narrow fiord of Indian Arm abuts residential and recreational land that includes a provincial park; Port Moody has shorefront industries, residences and parkland; Burnaby's shore is industrial, with some parkland. Vancouver has major port facilities and other commercial buildings along its shore, with Stanley Park its natural jewel; False Creek is a tourist centre with multifamily residences, and English Bay and the Spanish Bank beaches are solely recreational.

Burrard Inlet is the second largest harbour in Canada, after Halifax Harbour. The Port of Vancouver has grown consistently since the 1860s and very rapidly since the early years of World War II. Port facilities at Deltaport on Roberts Bank, south of the Fraser River, are considered part of the Port of Vancouver and make the port the largest in Canada in terms of foreign trade. Though its status varies year by year, in 1998 (the latest year for which statistics are available) it was the third largest port in North America, after New Orleans and Houston.

Burrard Inlet is deepest in the northern section of Indian Arm, south of Croker Island, where it reaches about 219.5 metres (120 fathoms). The entrance to the inner harbour through First Narrows has been dredged several times, helping to reduce the strength of dangerous riptides affecting vessels passing through.

The port is the responsibility of the federal government, and since 1913 several commissions and boards have been in charge of its administration. The Vancouver Port Authority, consisting of representatives from industry and government, took over in 1999. More than 70 million metric tonnes of cargo pass through the port yearly, over half of it dry bulk. In excess of 700,000 cruise ship passengers pass under Lions Gate Bridge each year on their way up the Inside Passage to Alaska. The port is a strategic and vital adjunct to the economic life of the city and provides a significant number of jobs directly and indirectly.

Geology

About 30,000 years ago a river, the precursor of Indian Arm, flowed south from the mountains, then turned to the west, forming the bed for Burrard Inlet. The Indian, Seymour and Capilano Rivers were the river's main feeders. The climate was gradually cooling, and snow began to fill valleys high in the mountains across what is now British Columbia. Small glaciers formed and expanded down the mountainsides, eventually meeting and

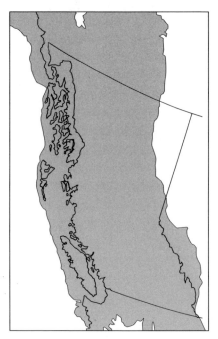

moving toward the lower levels. Along the Coast Mountains the advancing ice spawned meltwater streams that tumbled to the riverbed below, adding not only water but also rock sediments from the grinding action of the ice, gradually filling the beds of Burrard Inlet and the Strait of Georgia, forming a great plain intersected by a meltwater river.

The glaciers that gouged and clawed their way down the mountains, along Howe Sound and Indian Arm from the north and

About 30,000 years ago the weather in what is now British Columbia began to grow colder. Frequent and heavy snowfalls caused glaciers to form and expand from the mountains into the valleys, until the layer of ice was so thick that most of the mountains were covered. *Courtesy John J. Clague, GSC* through the Strait of Georgia from the west, joined to move south beyond the present United States border. About 15,000 years ago a glacial blanket buried nearly all of British Columbia, depressing the land surface. At the height of this period known as the Fraser Glaciation nearly 2,000 metres of ice covered the entire Vancouver area, including Grouse Mountain and the neighbouring peaks.

Seventy kilometres to the north of Vancouver's site Mount Garibaldi exploded, building itself upon the glacier and emitting clouds of steam and ash that were carried great distances. Streams transported some of the volcano's rock fragments to where they remain today, in a sediment deposit below the 18-metre elevation level in the cliffs at Point Grey.

After several thousand years, melt began. A frigid sea covered the land that now lies less than 200 metres above the water surface along the shores of Burrard Inlet. As the weight of the ice lifted, the land gradually rebounded, eventually emerging as some of the present shoreline.

Densely packed sandstone, overlaid by glacial detritus and stream deposits, formed the base of the future city of Vancouver and its suburbs.

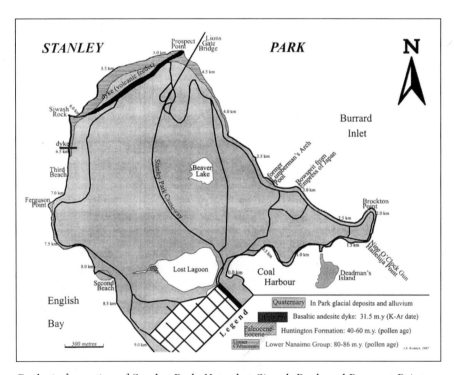

Geologic formation of Stanley Park. Note that Siwash Rock and Prospect Point are part of a 32-million-year-old volcanic dike. *Courtesy Jim Roddick, GSC*

Siwash Rock, a basaltic remnant of ancient volcanic action. *DA*

In Stanley Park a 32-million-year-old volcanic dike, a thin body of volcanic rock that cuts through the sandstone and rises above it, is the basaltic remnant of ancient volcanic action. Siwash Rock and Prospect Point are part of the formation. Burnaby Mountain, also rising above the sandstone, is composed of a thick section of solid conglomerate made up of rounded granite boulders and other rocks eroded from the North Shore mountains 65 million years ago.

Ice finally freed the Point Grey area and left behind the 62-metre-high sand cliffs that border Point Grey and Spanish Bank near the University of British Columbia. Sediment washed ahead of the ice lobes had formed the high promontory. The surface layer of silt, sand, gravel and boulders (glacial till) was laid down directly under the glacier and forms the base upon which the university buildings rest.

The Fraser River's close proximity has led many people to speculate that Burrard Inlet was originally part of that river system. Geologists have not been successful in locating deposits of sediment similar to that in the Fraser River delta that indicate a westerly current flow. These sediments should exist near Port Moody and at the westerly mouth of Burrard Inlet if an ancient water route tied the river and inlet together.[1]

As the ice receded, as the sea rose and then fell, and as the land rebounded from the massive ice pressure, the climate warmed, soil developed, and lodgepole pine, Douglas fir and spruce clothed the hillsides and valleys.

Aboriginal People

Aboriginal people believe that they have lived on the Pacific Coast since time immemorial. The earliest archaeological evidence for human occupation around Burrard Inlet dates from middens, or refuse heaps. Archaeologists have found several ancient sites, some around Burrard Inlet, deposited directly on the glacial gravels, indicating the first camps made on the land. In 1971 students from Simon Fraser University excavated segments of the Belcarra Midden on Indian Arm at Belcarra Park. They found that the bottom layer of broken shells, bones, stone tools and projectile points was lying directly on top of the glacial till and dated from between 1200 B.C. and 200 B.C. Apparently about 500 years elapsed between the time that earliest site was abandoned and the aboriginal people returned to develop the next encampment.[2]

More than 1,700 years ago a group of aboriginal people, the Tsleil-Waututh, settled at Belcarra, one of the few flat areas on Indian Arm. The view west along Burrard Inlet made the site easily defensible. They named it Tum-ta-mayh-tun ("the biggest place for people"). The land was a hunter's paradise. The SFU archaeologists found the remains of many animal bones—deer, elk, mountain goat, black bear, mink, otter, beaver, seal and sea lion. The waters around the camp abounded in sea life as evidenced by the accumulation of shells, bone fish hooks and antler harpoon heads in the midden. The Tsleil-Waututh made this site their late fall and winter home.[3] One group camped in summer on the Indian River at the north end of Indian Arm. Small shell middens indicate that others camped on Bedwell Bay and along Burrard Inlet near Port Moody.

Archaeologists discovered large but shallow middens at Noon's Creek and Pigeon Cove, at the far eastern end of the inlet, which also appear to have been seasonal camps.[4] The deposits are mainly crushed shells of clams, mussels and oysters, although some fish bones have also been found. (A young adult female skeleton was excavated at Pigeon Cove, its skull artificially deformed from binding during infancy.[5])

Dozens of archaeological sites have been recorded in North Vancouver, although relatively few have been thoroughly investigated.

Another group of Salish people settled around what is now Squamish, establishing villages on the Squamish and Cheakamus Rivers and at the head of Howe Sound. They were the ancestors of the Squamish people, and their territory eventually extended throughout Howe Sound and the western part of Burrard Inlet. Some believe Point Grey was the southern boundary; others feel the Squamish territory stretched to Musqueam at the mouth of the Fraser River. The Squamish and Musqueam (X'muzk'i'um) people both claim that the land between Burrard Inlet and the Fraser River was theirs.

The Squamish established seasonal camps at several sites on the shores of Burrard Inlet. The largest was Whoi-Whoi ("masks"), near what is now Lumberman's Arch in Stanley Park. The kitchen midden they left there was a mass of shells about 2.5 metres deep and several hectares in area. It appears to be one of the oldest in the vicinity: the bottom layer of ashes, soil, broken shells and ancient cedar and fir stumps lay directly on top of the glacial till.

Although aboriginal people apparently had no name for Burrard Inlet, their villages along its shores were identified specifically. Homulchesun was hidden in the trees on the east bank of the Capilano River at its mouth. Stuck-Ale, described by Squamish elder August Jack Khahtsahlano as a rude word for "smell" in the Salishan language, was at Skunk Cove, now Caulfeild Cove in West Vancouver, and was named for the unpleasant odour in the area at the time. Early settlers found oil seeping from the earth there and surmised that the odour came from accompanying natural gas.

Other villages were located at Jericho Beach (E-Eyalmu, meaning "good camping ground") and Locarno Beach; at Snauq near the entrance to False Creek under the south end of the present Burrard Bridge; and at Prospect Point in Stanley Park, where Chay-Thoos ("high bank") was a small clearing at First Narrows. Archaeologists have studied other shell midden sites at Cates Park, Stanley Park, Jericho, Locarno and Point Grey beaches, two in West Vancouver east of Point Atkinson and one just east of the Capilano River, finding stone and bone artifacts, stone hearths and burial sites.

The land and sea provided the earliest people's clothing, shelter and food. Their garments ranged from simple woven cedar shoulder covers to articles made from animal hide. They wore their black hair long, and the men kept theirs in place with buckskin headbands, sometimes inserting one or two feathers in the back. The women in later years wove blankets from mountain goat hair—warmer than cedar in cold weather. At Belcarra archaeologists discovered several bone blanket pins, some with carving, that were used to hold the coverings in place.[6] The women dusted clay into the woven hair to whiten it; a favourite source of the whitest clay was the bed of a stream named Stait-wouk ("fine clay"), at what is now Second Beach in Stanley Park. They rolled handfuls of the clay into loaves and baked them in a fire until they turned chalk white. Evidently visitors from other aboriginal nations travelled great distances to this location, the only known source of such pure white clay.

When the families moved to their summer camps they lived in temporary shelters constructed of posts and cedar mats. They usually built their winter homes within the shelter of trees to provide the safety of concealment. Upright cedar posts supported large, horizontal cedar slabs. Small cedar branches twined together fastened the uprights in position. The high side of the shed roof usually faced the water and sloped to the back. At the two ends of the house, doorways allowed access to the spacious, earth-floored single room. Houses used for potlatches were much larger.

While the men hunted or fished and the children and dogs played noisily around the camp, the women swept out their living areas with cedar

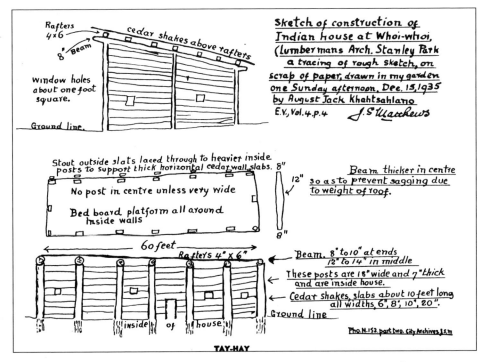

Sketch of construction of Squamish communal lodge at Whoi-Whoi, near the present Lumberman's Arch in Stanley Park. The lodge, known as Tay Hay, was 30.48 metres long. *CVA Major Matthews Collection Add. MSS 54, Topical files Khahtsalahno, drawings 504-E-5 file 61*

boughs to begin their daily tasks. In spring they collected inner cedar bark, pounded it with stone or bone tools, then used the shredded material to make essentials for their families' lives—rope for fishing, soft clothing, blankets, baskets and mats.[7] They collected berries, roots and other plant parts, pounding some into flat cakes and drying some to store for winter.

Several families occupied their own area in each home, sharing the space but cooking over separate fires. Roof boards slid aside to vent the smoke. Each family gathered around its fire to eat, sitting on wooden blocks or cedar-bark mats. Their utensils were small stone knives and goat-horn spoons, and they drank from alder-root cups.

The women roasted meat, often venison, by placing it between two sharp sticks stuck into the ground next to the fire. To boil food they used "boiling stones," specially selected for their shape, size and smoothness. These were heated in the fire until red-hot, placed in cedar troughs or tightly woven baskets partially filled with water, then covered with mats. As the stones cooled, more were added.[8] The cooks used mountain goat-horn ladles to move the food to large wooden plates that could be as long as 1.5 metres.

The men fished for salmon, flounder, sturgeon, smelt, trout and herring and hunted bear, deer, elk and beaver. The fish and strips of meat were smoke-dried over hemlock or alder and stored for winter.

Clams and mussels made up an important part of the people's diet; the old saying "When the tide is out, the table is set" aptly describes their dependence upon the sea for food. The shoreline at Whoi-Whoi was one of the most popular spots for clam digging at very low tides. The people came in their canoes from great distances to gather shellfish. At night the water reflected the flames from their pitch torches as men and women, with baskets on their bent backs, gathered the ocean's bounty.

The village of Snauq, at what is now False Creek, fronted on a favourite fishing ground. The Squamish men, and sometimes the Musqueam from near the mouth of the Fraser River, built converging fish fences on the huge sandbar with the wide, open end to the west, gradually narrowing to the east. They constructed nets made of supple branches woven around sharp stakes pounded into the mud, which dried at low tide. When the water rose it brought with it smelt, flounder and perch. As it receded, the fish were trapped by the corral and were easily collected.

Coal Harbour and the neighbouring waters abounded in millions of herring. To catch them, the men made fish rakes from cedar poles and pounded sharpened hardwood or bone stakes through one end. Standing in their canoes, they swept the rake through the water, catching several herring on the tines, then dumped the fish into the boats.

The people treated salmon with reverence. At the yearly First Salmon Ceremony, children carried in the specially prepared fish. Everyone ate with solemn care, then followed a time-honoured ritual as they returned the bones to the water. They believed the salmon lived in their own world as people, but appeared each year as fish to provide their flesh to humans.

Burrard Inlet was popular with duck hunters, who followed old traditions for attracting the birds. In the evening the hunters placed a cedar slab covered with mud across the gunwales of their canoes, then built a fire on top of the mud. At dusk they paddled quietly, waiting. When the flames encouraged the ducks to investigate, the hunter in the bow steadied his spear, attached to the end of a long pole. A sharp, expert jab and one more duck was ready for cooking.

As the years passed the Salish people continued to carry out their traditions in marriage, birth and death. They reverently placed the remains of their dead in trees, on islands where possible, or laid the bodies on the unprotected earth and covered them with cedar slabs. Deadman's Island in Coal Harbour and Eagle and Defence Islands in Howe Sound were favourite resting places. Archaeologists found many human remains along the north shore of Stanley Park.

Several legends involving Burrard Inlet have been passed down through the years by the aboriginal people. One story recounts how great spiritual beings turned a courageous young chief into an upright rock on the shore of what is now Stanley Park, to stand as an everlasting example to "clean fatherhood." The Squamish called it Slah-Kay-Ulsh ("he is standing up"). Later settlers called it Siwash Rock. Another legend tells how the spirits changed a young man, greedy for white man's gold, into a two-headed sea serpent that stretched across the inlet from Brockton Point to North Vancouver. Loathed by the people, the serpent was finally killed by a strong young brave.

Generations of aboriginal men searched in Indian Arm for a lost island where a revered medicine man was believed to have left his courage and fearlessness. According to another legend, Deadman's Island was the site of a great massacre of many warriors who died to save their families, held as hostages on the island. The Squamish named it the Island of Dead Men.[9] Images from the distant past remain in the form of pictographs on the mainland shores of Indian Arm—near the Buntzen Power House, at Brighton Beach, North Sunshine, Deep Cove, Farrer Cove and on Croker Island. These drawings painted on rock surfaces provide us with some insight into the lives of the early residents. Archaeologists have recorded human figures, animals, birds, fish, a canoe and abstract designs. As the years pass, the figures gradually fade as lichens cover the rocks and thin white minerals from water seepage form on the surfaces.[10]

CHAPTER 1
EARLY EXPLORATION: 1791–92

From Noon Breakfast Point [Point Grey]... the Continent takes a
Rounding turn to the Eastward forming a very Narrow Inlet with the
Opposite Shore. On its south Side is a Village from which we were vis-
ited by About thirty Indians, their Conduct was Friendly & inoffensive.
From them we procured an excellent Supply of Smelts in exchange for
some trinkets.

—Peter Puget, "A Log of the proceedings of HMS *Discovery*"

I n the seventeenth century, the principal sea route from Europe to
Asia and the South Pacific lay around the Cape of Good Hope and
across the vast Indian Ocean. Voyages were long, dangerous and
expensive, so it is not surprising that European nations sought a more
direct path to the East. One possible route was the so-called Northwest
Passage linking the Atlantic Ocean to the Pacific via a strait of water
thought to exist across the top of North America. For many years explorers concentrated on finding the Atlantic or eastern entrance to this fabled
passage, but in the last quarter of the 18th century attention shifted to a
possible Pacific entrance, and a series of maritime expeditions began visiting the coast of what is now British Columbia.

The Spanish were first on the scene, sailing north from their bases in
Mexico to assert their claim to the entire coastline as far as Alaska. They
were challenged by the British, who sent naval explorer James Cook to the
coast to pursue the search for the Northwest Passage. As a direct result of
Cook's 1778 visit to Nootka Sound on the west coast of Vancouver Island
a lucrative trade in sea otter pelts began, attracting merchant traders from
several countries.

Alarmed, the Spanish redoubled their efforts, opening a naval base in Nootka Sound in 1789 and forcibly asserting their sovereignty over the area. When Great Britain threatened to go to war in defence of its right to trade, Spain backed down and in 1790 signed the Nootka Convention, giving up its exclusive claim to the coast.

Meanwhile, British and Spanish mariners extended their search for the entrance to the Northwest Passage to the east of Vancouver Island, into Georgia Strait.[1]

The First Spanish Visitors, 1791

In 1791 Spain sent Francisco de Eliza, the commandant at Nootka, on an expedition into Juan de Fuca Strait where he anchored at Puerto de Quadra on the Olympic Peninsula, now Port Discovery. From here he dispatched one of his smaller ships, the schooner *Santa Saturnina* under the command of Jose Maria Narvaez, to follow the mainland coast northeast, between 48 and 50 degrees north latitude, charting and surveying along the way. Eliza intended to use this information to develop an exact plan of the coast and islands of what is now the Strait of Georgia.

Narvaez's vessel was small, only 11.3 metres in length with a four-metre beam, making islands and shoreline more easily accessible than with a larger vessel. He had a crew of 15 to 20 men including the pilot, Juan Carrasco, and a longboat for use in shallow water. Narvaez charted the shoreline through the Strait of Juan de Fuca and then north, passing Birch Bay, Crescent Beach and Point Roberts and entering the large body of water that earlier in the year another of Eliza's explorers, Pantoja, had named El Gran Canal de Nuestra Senora del Rosario la Marinera ("The Great Channel of Our Lady of the Rosary of the Seafarers"), now the Strait of Georgia.

As the *Santa Saturnina* moved northward, Narvaez and his crew noted a large expanse of fresh green water, evidently flowing from the mouth of a great river they could not locate because of sandbars and low, shrubby ground at its mouth. They anchored at the base of a large bluff on the northern shore of the waterway, marking the chart with an anchor symbol. Narvaez named this point of land Islas de Langara, believing Point Grey to be a group of islands at the river's entrance.

Because Narvaez did not leave a log, or it was lost, historians have had to infer his next movements from his charts and Eliza's notes. The ship moved into what is now Burrard Inlet, carrying the men who have long been considered the first Europeans to see this area. Narvaez's chart shows the opening between Point Grey and the North Shore and labels it Boca de Florida Blanca (Mouth of Florida Blanca), named for Count Floridablanca, a minister of the king of Spain, so perhaps Narvaez went with his longboat to scout the location as a possible river mouth.

He must have continued by boat along the shore of Stanley Park, because he evidently named either Ferguson Point on the park's west shore or land at the mouth of the Capilano River as Punta de la Bodega, and he marked three small squares denoting aboriginal villages at each of three locations—near the Capilano River, at Jericho, and beside Point Atkinson. Surprisingly, he did not discover the opening at First Narrows (which was well hidden by overhanging trees), so he did not enter the inner harbour.

Returning to his ship, Narvaez followed the shoreline to the west, naming Howe Sound Bocas de Carmelo and Bowen Island Isla de Apodaca, then on to Texada Island, across to Parksville, into Nanaimo Harbour and south along the outside of the Gulf Islands. The ship apparently was running short of food, and on July 22 Narvaez returned to Port Discovery to rejoin his commander Eliza, bringing to an end the first known visit by Europeans to Burrard Inlet.[2]

The English, 1792

The following year the British sent two ships to explore the waters east of Vancouver Island. Captain George Vancouver led the expedition. He had joined the British navy in 1771 at the age of 13. Between 1772 and 1775 he served as midshipman with Captain James Cook on his second voyage to the South Pacific and the Antarctic, and from 1776 to 1780 sailed with Cook to Alaska and the west coast of Vancouver Island. In 1790 he was appointed commander, and he was assigned to the ship *Discovery* the following year, after the signing of the Nootka Convention.

Vancouver's orders directed him to proceed to Nootka Sound and receive from the Spanish the land and buildings they had seized from the English there in 1789. He was also to survey the western coast of North America north from 30 degrees latitude, paying particular attention to waterways that seemed to lead to the continent's interior and the Northwest Passage, but not to waste time on rivers that did not appear navigable. The *Discovery* carried a complement of 100 men. Travelling with her was the armed tender *Chatham*, commanded by Lieutenant William Broughton and carrying 45 men.

Crossing the Pacific Ocean Vancouver's expedition visited Australia, New Zealand and the Sandwich Islands, arriving off the coast of California in the middle of April 1792 and beginning the survey there. Vancouver arrived at Port Discovery at the end of the month and began his exploration of the coast, naming islands and waterways in the vicinity of the Strait of Juan de Fuca, Puget Sound and the mainland shore to Bellingham Bay and claiming possession of the coast for King George III of England. He also named the "Gulph of Georgia" after the king.

Continuing along the mainland coast, the ships anchored in a protected bay with a sandy bottom (Birch Bay), just south of the 49th parallel. Outfitting the ships' yawl and launch with a week's supply of necessities, Vancouver travelled in the yawl with a crew of about 13 men; Second Lieutenant Peter Puget was in charge of the launch and about 10 men. These boats, equipped with oars and sails, were carried aboard the *Discovery* and lowered when needed to explore bays and inlets.

The crews left at 5:00 a.m. on June 12, rowing north to explore the shoreline. The men were unaware that they were tracing the same course as Narvaez the year before. Because of a strong wind they sought overnight protection across the Gulf of Georgia on one of the Gulf Islands, possibly what today is known as Galiano. Finding only steep rocks along the shore, they stopped at 1:00 a.m. to cook a meal, then spent an uncomfortable night in the boats. Peter Puget wrote in his log: "This disappointment we much regretted as the People had been incessantly on the Oars Ten Hours and an Half."

Quitting their anchorage at 5:00 a.m. on June 13, the men headed back across the gulf toward a high bluff, where they landed at noon. Puget called this spot Noon Breakfast Point, but Captain Vancouver named it Point Grey after his friend Captain George Grey of the Royal Navy. Somewhat refreshed, the men rowed eastward across the outer harbour. Vancouver observed:

> From point Grey we proceeded first up the eastern branch of the sound, where, about a league [4.8 kilometres] within its entrance, we passed to the northward of an island [Stanley Park] which nearly terminated its extent, forming a passage from ten to seven

fathoms deep, not more than a cable's length [185 metres] in width [First Narrows].

When surveying the inlet, Vancouver probably followed the practice of rowing along the right-hand side of the channel, keeping a record of his course with a compass and estimating the waterway's width as he travelled. The men made sextant observations on shore. All of this information was later recorded on a plotting sheet on board the *Discovery*. As the boat headed toward the middle of the inner harbour, Vancouver noted:

Detail of Captain George Vancouver's chart of Burrard's Canal, 1792.

> Here we were met by about fifty Indians, in their canoes, who conducted themselves with the greatest decorum and civility, presenting us with several fish cooked, and undressed, of the sort already mentioned as resembling the smelt. These good people, finding we were inclined to make some return for their hospitality, shewed much understanding in preferring iron to copper.[3]

Drawing of Captain Vancouver and his crew in one of the ship's boats, 1792. *UBC BC1060*

The aboriginals were probably Squamish people from the village of Homulchesun beside the Capilano River. Puget noted that about 30 Natives (probably from the village of Whoi-Whoi in Stanley Park) paddled out to his boat from the south shore and engaged in bartering. The Squamish were very interested in watching the sailors fire muskets, and examined the men's white skin curiously. Puget commented:

> ...we contrived by Signs to convince each other of reciprocal Friendship. May we not from the Circumstances of the Musquet infer, that their tribe heretofore were unacquainted with Europeans, else why betray so much Astonishment-Altho Indians familiarized to Fire Arms in general shrink from the Report as if to avoid the Effect. The Ideas of these People could only be understood from the Expression of Countenance—& evident Signs of Fear—I therefore have no Doubt but we are the first Europeans who have penetrated thus far into the Streights, though it has been alleged that the Copper Ornaments in general Use with most of the Tribes we have met must have been procured from Visitors...I have no hesitation in venturing an opinion, that we are the Discoverers of this part of the Fuca Streights.[4]

The canoes accompanied the ships' boats for some distance east, then most returned to their villages. The exhausted Englishmen camped on the south shore, probably at the location of the present Barnet Beach Park.[5] Captain Vancouver noted:

> We landed for the night about half a league from the head of the inlet and about three leagues from its entrance. Our Indian visitors remained with us until by signs we gave them to understand we were going to rest.

Again steep, rocky cliffs lined the shore, leaving very little space for sleeping. Although most of the men slept in the boats for the second night, a few chose to stay near the heat of the cook fire. Vancouver in his log describes the result:

> Some of the young gentlemen, however, preferring the stony beach for their couch, without duly considering the line of high

The mouth of Indian Arm today, a view not unlike that seen by Captain George Vancouver and his crew when they set up camp in 1792. Boulder Island in foreground, Belcarra at centre right and Deep Cove centre left. *MP*

water mark, found themselves incommoded by the flood tide, of which they were not apprized until they were nearly afloat; and one of them slept so sound, that I believe he might have been conveyed to some distance, had he not been awakened by his companions.

Leaving at 4:00 a.m. on June 14, Vancouver decided not to explore Indian Arm because, as he noted in his log, he had "a grander object in contemplation" and felt that this channel was not navigable for shipping. Retracing their route the explorers headed west, catching a breeze for their sails, but this time they did not meet any aboriginal people. Vancouver named this inlet Burrard's Channel, later shown on his chart as Burrard's Canal, after his friend Sir Harry Burrard of the navy. (Evidently the Burrard family pronounced the name with the accent on the first syllable, not as the inlet's name is commonly pronounced today.)[6]

Stopping for breakfast about two kilometres east of Howe Sound, near Cypress Creek, the men then caught a favourable wind and again were able to use sails. Vancouver named the northwest point of Burrard's

Sir Harry Burrard Neale, a friend for whom Captain Vancouver named Burrard's Channel. Harry Burrard was born in 1765, entered the navy in 1778 and became Lord of the Admiralty in 1804. He added 'Neale' to his name for his wife's family. *National Maritime Museum Greenwich Collection, neg. A8600*

Channel Point Atkinson after another particular friend, Thomas Atkinson. The boats rounded the point and proceeded to explore and chart the fiord leading north, which Vancouver named Howe's Sound in honour of Admiral Earl Howe. The surveyors continued northwestward along the coast as far as Jervis Inlet before turning back on June 22 to rejoin the *Discovery* and the *Chatham* at Birch Bay after 11.5 days on the water.

The Spanish, 1792

Spain's continuing interest in discovering the Northwest Passage led in 1792 to another expedition through the Strait of Juan de Fuca and north, following part of Narvaez's 1791 route. Two officers, Dionisio Alcala Galiano and Cayetano Valdes, commanded the schooners *Mexicana* and *Sutil*. These newly constructed ships each carried a crew of 24 men and food and water for 100 days. Part of their cargo was copper, iron and other items to distribute to the local people.

The ships left Nootka Sound on June 5, heading south, then followed the shoreline eastward through the Strait of Juan de Fuca and nearly duplicated Narvaez's and Vancouver's courses. Stopping at Neah Bay at the entrance to Juan de Fuca Strait, they met other Spaniards from Nootka who were building a fort. They also met some aboriginal people who told them about two English ships inside the strait. Passing Birch Bay, the sailors observed lights from vessels that they took to be the English, but because they were travelling at night and wanted to reach the Boca de Florida Blanca at daybreak they did not approach.

They anchored at a sheltered spot between Gabriola Island and Nanaimo Harbour to avoid a strong wind and stayed in the area for seven days. Heavy rains forced them to stay at anchor for the first few days and they took the opportunity to replenish water and other supplies, then explored some of the neighbouring islands and their bays. On the morning of June 19 they headed east toward what they later called the Punta de Langara (Point Grey). With a fresh following breeze they reached and anchored at the mouth of the Fraser River.

Seven canoes, each with two or three occupants and probably from the Musqueam village on the river, came out to greet them. The aboriginals wore no clothing except for a few with hats, and most were marked with body paint. Galiano commented:

> The features of these natives were better proportioned than those of the other Indians we had seen in all the channel, and the shape of the face more perfect, and so they very much resembled Europeans. Their muscles, if not more developed, were of better form than those of the inhabitants of Nutka and they were not so white, but their liveliness, grace and talent engaged all our attention. They displayed an unequalled affability together with a war-like disposition.

The Spaniards were impressed by the Musqueam, although the aboriginals did appear warlike. They were carrying spears with iron tips, bows and arrows, and war clubs that they refused to exchange for knives or seashells.

As the tide was running out, the captains decided to move their ships to a safer moorage. Sounding the depth constantly they advanced cautiously, eventually anchoring off the northern shore of Punta de Langara in the area now known as Spanish Bank. They renamed the inlet Canal de Floridablanca. Again aboriginals met them in canoes and, again, Galiano and his crew were impressed with their friendliness and their ability to repeat Spanish words. One sailor combed and decorated an aboriginal man with a ribbon. This so pleased him that he embraced the sailor warmly. The crews appeared to enjoy this meeting and, in a lighthearted mood, began to sing a well-known French song, "Malbrough s'en va t'en guerre."[7] The Natives easily picked up the tune and sang along, continuing on their own after the sailors stopped. By several signs, the local people indicated that the Spaniards would find food and water if they continued down the channel.

The English and Spanish

At seven o'clock in the morning on June 22, Spanish lookouts spied two vessels approaching their ships. They were Captain Vancouver's boats, returning to Birch Bay from their exploration of the coast. Vancouver and Lieutenant Puget joined the Spanish on board the *Sutil*, meeting Galiano and Valdes.

In his log, Vancouver admitted that he experienced "no small degree of mortification" when he found that Narvaez the year before had visited much of the shoreline the English had just charted and had given the Gulf of Georgia a Spanish name. He also was dismayed at the small size of the Spanish ships and their living quarters, remarking that "they were the most ill calculated and unfit vessels that could possibly be imagined for such an expedition." His *Discovery* was nearly 35 metres long with an 8.5-metre beam; the Spanish vessels were just over 14 metres with a four-metre beam.

As Captain Galiano spoke some English they were able to discuss over breakfast details of their explorations and make plans for a second meeting within the next few days. The English in their two small boats then wearily headed back to their ships and reached them on June 23, having rowed and sailed 531 kilometres. Before leaving their moorage and heading for their rendezvous with the Spaniards, they officially named the harbour Birch Bay for the numerous black birches growing in the vicinity.

Vancouver had informed the Spanish that he and his men had explored to the farthest end of Burrard Inlet but had not followed and charted the northern arm. The Spanish, wanting to obtain details of this waterway, sent the ships' two second officers, Secundino Salamanca and Juan Vernaci, in two boats to explore the east-west channel and the inlet heading north (Indian Arm).

The men rowed through the narrow opening at First Narrows and along the length of the inlet. By 4:00 p.m. they had reached what they called a basin or lagoon, at what is now Port Moody, then headed back and entered the channel leading northward, in their words "the northern arm of the canal."[8] They were the first Europeans to travel the length of that magnificent fiord. They did not see any villages on their way, evidently missing the camps at the Capilano River, on the south shore at Stanley Park and at Belcarra on the east shore of Indian Arm.

The officers reported that they found a river "of very little consequence" at the head of the inlet. They were unable to take their boats up the narrow waterway but were impressed with the beauty of the location. They observed a small village and apparently surprised the people there as the women ran away and hid in the trees. A few men approached the Spaniards in a canoe, staying for a short time, but they soon disappeared into the woods. The officers must have made some attempts at conversation as they reported that the aboriginals called the area "Sasamat." The Canal de Sasamat appears on their map.[9]

While awaiting the return of the boats, Captain Galiano in a pensive mood had reflected:

Although in these places we do not find that pleasant view which a diversity of trees and young plants presents, nor the elegance of flowers and beauty of fruits, nor the variety of animals and birds; while the ear also misses the pleasure of the song of the latter, yet the observer will not fail to find many opportunities to admire the works of nature and divert his thoughts in contemplating the enormous masses of the mountains. These are clad with pines and crowned with snow, which when it melts forms most lovely cascades. When these reach the end of their course with an amazing velocity, they break the silence of these solitudes, and with their united waters form copious rivers, which serve to water the plants on their banks and in which breeds a quantity of salmon.

After the boats had returned from their surveying expedition to Indian Arm, the schooners set sail to join the English ships off Point Grey.[10]

About 60 years elapsed before the Squamish people again saw white men on Burrard Inlet. Doubtless many stories of the strange white-skinned visitors were passed along from parent to child. Andrew Paull, secretary of the Squamish Indian Council for many years, told this story in 1932:

It seems that it was a tradition among the Indians of early days that a calamity of some sort would befall them every seven years. Once it was a flood. On another occasion disease wiped out Whoi-Whoi. Again, it was a snow storm which lasted for three months. The wise men had long prophesied a visitation from a great people, from a very powerful body of men. Capt. Vancouver came in 1792, a year which coincided with the seventh year, the year in which some calamity was expected, regarding the form of which there was much trepidation, so that when strange men of strange appearance, white, with their odd boats, etc., etc., arrived on the scene, the wise men said 'this may be the fateful visitation, what may it bring us', and took steps to propitiate the all powerful visitors.... As your great explorer Vancouver progressed through the First Narrows, our people threw in greeting before him clouds of snow white feathers which rose, wafted in the air aimlessly about, then fell like flurries of snow to the water's surface and rested there like white rose petals scattered before a bride. It must have been a pretty welcome. Then there were presents of fish; all to invoke the all powerful arrivals to have pity on them—it was the seventh year. You see there was motive behind it. They were expecting a calamity and were anxious to do anything to avoid it.[11]

Although the outer coast attracted hundreds of traders collecting the extremely popular sea otter skins, the white men seldom entered the Strait of Georgia as the sea otters were not prolific there, and so Burrard Inlet remained for another half century the unchallenged possession of its aboriginal inhabitants. The calamity that the Squamish were predicting could have been based on the fear of another smallpox epidemic. The first one had reached the communities around the strait in 1782 with devastating results. Entire villages disappeared, and the aboriginal people remembered smallpox with a superstitious dread.[12]

CHAPTER 2

THE FIRST COMMERCIAL ENTERPRISES: 1850–70

Burrard Inlet differs from most of the great sounds of this coast in being extremely easy of access to vessels of any size or class, and in the convenient depth of water for anchorage which may be found in almost any part of it; its close proximity to Fraser river, with the great facilities for constructing roads between the two places, likewise adds considerably to its importance.

—Captain George Richards, *Vancouver Island Pilot*, 1864

I n the early 1850s Burrard Inlet was a pristine environment, home to several hundred aboriginal people, with very few white visitors. Vancouver Island, a British Crown colony, had been granted to the Hudson's Bay Company in 1849. Through Chief Factor James Douglas, later governor, the company encouraged white settlement in Fort Victoria and other parts of the island. A major coal find at Nanaimo in 1852 excited the British government's attention with the implications for cheaper and readily available fuel for ships. The discovery of gold on the Fraser River in 1858 caused a stampede of thousands of hopeful miners to Victoria, the port of entry to the goldfields, eventually contributing to a population increase on the island. That year the mainland was recognized by Britain as the Colony of British Columbia. The transformation of the north Pacific area, including Burrard Inlet, was under way.

Although gold was the magic word in the interior of British Columbia, coal was the mineral that attracted the initial interest of outsiders in Burrard

Inlet. The first person who arrived in search of good coal was John Muir, an early Sooke pioneer and coal miner who, in 1851, was sent by the Hudson's Bay Company to investigate the extent of the deposits. He reported to Governor James Douglas that they were surface deposits of insufficient size and quality to interest the company, and discouraged further interest.[1]

On June 22, 1857, W. Colquhoun Grant presented a paper to the Royal Geographical Society in which he mentioned a coal seam a few centimetres thick "between Burrard Canal and Home Sound [Howe Sound?], i.e. on the southern shore of Home Sound close to the entrance," but did not comment on its quality. Grant, a former lieutenant colonel of cavalry, had settled at Sooke on Vancouver Island in 1849 and explored the island and parts of the mainland.[2]

Despite Muir's earlier negative report on the quality of the coal, on June 12, 1859, Captain George Richards, in Burrard Inlet on the English survey ship HMS *Plumper*, sent his senior engineer, Francis Brockton, in

The British survey ship *Plumper*, in a drawing that appeared in the *Illustrated London News* in 1862. Its captain, George Richards, charted all of Burrard Inlet in 1859–60. *CVA OUT. P.1097.638*

a boat to investigate the veracity of stories he had heard about the coal on the inlet. Returning to the *Plumper*, Brockton reported "an apparently extensive vein on the south shore, about one-and-one-half miles within the first narrows."[3] Richards promptly visited the location himself and had his men take more than two tonnes of coal back to the ship, where he found that it burned well in the galley stove.

The colonial government was very anxious to uncover new sources of coal, hoping for another major mine to equal the one at Nanaimo, so Captain Richards sent samples to Governor Douglas in Victoria and to Colonel Richard Clement Moody, chief commissioner of lands and works, in New Westminster. The coal find seemed so important that Richards named the site of his discovery Coal Harbour, and what is now Stanley Park he called Coal Peninsula. Within two weeks Richards was advising that the specimens obtained "did not produce sufficient heat to generate steam [in the ship's boilers]" because of prolonged exposure to salt water, but he remained optimistic that "coal of a superior description and in large quantities will be obtained."[4]

Lieutenant Robert Burnaby, Colonel Moody's 31-year-old private secretary, heard the news of the find and shared it with his friend Walter Moberly, a 27-year-old civil engineer who had been surveying for the British Columbia government. They decided to investigate for themselves. Early in August they and a small group of men with picks and shovels took a canoe from New Westminster down the Fraser River to its mouth and around Point Grey, into False Creek. The next day they paddled through First Narrows and camped on the south shore at Coal Harbour, then started an investigation into what would be the first attempt at a business enterprise on those shores.

The following morning Moberly and Burnaby left their team of prospectors digging for coal and went in search of the gold that aboriginal people had told them could be found in the river at the head of the north arm (Indian Arm). After paddling up the arm they beached their canoe and hiked along the riverbank, pushing through trees and bushes, finally scrambling up a rocky cliff beside the arcing spray of a high waterfall. Although the scenery was spectacular, the search for gold was a disappointment. They retraced their steps, launched the canoe and began the return trip to Coal Harbour. As evening approached the paddlers headed for the arm's eastern shore, where they lit a fire and contentedly enjoyed the fiord's peaceful, rugged beauty. Moberly recalled that night many years later:

> Making a trip up the north arm, we camped on a rocky point and tied
> our canoe to a tree, only partially hauling her on the rock. Burnaby
> and I slept in the canoe, and I awoke with an unpleasant sensation,
> finding my feet were much higher than my head. I could not under-
> stand the situation at all, but could see Burnaby fast asleep at the
> other end of the canoe, which would apparently be soon standing on
> end. Satisfying myself that I was not dreaming, I crawled carefully to
> the other end, when the canoe suddenly resumed its horizontal posi-
> tion and Burnaby awoke. We found when we went to bed that the
> tide was in, but as it ran out of course the canoe kept tilting over, and
> we had but narrowly escaped a bath a little before our usual hour.[5]

Next morning the men headed back to the coal seam. Rather than finding
the quiet scene they had left, they were surrounded by more than 100
canoes paddled by Squamish men who were obviously angry and ready for
action. Moberly, Burnaby and their aboriginal guides cautiously wound
their way past the canoes to shore, where an anxious Moberly sent off a letter to Magistrate Spalding in New Westminster with a Frenchman who was
trading with the aboriginals. "We are in a state of siege here," he explained.
"The Indians say the soldiers have taken two Squamish Indians and are
going to hang them [for a murder]."[6] Apparently a white man had been
murdered at O'Donohue's mill on the Fraser River and Captain Louard of
the Royal Engineers had captured the Squamish men believed to be
responsible, on Sea Island. Thinking the pair were about to be hanged, the
Squamish on Burrard Inlet were indignant and had gathered to protest.

At Nanaimo, Captain Richards received orders to depart immediately
in the *Plumper* for Burrard Inlet to settle the problem and, if necessary,
rescue the Burnaby/Moberly party. When he arrived on August 20 he
found that the confrontation had been exaggerated and the men needed no
assistance. The visit was, however, not wasted. Moberly recalled:

> ...the presence of the bluejackets enabled us to spend a jolly
> night. They landed, as we had done, at the foot of what is now Bute
> street, and later brought a keg ashore. Then we lit a roaring fire of
> logs as night came on, and our party and the English sailors spent
> one of the jolliest nights I remember. Many rollicking old sea songs
> were sung and many a rousing chorus echoed through the forest
> and many a toast was drunk.[7]

The digging continued, but with difficulty. Burnaby wrote to Governor Douglas on August 28 that his crew needed tools and a pump. The sandstone was very hard and water from springs interfered. Results were inconclusive though not unsatisfactory, but an attempt to establish a mining syndicate went nowhere. Although coal on the inlet was a prime topic of discussion among potential entrepreneurs during the next few years, only the colonial government made a firm plan, and had the quality of the coal seam checked again.

Sewell Prescott Moody, who had set up a sawmill at New Westminster, and his partner George Dietz, another entrepreneur, were the first to make a formal application to the colonial secretary. On November 24, 1864, they requested a grant of 640 acres (259 hectares) of land for coal mining on English Bay where it meets False Creek in the neighbourhood of the Kitsilano aboriginal settlement.[8] With the governor's approval for the land grant, dependent upon a one-sixteenth royalty on all coal produced, Moody and Dietz formed the British Columbia Coal Mining Company (BCCMC) on July 22, 1865. The board of directors included John Robson, editor of the New Westminster *British Columbian*, who encouraged the sale of shares through articles in his newspaper.

Captain Edward Stamp was in the process of establishing a sawmill on the south shore of Burrard Inlet at this time, and he objected that the coal company's grant interfered with his logging. As a result the BCCMC gave up its rights to the land on English Bay and instead received a 400-acre (161.8-hectare) coal reserve near Coal Harbour at the foot of what is now Burrard Street. During the winter of 1865–66 the BCCMC's coal bore went as deep as 152 metres without making a major find. Finally, in March 1866, a notice in the *British Columbian* advised that the British Columbia Coal Mining Company had called a meeting to wind up its affairs and that no further expenditures would be made.

This was not the last attempt to find a productive coal seam on Burrard Inlet, but many years passed before other investors ventured into the business.

The Colony of British Columbia

While the search for coal had been going on in Coal Harbour and English Bay, the Colony of British Columbia officially came into being on November 19, 1858. James Douglas, already governor of Vancouver Island, became governor of the mainland colony as well and took office at the ceremonies held in New Fort Langley on the south shore of the Fraser River. Heavy rain forced the swearing-in ceremony inside, to the echoes of an 18-gun salute. English law was instituted.

In 1864, Douglas retired and Frederick Seymour took over as governor of British Columbia. The mainland colony followed the same boundaries as the present province, except that Vancouver Island remained a separate colony until August 1866.

British Columbia was created in response to the discovery of gold in the gravel bars of the Fraser River in 1858. The government realized that the large influx of prospectors heading for the interior needed laws dealing with their specific governance. The threat of possible American expansion also made formation of a formal government a priority.

In 1859 a group of Royal Engineers under the command of Colonel Richard Moody arrived from London to build roads and trails and assist in maintaining law and order. Moody convinced Governor Douglas that the location of the capital at Derby, near Fort Langley, would be indefensible in the event of an American invasion. The capital was moved to the north bank of the Fraser River and originally named Queensborough, later changed by Queen Victoria to New Westminster. The Royal Engineers began the task of clearing the site and erecting the first buildings.

Moody realized that a trail from New Westminster to Burrard Inlet was essential. He predicted that the inlet would become a popular harbour, especially for ships deterred by the sandbars of the Fraser River. He was also aware that the inlet could provide a route for invading American ships, and he wanted access for British troops from New Westminster. He ordered the Royal Engineers to build a trail from their camp at Sapperton, just east of New Westminster, to the head of Burrard Inlet at what became Port Moody. In 1861 the trail was widened to make a wagon road and called North Road. That winter it proved its value when the Fraser River froze. A steamer from Victoria was rerouted to Port Moody, the first delivery on the inlet, and mail was transported along the road to New Westminster.

Concern about an American invasion was so strong that the government decided to establish military reserves along the shores of Burrard Inlet. When HMS *Plumper* began charting the inlet in 1859, Captain Richards was under orders to establish reserves at Point Grey, on English Bay (now Jericho), at the first narrows on the south and north shores, on the south shore at what would become the town of Granville, on the north and south shores at the entrance to Port Moody, and three reserves around Port Moody's shoreline. Government plans included a battery of heavy guns on the north side of Point Grey to combine with others at Point Atkinson to protect ships at anchor in English Bay.[9] They also included the positioning of cannon at the height of land at Barnet, the military reserve opposite Indian Arm, with guns that could be raised by machinery to hurl shells the length of the inlet to deter enemy ships from entering First Narrows. Other plans included construction of fortifications and cannon on all of the reserves' heights.

The reserves were put in place, but the only aspect of the greater plans that was implemented was Moody's trail from New Westminster to the reserve at Jericho on English Bay, for the movement of soldiers.

Moodyville

Besides those connected to coal mining, the only other white men attracted to Burrard Inlet were a few prospectors heading for the goldfields and the odd trader wanting to do business with the aboriginal people. That changed with the arrival of the first loggers, when the shores of the inlet began to echo with the sounds of axe and saw.[10] It was the size and quality of the trees that attracted men to the logging and sawmill business. Giant cedars and firs grew thickly down to the shoreline, where they could easily be transported by water to sawmills.

In 1862 Thomas Wilson Graham, a builder and architect, George Scrimgeour and Phillip Hick pre-empted lots 272, 273 and 274, a total of 480 acres (194 hectares) of prime timber property on the north shore of Burrard Inlet, about two kilometres east of First Narrows. At this site they constructed a sawmill powered by two water wheels driven by a 50-horse-power water-head, drawing water 3.2 kilometres by flume and ditch from Lynn Creek, about three kilometres away. Two circular saws, a 22-inch planing machine and other equipment gave a mill capacity of 40,000 board feet per 24 hours. Oxen pulled the logs to the mill. The men were ready for business by May 1, 1863, when they advertised in the *British Columbian* that Pioneer Mills was "now prepared to furnish Fir, Cedar, Spruce Lumber, also Tongued and Grooved flooring to be delivered at the mill, New Westminster or Victoria, Vancouver Island, at prices lower than Puget Sound lumber."

On June 10 the three men signed an agreement for a mortgage with Chartres Brew, a New Westminster magistrate and first chief inspector of the provincial police, in the amount of £400, with interest at the rate of five percent a month, repayment due on June 10, 1864. The *Flying Dutchman* carried the first lumber from the mill on August 13, 1863, to New Westminster: a cargo of planks for use as a river levee to protect the capital from Fraser River flooding. The commercial life of Burrard Inlet had begun.

The mill opening piqued the curiosity of colonists, some of whom sailed to the inlet from New Westminster to visit the property and enjoy a party atmosphere. On a second trip, in late August, visitors also saw HMS *Sutlej*, a British naval vessel whose captain was examining Burrard Inlet as a potential site for a naval base (which was established at Esquimalt instead).

Graham's company, Pioneer Mills, was short-lived due to transportation difficulties and competition from sawmills on Vancouver Island and the Fraser River and at New Westminster. When the owners failed to make their mortgage payments, Chartres Brew foreclosed and advertised the land and buildings for sale at a public auction on December 16, 1863. The sale included "one million feet of cut and prepared logs and 2.5 yokes of oxen."

John Oscar Smith bid $8,000 for the outfit, besting by $100 Sewell Moody, the only other bidder. Smith had been a New Westminster grocer, then an employee of Captain William Irving on his Fraser River steamer *Reliance*. He renamed the property Burrard Inlet Mills, and advertisements appeared in the *British Columbian* and *The British Colonist* newspaper in Victoria in March 1864. By April the mill had shipped its third cargo, but Smith must have been experiencing financial problems, because on May 14 he signed a mortgage held by Irving, his former employer, for $6,626.70, due for repayment by December 16 that year with interest at two percent per month. During the summer of 1864, Smith contracted with the Duncan & George agency in Victoria to carry an assortment of Burrard Inlet Mills' rough and dressed lumber, making it more readily available for builders and contractors on Vancouver Island. Although Smith had made shipments to Victoria, Nanaimo and New Westminster, until this time he had shipped none to foreign markets.

On August 27, 1864, *The British Colonist* noted:

Burrard's Inlet,—We are pleased to notice the progress which Mr. J.O. Smith, the enterprising proprietor of the Burrard Inlet Mills has been recently making. Lumber from his mills is now finding a general market, and we understand that the brigantine *Brewster* which arrived yesterday from San Francisco, has been chartered to load lumber at these mills for Valparaiso, Chile. Now that Mr. Smith has inaugurated a foreign export trade we hope to see the official returns from British Columbia exhibit a rapid increase in their exports until they shall have assumed proportions commensurate with the material wealth of the country.

On September 1, Captain Carleton sailed the two-masted *Brewster* to New Westminster, the port of entry, where she was cleared to enter Burrard Inlet. However, on September 3 *The British Colonist* announced:

> For Valparaiso,—The brig *Brewster* which cleared a day or two ago for Burrard's Inlet to load with lumber for Valparaiso, will instead load in this port [Victoria], there being a sufficient quantity of lumber in the hands of the company's agents, Messrs. Duncan & George. She will take 240,000 feet.

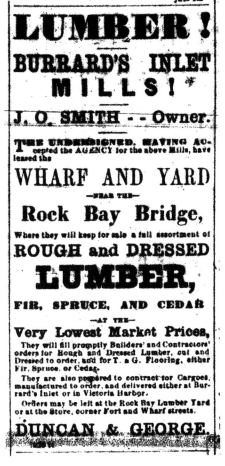

Announcement that the Duncan & George agency in Victoria would be stocking lumber from Oscar Smith's Burrard Inlet Mills. *Daily British Colonist*, August 8, 1864

The newspaper noted on September 15 that the *Brewster* had finished loading the lumber for Valparaiso and was moored to the Hudson's Bay Company wharf, ready to sail. SS *Caledonia* towed her out of the harbour on the morning of September 17, carrying the first foreign shipment of Burrard Inlet timber.

The previous day, the barque *Ellen Lewis* under the command of Captain Hellon had entered Burrard Inlet and begun loading lumber directly from the mill. The cargo of 277,000 board feet of lumber and 16,000 pickets took nearly two months to stow aboard. The *Ellen Lewis* sailed for Adelaide, Australia on November 9, 1864,[11] the first ship to load lumber on the inlet for a foreign port but the second to carry a cargo of Burrard Inlet lumber abroad.

Overextended financially, Oscar Smith could not meet his creditors' demands. He announced a sale to foreclose his mortgage by auction, to be held on January 29, 1865. On that day Sewell Moody was the successful bidder, obtaining the property for $6,900—$1,000 less than he had bid one year before. Again William Irving held the mortgage. The handwritten indenture stated that the premises were "knocked down to the said Sewell Prescott Moody, James Vanbremer [sic], James S. Howe, John Polmere and Moses C. Ireland for $6900, being the highest sum bid for the same." The sale included the "sawmill with its appurtenance and the houses and tenements with their appurtenance." In February, Burrard Inlet Lumber Mills, more popularly known as Moody's Mill, opened for business. It would become the first successful enterprise on the site.

Sewell Moody (no relation to Colonel Moody), a quiet, intelligent, determined man, was born in Maine around 1837 and arrived in New Westminster in about 1861. He became an importer, then attempted an unsuccessful venture as a sawmill operator. He originally became interested in Burrard Inlet when he and George Dietz attempted to develop a coal mine there in 1864.

With their new mill business barely under way, Moody and his partners wrote to Governor Frederick Seymour on February 16, 1865, to request the appointment of James Howe as a customs officer on Burrard Inlet. Until this time ships arriving in and leaving the inlet had to pass through customs at New Westminster. The men explained:

> ...that it would cause great inconvenience and delay to your Memorialists, if all vessels had to come to New Westminster to enter and clear as well as a heavy additional charge for freight, thereby preventing your Memorialists from successfully competing with the Lumberers on Puget Sound.[12]

The request was granted. At that time customs duties were 12.5 percent on lumber and many other items.

The mill owners also recognized the need for access to more trees, and added to their acreage. On November 30, 1865, they received a 21-year

Sewell Prescott Moody, circa 1870. In 1865 he became the third owner of the sawmill on the north shore and renamed the business Burrard Inlet Lumber Mills. *CVA PORT. P.861*

timber lease for an additional 18,559 acres (7,511 hectares) and the following January an additional 2,634 acres (1,066 hectares).

The company established an agency in New Westminster to encourage local buyers, but also began shipping to foreign markets. Employees took six weeks to load lumber on the barque *Glimpse*, which headed for Sydney, Australia in May 1865. They shipped another 300,000 feet on the *Envoy* in May for delivery to Adelaide, Australia. The company sent beams 70 inches long and 20 inches square to New Westminster for construction of the bell tower at Holy Trinity Church there. The mill's growing reputation for producing the best lumber on the coast, coupled with an exceptional harbour, led to cargoes leaving for Mexico, China, Peru, Hawaii and other destinations abroad.

The mill site was developing into a small community that became known as Moodyville. The *British Columbian* in June 1866 described the setting:

The beautiful sunny, side of the slope is now dotted with the neat cabins of hardy woodmen . . . wharf accommodation and a dozen ships . . . a large store built on the wharf is well stocked with general merchandise for employees and visitors. A new building is being constructed as a lecture and reading room for employees of the mill.

The new building was the Mechanics Institute, which opened for members in 1869. Moody allowed no alcoholic beverages in Moodyville, worried about the problems they could cause not only with the white men but also with the aboriginal people who worked at the mill and lived nearby.

The business prospered, but in 1866 James Van Bramer withdrew from the partnership. Moses Ireland had left in 1865. George Dietz, who had worked with Moody on the coal project, and Hugh Nelson, later lieutenant governor of British Columbia, joined Moody as partners in S.P. Moody & Company, later referred to as Moody, Dietz & Nelson. In 1868 they added a steam-driven mill to the water-powered plant. The new building was 61 metres long and supposedly 100,000 board feet of lumber could be produced a day. After the two wharves leading to the mills were joined, a dozen ships could moor there at one time.

The next year a telegraph line from New Westminster that had reached as far as the hotel at Brighton on the south shore was extended across the inlet to the company offices. Messages cost 25 cents each, later raised to 50 cents. By 1869 the town of Moodyville was well established, the mill's business was increasing, and on July 22 Sewell Moody allowed himself the time to get married. He and his family settled in a comfortable home in Victoria, but Moody spent a great deal of time in Moodyville and made business trips to the United States.

Stamp's Mill

With news spreading about the outstanding quality of Burrard Inlet timber, it was not long before interest developed in opening a second sawmill, this time on the inlet's south shore.

Captain Edward Stamp, born in England in 1814, was a master mariner who on a trip to the Pacific Coast became interested in the prolific timber stands on Vancouver Island. In 1858 he opened a store in Victoria. Three years later he started the first export sawmill in BC, named Anderson Mill after its principal backer (the Anderson family of London), on the Alberni Canal on the west coast of Vancouver Island. Although he shipped out several foreign exports, the business was not successful and Stamp resigned as manager in 1863. The mill closed in 1864.

Stamp returned to England and arranged financing for the British Columbia and Vancouver Island Spar, Lumber and Sawmill Company. Back in British Columbia in 1865, the year Sewell Moody purchased the North Shore mill, Stamp applied for 100 acres (40.46 hectares) of land at $1 per acre for a sawmill, to be located on the government military reserve in what is now Stanley Park, just west of Brockton Point near Lumberman's Arch. A letter to the colonial secretary on June 3, 1865 from J.B. Launders, the surveyor assigned to establish Stamp's site, mentions one of the problems in locating this mill near the Squamish village of Whoi-Whoi, long occupied by First Nations people:

> On referring to the sketch appended it will be seen that the north-west corner occurs in the centre of an Indian village, (Whoi-Whoi), to clear which would only give the sawmill ninety acres. By the appearance of the soil, and debris, this camping ground is one of the oldest on the Inlet. The Indians appeared very distrustful of my purpose, and suspicious of my encroachment on their premises. The sawmill claim does not in any way interfere with the proposed site of the fort [planned for the reserve].[13]

The very strong tidal flow made the location unworkable for loading ships and storing logs on the water. Stamp received permission to purchase an alternative 100 acres on a point of land farther east along the shore that he described as halfway between the then mill site and the end of the new Douglas Road, which had recently been completed from New Westminster and ended near Second Narrows. This location was ideal for his shipping and towing needs. Today Centennial Pier occupies the site, at the north end of Dunlevy Avenue just east of the SeaBus terminal on the Vancouver waterfront.

When the mill machinery arrived from England, some parts were missing and Stamp was unable to cut lumber. He did, however, send a load of spars, logged by Jeremiah Rogers on English Bay, to Ireland in November 1865.

Captain Edward Stamp, circa 1870. He established Stamp's Mill on the south shore in 1865. *CVA PORT. P.264*

While waiting for his machinery and construction of the sawmill, Stamp had a towboat built in Victoria for $50,000, the 44.5-metre side-wheeler *Isabel*. Launched on July 25, 1866, she was the first towboat on Burrard Inlet and was kept busy towing sailing ships through First Narrows and carrying passengers and freight between Victoria and New Westminster. Moody's Mill also benefitted from the boat's availability.

In June 1867, the steam-powered Stamp's Mill (as it was commonly called) opened as the second sawmill on Burrard Inlet. The *British Columbian* reported that the mill was expected to turn out 30,000 board feet a day. The site had a boarding house and other accommodation for the workers and their families, but it was surrounded by shacks and makeshift huts. The area became known for drinking parties attended by sailors in port and the local men. Liquor was available at the rough wooden building housing the nearby Globe Saloon, whose proprietor was John "Gassy Jack" Deighton, and at the Brighton Hotel four kilometres east of the mill property.

In January 1869, Stamp resigned as manager after repeated disagreements with his backers. He had been active in politics and had become a member of the colony's first legislative council in 1866. After leaving the sawmill he opened a salmon cannery at Sapperton, but died of a heart attack in 1872.

Captain James Raymur took over as manager after Stamp's resignation. With the British owners evidently in financial trouble, the business was sold "by way of mortgage"[14] for $20,000 on May 31, 1869 to Dickson, De Wolf and Company of San Francisco, with arrangements to "make further advances from time to time." Financial problems continued. The business closed for a short time, and the mill was sold for $20,000 on February 23, 1870 to an English firm, Heatley and Company.

Reopened in August 1870 as Hastings Sawmill Company, commonly referred to as Hastings Mill, it was named after British Rear Admiral George Hastings, who at that time was in charge of the Esquimalt naval base on Vancouver Island. Probably management felt that the connection with such a distinguished name would help their business image.

Jeremiah Rogers

By 1868 six logging camps on Burrard Inlet were supplying logs and spars to the mills. Jeremiah "Jerry" Rogers, a New Brunswick logger, had begun cutting timber for Captain Stamp around the government reserve at Point

Grey and at English Bay in 1865, and supplied Stamp's Mill with world-renowned quality spars. Some of them were 180 feet (54.8 metres) long and had to be shortened to the regulation length of 150 feet (45.7 metres). Rogers' location on the south shore of the outer harbour made towing the timber to the mill a fairly easy task, as long as the tide was navigable through First Narrows. Captain Charles Henry Cates of North Vancouver recalled in 1958 stories of a nonmotorized method of moving the logs:

> Some of the old fellows used to tell me that they would wait until the tide was right, take a big rowboat and a couple of Kedge anchors [ahead of the boom] and go out and dredge their anchors along the bottom [winch the boom up to the anchor and repeat the process] and bring the boom over from English Bay in through the First Narrows and up to either the Hastings Mill or Moody's Mill without any tug at all, just with the rowboat and Kedge anchor. That was the way the timber was first moved, but of course it was not very long before the logging camps got a little too far away for that, and smaller harbour tugs...were used to bring the timber to the mill.[15]

On land, Rogers used oxen to haul the logs to the water along skid roads made of narrow logs laid crosswise. The teamster, or bull puncher, used a goadstick and cusswords to encourage the slow beasts to move along. The oxen's hooves were so thin that they were in difficulty on the rough logs and had to be shod. The men wrapped a broad leather band around the animals' bodies, winched them off the ground with a hand windlass, then nailed on the shoes. To make the hauling easier, a "greaser" swabbed the skids with dogfish oil, or added sand on a downhill slope to slow the logs. Waving his arm back and forth, he spread the oil liberally across the logs—and himself. The greaser always smelled so strongly that the rest of the loggers were only too happy to give him his own cabin.[16]

Looking for a faster method of hauling timber, Rogers heard about the Thomson Patent Road Steamers that had been brought from Scotland to move freight on the Cariboo Road. They were unsuccessful in the interior, because they were not powerful enough to handle the steep hills, were too heavy for the culverts and frightened the pack animals and stage horses. Rogers bought one in 1873, replaced its road wheels with railway wheels, and used it on a narrow track he built between the waterfront at Jericho to approximately the intersection of today's Arbutus Street and 33rd Avenue. The abandoned wheels rusted on the ground at the intersection of McDonald Street and 1st Avenue until 1907.[17] It was the first successful logging railway in BC, and with it Rogers ushered in a new logging era.

Rogers opened more logging camps as he needed new supplies of trees, and in 1872 he expanded to the North Arm of the Fraser River. His camps were in isolated locations; being a good-hearted employer, he used to hold a huge Christmas dinner at Jericho for all of his workers. The occasion was described by Wymond Walkem in an article, "Christmas Thirty-Eight Years Ago":

> Jerry Rogers was always proud of his Christmas dinners. They were high class, and put on the table with great ceremony. Sometimes a miniature barbecue would be furnished the boys, as the old man affectionately called his workers. Such a dinner!...Venison fat and juicy-sucking [sic] pigs and turkeys;...ducks and geese, both wild and tame, and a huge sirloin of George Black's [butcher] best bunch grass product. A monster plum pudding with a sprig of holly, and aflame with brandy, wound up the feast...Small stowage, Jerry called it. How the old man's eyes would twinkle as he watched the feast, and listened to the occasional sallies of wit which burst from different parts of the table.[18]

In August 1873 Rogers added an important asset to his business, the 22-metre sidewheeler towboat *Maggie Rogers*, named for his daughter Maggie. Supposedly she was the first steamer built on the inlet. At the same time he signed a contract to provide the largest spar shipment ever made from the colony.[19]

Jericho Beach on English Bay immortalizes the memory of Rogers; two plausible explanations for the name have been suggested. Initially he named his business Jerry & Co., which could have become Jerico, then Jericho. Alternatively, the site of his camp Jerry's Cove could have been shortened to Jericho. Rogers built a home at Jericho in about 1870; it was renovated by the Jericho Country Club in 1905 for use as its clubhouse.

This famous lumberman died of a stroke on October 24, 1879, at the age of 61.

The Small Businesses

Although several pre-emptions had been staked along the south shore and at False Creek since 1860, the wooded shores of Burrard Inlet were largely undisturbed in 1862 when three young men from Yorkshire, England, landed at New Westminster, intent on searching the Cariboo for gold.

John Morton, 28 years old, was strolling along a street in the small settlement when he spied a lump of coal in a shop window. Coming from a family of potters, he knew that coal often appeared in clay beds, and he was keen to visit the coal source. With the help of an aboriginal man he hiked and canoed to Coal Harbour, where he did find clay. He returned to New Westminster and he and his cousin Samuel Brighouse and a friend they had met on the ship, William Hailstone, first tried their luck in the Cariboo.

Unsuccessful at finding gold, they returned to Burrard Inlet and pre-empted 500 acres (202.34 hectares) of what later became district lot 185, taking in all of what today is the West End of Vancouver, reaching from Burrard Street to Stanley Park and from the inlet to English Bay. For this property they paid just over $1 per acre. The three men cleared some of the land and built a cabin and small barn at what is now Hastings Street, between Burrard and Thurlow. Besides operating a small farm, they became the first small-business operators on the inlet. They built a kiln and produced the first bricks made on the mainland of British Columbia. Their land became known as the Brickmakers' Claim.

Although Morton's grindstone attracted many aboriginals to the property, the brick business was slow because of the partners' distance from potential customers. They were dubbed

Royal Engineers' 1859 survey of the first land pre-emption that actually led to settlement on Burrard Inlet, the Brickmakers' Claim. The map notes the coal and clay deposits at lower left. *CVA FC 3847-49*

"the Three Greenhorns" because people generally felt the trio had wasted their money on useless land.

Needing money, they tried unsuccessfully to sell lots on their property, which they called New Liverpool, claiming that it would become a major city. After receiving their Crown grant of land, which was earned by living on and improving the property, Morton went to search for gold in California, Hailstone returned to England, and Sam Brighouse eventually became a man of means. They were truly Burrard Inlet's first white settlers.[20]

John "Navvy Jack" Thomas, a dark-haired Welshman, set up the first ferry service on Burrard Inlet in the spring of 1866. Having operated a riverboat on the Fraser River during the gold rush, he was well experienced on the water. He carried freight and passengers in his 9.14-metre sloop on a triangular route from the end of the Douglas Trail, which went from New Westminster to the inlet at Brighton, to Moodyville and then to Stamp's sawmill. When needed, he also used his rowboat to provide a private water-taxi service for one or two passengers.[21]

Captain James Van Bramer, no longer one of Sewell Moody's partners, offered an improved ferry service in October 1866 with his steamer the *Sea Foam*, following the same route as Navvy Jack Thomas. Although Stamp's Mill was only about 4.8 kilometres away, no trail existed between the mill and Brighton until 1876. The Burrard Inlet Stage Line carried passengers from New Westminster to Brighton two or three times a week by July 1867, and the service was upgraded to daily trips in October, adding to the *Sea Foam*'s business. In November that year ferry service was interrupted when the ship's steam pipes exploded while passengers were boarding, injuring three people. One year later a fire destroyed the upper works. Ferry service resumed on the *Sea Foam* the following spring. The New Westminster *Mainland Guardian* reported on April 13, 1870, that the boat was "quite a nice comfortable and airy conveyance."[22]

People were discovering that Burrard Inlet was an appealing place to visit, and the number of workers was increasing with the development of the mills and logging. Accommodation and entertainment were needed, and in August 1865, Oliver Hocking and Fred Houston recognized the business potential. They erected the inlet's first hotel on the south shore at the terminus of the Douglas Road, just west of the present Second Narrows and surrounded on three sides by forest. On August 12 the *British Columbian* promoted the enterprise:

Our outer harbour is rapidly rising in importance as well as attractiveness. Messrs. Hocking and Houston are shrewd enough to see that 'Brighton' will soon be a favorite resort for pleasure seekers, and they are making such improvements as will add to the natural attractiveness of the place. Pleasure boats are being provided, additions to the Brighton Hotel are going up, beautiful grounds and picturesque walks are being laid out and it is rapidly assuming the appearance of a fashionable watering-place. Even now it is almost daily visited by pleasure seekers. Amongst others, His Excellency the Governor rode over this week and honored the Brighton Hotel with a call, and appeared to take much interest in the improvements going forward and in contemplation.[23]

The resort area became known as New Brighton. Hocking and Houston contructed a wharf for the convenience of ferry passengers (and also built nearby an enclosure for hogs, which vied with the natural scents in "the beautiful grounds"). The name was changed in the spring of 1869 to Hastings Hotel, with a post office added. After Maximilien Michaud bought the hotel that year, it was always referred to as Maxie's.

The government offered surveyed lots at auction in the summer of 1869. With the beginnings of development around the hotel, the townsite's name was changed from Brighton to Hastings.

Navvy Jack Thomas was not discouraged when James Van Bramer put him out of business with the superior *Sea Foam*. He immediately started another, very profitable enterprise that was to make his name part of the construction community's vocabulary. From his office, a shack on the waterfront at Gastown, he took orders for a quality sand and gravel mixture used in making cement and still referred to today as "Navvyjack." He dug the gravel from the beach west of Capilano Creek, probably anchoring his sloop in Swy Wee Lagoon, a safe moorage near the boundary of the aboriginal settlement. Future settlers would refer to the tiny inlet as Ambleside Slough, and many years later the municipality of West Vancouver filled it in to make Ambleside Park, keeping the lagoon as the only remaining part of the slough.[24]

Yorkshireman John Deighton, commonly known as "Gassy Jack" because of his glib tongue, was one of the first entrepreneurs on the south shore and probably the best known. He had been unsuccessful with gold prospecting and ill health had cut short his career as a Fraser River pilot. He decided that the men at Stamp's Mill needed a reliable source of liquid refreshment and he hoped to finally find business success with a saloon. In New Westminster in September 1867 he loaded a canoe with his wife, a Squamish woman from Burrard Inlet, her mother and cousin, blankets, pots and pans, tools, two chairs, a yellow dog and one barrel of whiskey. Six dollars was all the money he had.

They landed on the inlet's south shore at an area the aboriginals called Luck-Lucky, meaning "grove of beautiful trees," just west of Stamp's Mill. The eager mill workers were happy to assist Deighton and within 24 hours built the first saloon, a 3.65-by-7.3-metre board-and-batten shack just a few metres from the high-tide line. From the front door two planks on the ground formed a sidewalk leading to the mill. Gassy Jack called his new establishment the Globe Saloon, after one of the same name that he had owned for a short time in New Westminster. He was in business, with the Union Jack flying from his roof. Building a floating log wharf, Deighton made his services available to thirsty workers arriving by boat and canoe from other parts of the inlet. He later imported fighting cocks to entertain and attract his customers.

The business was doing well, but he was only a squatter. His effort to lease land failed, so he decided to open another saloon on the north shore. The site he selected in 1869 was easily accessible from the water, but otherwise poorly located on land that was part of the Squamish village of Ustlawn west of Moodyville. His land application was turned down after the Squamish appealed to the government, and he returned to his Globe Saloon in Gastown, the small community named for him.

Surveyors were busy during late 1869 and early 1870 staking townsite lots, leaving the saloon sitting in the middle of the intersection at Carrall and Water Streets. On March 1, 1870, the government named the six-acre (2.42-hectare) site Granville, after Earl Granville, British colonial secretary. Jack bought lot 1, block 2 for $135, half down. Only two other lots sold, one to Ebenezer Brown, saloonkeeper, the other to Gregorio Fernandez, a merchant. They each paid $100, but everyone else thought the land too expensive.

Jack's new Deighton House had two storeys, a barroom and billiards room, and bedrooms on the top floor. A spreading maple tree shaded the veranda. On July 20, 1871, when British Columbia joined the Dominion of

Canada as a province, the first Dominion flag on the inlet flew from the hotel's roof. The business prospered but Jack's ill health continued. He died on May 29, 1875. The hotel stayed in business until the Great Fire of 1886 consumed the building along with the rest of the new City of Vancouver.[25]

Business development around the inlet, especially the sawmills, was attracting workers from many ethnic backgrounds, including Chinese, many of whom came north from the California gold rush, and Hawaiians (Kanakas). Some Squamish people, who already lived in villages on the shore or moved from Squamish, took advantage of the available jobs. The so-called "rancherie" east of Hastings Mill was the home of many aborigi-

Squamish huts built of cedar slabs at what is now Lost Lagoon but was then part of Coal Harbour, 1868. *CVA STPK. P.112 N.4#1*

nal mill workers. Ustlawn, meaning "head of the bay," was situated on the north shore, quite close to Moodyville's western boundary and convenient for employment at the mill. The aboriginals built the first mission church on the inlet there in 1869. It was consecrated as Our Lady of Seven Sorrows in April 1873, and was not replaced by a larger structure until 1884.[26]

Meanwhile, settlers were discovering the land around the inlet, and the first pre-emptions were filed for hopeful farmers who would log their land, perhaps earn some money from the mills, and watch the growth of the communities around the shore.

CHAPTER 3

THE FOUNDATIONS FOR MATURITY: 1870–90

*We had two strings of [15] Indian canoes, each string . . . towed by a
steam tug. In the centre of each canoe was a small mast, and a line of
[coloured] Chinese lanterns were suspended from the mast top to the
prows and sterns. After dark the two strings of canoes, with lanterns
lighted, were towed to and fro over the waters of the Inlet, passed,
repassed, and circled around. The bands on the warships were playing, the sea was glassy smooth, the crowd watching lined the shore,
and Water Street.*

—A.E. Beck, describing Dominion Day celebrations on Burrard Inlet
in *Early Vancouver*, vol. 1

The years between 1870 and 1890 transformed Burrard Inlet from
a quiet backwater to a roistering centre of trade. Moody's and
Hastings Mills were enlarged and modernized and production
increased as demand grew worldwide for the flawless timber being har-
vested around the inlet's shores.

The greatest impact on the area came from the completion of the
Canadian Pacific Railway (CPR) line across Canada. Port Moody sprang to
life as the original western terminus for the railway. When the CPR selected Granville townsite instead, that sleepy town came to life with loggers,
surveyors, builders and land speculators. In 1886 Granville became the
City of Vancouver, but shortly afterwards the entire site burned to the
ground. The CPR gobbled up thousands of hectares of surrounding land,
establishing itself as the pre-eminent influence on the city's early development. By 1890 a dramatic increase in foreign trade reflected the railway's

impact on the inlet. Trains were arriving from and leaving for eastern Canada, carrying passengers and cargoes from around the world.

Point Atkinson Lighthouse

Burrard Inlet's increasing popularity as a safe harbour, and the sawmills' proficient output in the inner harbour, attracted more and more ships. The strong tidal rips and dangerous rocky shores near the outer entrance at Point Atkinson encouraged the Canadian government to investigate the possibility of erecting a lighthouse in the vicinity. While Passage Island at the southern end of Howe Sound was the initial choice, Point Atkinson was selected due to its prime location at the mouth of the inlet.

In 1872 the Marine Department in Ottawa contracted Arthur Finney to build the lighthouse and lightkeeper's home for $4,250. Finney and his crew boarded the steamer *Leviathan* at Nanaimo in May 1874 and headed for their construction site. They took only one month to complete the building, but when the light itself was received from England it was not appropriate and another had to be ordered. Six months later, in January 1875, the correct light arrived and was installed.

Edwin Woodward, the first lightkeeper, his wife Ann and their two children landed at the inhospitable point on March 17 to begin their four-year sojourn. The light shone from a white wooden tower attached to the roof of their house. At 27.5 metres above water level, its beam could be distinguished by ships as far as 22.5 kilometres distant.[1] The family's breathtaking views of the Strait of Georgia's rolling waters and the green islands in Howe Sound, and the peacefulness of the pristine forest, made their location appear to be idyllic. However, it was also lonely. The nearest social life was in Moodyville and Granville, reachable only by water. Ann Woodward was the first white woman to live in what is now West Vancouver and during her stay she saw only one other woman, a Squamish who passed in a canoe.

On April 25, 1876, her husband delivered their third child. Edwin wrapped his new 1.4-kilogram son, James Atkinson Woodward, in a blanket and laid the tiny baby aside while he tended to his wife. About five hours later Ann got out of bed and washed and dressed the baby. They were alone and no other assistance was available.

Edwin had to leave the family alone at intervals to row to Moodyville or Granville on business. Ann remained behind to keep the light working.

Their intermittent social life revolved around the steamers, sailboats and canoes that passed. Captain White of the tug *Etta White* often dropped off mail, and the government steamer *Sir James Douglas* called with supplies. James Woodward later liked to tell the story about a day when his mother was standing on the rocks and two men in a canoe passed by. They noticed her and one remarked, "My God, there's a white woman."

Edwin Woodward kept a garden, and often shot deer for meat. He arranged for the purchase of a cow that was delivered by being dumped overboard from a tugboat and pulled to shore, splashing and bawling, by means of a rope attached to its horns. Deer from the woods became attracted to the cow and would wander in to join it in the stable.

The loneliness became overwhelming for Ann, and she and her husband decided to leave their post in 1879. They were succeeded by the R.G. Wellwoods. In 1939 Hiram, the eldest Woodward child, was interviewed by Major J.S. Matthews of the Vancouver Archives and shared his memories of his family's departure. He recalled that his mother was very upset when Mr. Wellwood would pay her only $5 for the cow, but there was no other choice. However, when the new lightkeeper offered a mere 25 cents for her down pillows she refused, laid them out on the rocks and watched the feathers blow away and settle on the water (in fact, not far from where the Squamish had sprinkled their feathers in honour of Captain Vancouver 87 years before). The Wellwoods stayed only one year, then left because of the isolation and the constant wash-wash-wash of the waves on the rocks.

Walter Erwin took his family to the lighthouse in the fall of 1880, and they remained for 30 years, though in their early days the isolation was no less severe. On one occasion his wife Rhoda became seriously ill. Her husband sent a note by means of a passing canoe to a young married nurse, Emily Susan Patterson, a resident of Moodyville. Emily's granddaughter, Muriel Crakanthorp, later wrote a description of the event:

Shortly after five o'clock on a very stormy day in the fall of 1883, two Indians came to the door with a note from Mr. Walter Erwin asking my grandmother to come as soon as possible as Mrs. Erwin was dangerously ill and in great need of help. Grandma rushed upstairs and got her things together, and went down to the Indian ranch. The masters of the "Etta White" and "Leonora" having refused to put out, the Indians put her into a canoe with blankets, and put out. Two Indians went with her. Some begged her not to go as by this time a regular gale was blowing, but she knew nothing of fear. They made it as far as Skunk Cove, now Caulfeilds, but couldn't reach Point Atkinson as the gale was terrible just there, so they had to tramp from there, the distance being about a mile to the lighthouse through thick forest and rough hills. There was a very small path, but all this took place after dark, and it was very black. One Indian went ahead of her and one behind her and they made the Point Atkinson lighthouse after about four hours from the time they left Moodyville, none the worse for their trip. When she arrived Mrs. Erwin shouted "I knew you'd come; I knew you'd come". Mrs. Erwin scarcely knew her.[2]

Emily Patterson's bravery inspired Nora Duncan of Vancouver in 1936 to write a 14-stanza poem, "The Heroine of Moodyville."

The Erwins' problems were solved for the time being, but the future was to bring almost insurmountable difficulties for them at their isolated station.

The North Shore Pioneers

Although Point Atkinson's lightkeepers were isolated from the social life around the inner harbour, they did have one distant neighbour on the same shore. Navvy Jack Thomas had purchased a 160-acre (64.7-hectare) pre-emption for $160 from James Blake, a stevedore at Moodyville, in 1874 while the Point Atkinson lighthouse was still waiting for its light. His thickly wooded waterfront property extended approximately from today's 16th Street in West Vancouver west to Navvy Jack Point and north to Haywood Avenue, offering convenient access to the beach for his gravel-supply business. He reportedly sold his share in the Granville Hotel and concentrated on building his home and a barn on the North Shore.

The best fir and cedar on the market were available to him from the nearby mills, and the quality construction of his house has endured to the present day. It was painted white, with a large front porch and gingerbread trim. Now the property of the District of West Vancouver, it still stands at 1768 Argyle Avenue, a little south and west of its original location. Navvy Jack Thomas and his wife Row-i-a, granddaughter of Squamish Chief Ki-ep-i-lano, and their four children lived there for many years. They planted fruit trees and developed a vegetable garden, even attempting to grow tobacco and sugar cane. A pipe carried water from a nearby creek to the house, barn and garden.

Navvy Jack's close proximity to First Narrows proved to be an unexpected advantage to navigation. The sternwheeler *Yosemite* and her passengers were caught in heavy fog the morning of May 24, 1888. The captain decided to drop anchor and wait until visibility cleared before attempting the tricky passage between Prospect Point and the Capilano River shoreline. Suddenly the sound of a rooster crowing pierced the fog-blanketed air. Obtaining a bearing on the location, the captain lifted anchor and safely made his way to the dock at the inner harbour.

The Thomases had no close neighbours, as pre-emptions on all the North Shore lots had been suspended until the route for the new Canadian Pacific Railway was established, to prevent speculators from taking over the land. Applications for lots then flourished along the waterfront on the North Shore. Navvy Jack sold 120 acres (48.6 hectares) of his property in 1893, living on the remaining 40 acres (16.1 hectares).

Although he had played an important part in the life of early Burrard Inlet, he died in the town of Barkerville. Caught in the depression of the 1890s, he had decided to mortgage his home and become part of a business venture in the interior mining town. His land was sold to J.C. Keith (for whom Keith Road on the North Shore is named) in 1905 to clear the mortgage. The following year John Lawson purchased the property and he lived there for many years.[3]

During the 1860s and until 1878, when the pre-emption ban on North Shore properties was imposed, pioneers pre-empted several of the densely wooded waterfront lots there. One of the early settlers, John "Jock" Linn, a Scott, had come to British Columbia in 1859 as a Royal Engineer and worked under Colonel Richard Moody, building roads and clearing land. He received military and Crown land grants on February 10, 1871 for district lot 204, 150 acres (60.7 hectares) of land he had originally pre-empted in 1867 on the east side of what later became Lynn Creek, named for him. Old maps show that Lynn Creek was called Fred's Creek at that time, named for Frederick Howson, who had been the first pre-emptor of the same land in 1863.

The Linns built a small whitewashed board-and-batten cottage about 16 metres east of the creek near the inlet's marshy shoreline. Sitting on their front veranda they could look west along the inlet. Their children all attended school at nearby Moodyville and the family developed their land into a producing farm with a barn for their cows and horses, an orchard, a vegetable garden, and chickens. John Linn used to row to Moodyville and the south shore to sell his produce. After her alcoholic husband died in 1876, at the age of 55, Mrs. Linn continued to run and manage the farm with her children's help. She sold it for $21,000 in 1896.[4]

She had not been without family problems. Old Jack Green was a pioneer settler and store owner on Savary Island near Powell River when he and his helper, Tom Taylor, were shot to death in Green's cabin in the fall of 1893. Although the men's rifles lay beside them, appearing to have been the cause of their deaths, the police soon realized that murder had been committed and began a manhunt along the coast for someone known to the dead men. Hugh Linn, son of John Linn, was identified as the man who had purchased several bottles of liquor at a pub in the coastal town of Lund in Green's name the day after the murders. Other evidence linked Hugh to the murders, and the police finally located him living on an island in American territory with an aboriginal woman and her child. The American and BC police successfully raided his cabin, handcuffed him and took him to jail.

The woman claimed he had been keeping her against her will, and she and her son became willing witnesses for the prosecution. Linn was found guilty and sentenced to hang in New Westminster. He had apparently coveted treasure that Green was rumoured to have buried near his cabin. Over the years many treasure hunters have dug up the ground around the abandoned building, but no treasure has surfaced.[5]

The Linns' closest neighbours other than the people at Moodyville were the Burr family, whose land bordered the east shore of Seymour Creek. Hugh Burr, an Irishman, had pre-empted district lot 193 in 1867. He, his wife and their large family of daughters lived close to flat, grassy fields near the shore. They developed the first dairy farm on the inlet. Burr rowed across to the south shore to deliver milk and butter to Maxie's Hotel at Hastings, water conditions permitting. Moodyville, and the crews of ships loading lumber at its wharf, also provided a good market for his fruit, vegetables and dairy products. Joseph Burr Jr., a member of Hugh's family, had pre-empted the next lot to the east in 1867, and Hugh Burr obtained a second piece of land just east of that. The Burrs then owned all of the shoreline between Seymour Creek and the Burrard aboriginal settlement.

Meanwhile William Bridge, a former English seaman, pre-empted DL 271, about one kilometre west of Moodyville near the Mission aboriginal community. He planted an orchard and developed a pasture for cows, but it was not his dairy farm that caused ripples of concern at Moody's Mill. He was also selling liquor from his house. Sewell Moody and his partners George Dietz and Hugh Nelson were committed to preventing the sale of liquor on or near their land, and on March 16, 1874 they wrote to Robert Beaven, a government representative and future premier:

> A man named W. Bridge who has a license to retail liquor at his place about a mile below our mills is desirous of obtaining permission to build a trail from his place through our property to our mills and we have declined allowing him the privilege as we allow no liquor to be sold at our mills and do not wish in any way to encourage or facilitate liquor being brought here...We are apprehensive that he may apply for a road to be laid off through our land and we wish to protest against the granting of the same...

A note added to the letter mentioned that Bridge did not make an application.[6] After Bridge's death in 1883, his land passed to Tom Turner, his nephew, and became known as Tom Turner's Farm. Just to the west of the

Tom Turner's cottage on the shore just west of the present foot of Lonsdale Avenue in North Vancouver, circa 1890. He had an orchard and barn and sold his produce to Moodyville. *CVA OUT. P.225 N.157*

south end of the present Lonsdale Avenue, Turner built a cottage with a cedar-shake roof, and a barn, and developed a good-sized orchard and garden. He sold his produce at Moodyville and Hastings Mill, but his farm became best known to early residents as a pleasant picnic area. During the next few years, land all along the shore to the west was pre-empted.

As white settlement spread around the inlet, aboriginal people grew concerned at the alienation of what they considered to be their land. In 1876 the Canadian and BC governments appointed the Joint Commission for the Settlement of Indian Reserves in the Province of British Columbia. The commission began its work by revising and affirming 82 small reserves that had been laid out in areas of white settlement.[7]

In the winter of 1876–77 the commissioners visited Burrard Inlet, where the existing white settlements and sawmills prevented any extension of reserve land there: the commissioners were under instruction not to disturb established settlements. Instead they formalized six existing Squamish sites: Mission No. 1, 38 acres (15.4 hectares, now at Mosquito Creek in North Vancouver, originally gazetted on November 25, 1869); Seymour Creek No. 2, 147 acres (59.5 hectares); Reserve No. 3, 275 acres (111.3 hectares, now the Tsleil-Waututh reserve near Dollarton, also orig-

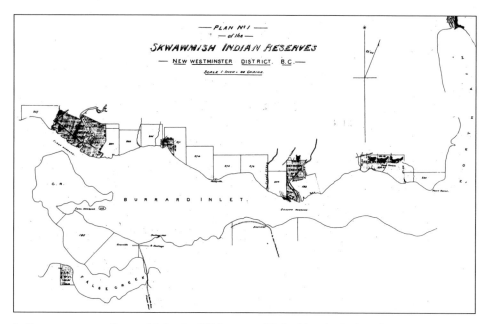

Indian reserves on Burrard Inlet in 1880, as established by the Indian Reserves Commissioners.

inally gazetted on November 25, 1869); Mesliloet Stream (now Indian River) No. 4, 33 acres (13.3 hectares, at the north end of Indian Arm and then called In Lai La Wa Tash); Kahpillahno Creek No. 5 (Homulchesun), 444 acres (179.7 hectares); and at the village of Snauq, No. 6, 80 acres (32.4 hectares, on the south shore at the mouth of False Creek). On an 1880 survey map no reserve was shown at Stanley Park, although a large midden had been found there. To compensate the Squamish people with more land in lieu of expanding their existing communities, the commissioners allotted two other reserves at the north end of Howe Sound in unsettled areas on traditional Squamish land, one of 2,000 acres (809 hectares) and the other 14,000 acres (5,666 hectares).[8]

Moodyville

The community of Moodyville was developing a broader social life and increasing lumber production. In January 1869 the first two-storey building on the North Shore was completed. The top floor became the home of Mount Hermon Masonic Lodge No. 493; many of the administrators at the mill were Masons. The lower floor became a community centre named the "Mechanics Institute—Burrard Inlet" and housed a library, reading room and museum. The minute book shows that on January 13, 1869, members elected the first officers and established rules. The joining fee was $5, with a 50-cent monthly charge.

The library was open each Saturday evening for two hours; the room was otherwise available free of charge for preachers of the gospel, of any denomination. George Dietz's donations to the library illustrate the academic content available to members; a handwritten list records "the Bible, Comstock's Philosophy, Comstock's Mineralogy, Hitchcock's Geology, Chemistry and Electricity, Chambers Manual of Chemistry, Biography of a Self-Taught Man, 2 volumes, Signers of the Declaration of Independence, Life and Essays of Franklin, Combs Moral Philosophy and Natural History of the Human Species." Sewell Moody was given $100 to buy books on his next trip to San Francisco. Papers and magazines were also purchased at regular intervals.

By February 1872 the institute had 28 paying members, all men, and the provincial government was providing a yearly allowance of $125. In 1875 members paid a librarian an annual salary of $125. An entry in February 1877 emphasized that liquor was still not welcome at Moodyville.

At least two instances were noted of liquor being brought into the reading room and handed around during the previous year; it was moved and resolved "that no liquor of any kind be brought into this Institution, or handed around by any person whatever, under any pretence." The last minutes appeared on April 12, 1884,[9] although the British Columbia Directory for 1885 reported that there were 56 members and the library contained 600 volumes.

Social life for the women revolved around their daily personal interactions and weekly church services. Although Saturday dances at the hotel at Hastings townsite were a high point of the week, they were only for "the boys" (the single workers) and their lady friends. No white "ladies" attended.[10]

John Bell, who lived in Moodyville for several years, recorded his memories of his mother's and grandmother's daily activities:

My grandmother had a large and a small spinning wheel with which she spun the yarn used for making sweaters and socks for the men. The job of carding the wool with two hand carders was uninteresting to me—I did not like that job but grandma said, "How would you like to go bare footed, or without a warm sweater? You finish that bunch of wool and you can go and get me some chips for kindling".

In the room where the spinning wheels were kept there was a wooden frame which lay on two wooden horses where quilts were made. A "crazy quilt" was one made up of any odd pieces of cloth sewn together for the top, somewhat on the order of a jigsaw puzzle. Between the upper and lower covers—carded sheeps wool was carefully layed—then it was quilted-sewn criss-cross up and down or tucked every 4 or 5 inches apart. Selected material with designed border and pattern, well chosen colours—a generous amount of wool and you have something to be proud of—well named "a Comforter".

Floor rugs were "hooked" on strong sacking or canvas. These were made from old clothes or remnants saved up. The cloth was cut into narrow strips and made into a "crazy rug" but usually in design or pattern of some sort. A rug to be proud of and fit for a sitting room had to have a special design, such as a dog lying on a green field in the centre and an artistic mosaic border. For such a rug one needs to dye the material.

Bear and panther also make good floor rugs but for some reason most of the women did not like [them]. "Smelly things—can't wash them".[11]

In 1869 the mill foreman, George Haynes, brought his sister Laura from Bangor, Maine to Moodyville to start the first school in the newly formed Burrard Inlet School District. A wood-frame building was constructed on the "Sawdust Pile" near the shore, the first school on Burrard Inlet. The schoolhouse was so close to the mill building that often classes had to be cancelled for the 13 pupils because of the smoke from burning sawmill refuse seeping in under the door and windows.

The next year a new building was constructed farther away. Mrs. Murray Thain took over in 1871 as teacher. In 1874 the school inspector reported that "... the teacher is most energetic in the performance of her duties and exercises great influence for good over the minds and conduct of the pupils." That year Mrs. Thain taught 39 children, most five to 16 years old and 12 of other ages.[12] The pupils were mostly white, aboriginal and Kanaka (Hawaiian).

A fire, the dread of every sawmill owner, cast a pall over Christmas 1873. The *Victoria Daily Standard* reported on December 23:

> Telegrams were received in town yesterday announcing that Messrs. Moody, Dietz and Nelson's lumber mill, Burrard Inlet, was destroyed by fire at four o'clock yesterday morning. The machinery is saved, so that the loss will not amount to more than from five to ten thousand dollars. There is no insurance.

Fortunately the water-powered mill was saved and continued to operate. The men rebuilt the steam mill and had it ready for business by the end of May 1874. The machinery from the old British man-of-war *Sparrowhawk*, which Moody had purchased to use in a tugboat, had been sitting on the dock and was installed in the new mill. The engine performed admirably for the mill's lifetime.

Sewell Moody left Victoria as a passenger on SS *Pacific* on November 4, 1875, heading for San Francisco on business. Off Cape Flattery his ship collided with another steamer and sank with the loss of nearly 300 people, leaving only two survivors. A few weeks later a piece of ship's timber washed up on the shore at Victoria. Written on it in pencil was: "S.P.

Moody all lost." Friends identified the handwriting as that of Sewell Moody. British Columbia had lost one of its leading businessmen.

At Moodyville the business continued to expand under restructured leadership. In April 1876 a newspaper reported:

> The Mill itself is a mammoth building upwards of 300 feet in length, 290 feet of which is roofed over and covered for the greater part with corrugated iron. The interior presents a complete network of shafts, bands and wheels by which the machinery is kept in motion, the while being driven by a powerful steam engine, which formerly belonged to H.M.S. Sparrowhawk. About 30 saws were in operation, and the way they converted immense logs of wood into lumber of various lengths and thicknesses was something marvelous. Over 100 men are employed immediately about the mill, and not less than 800 persons find employment in one

Moody, Dietz & Nelson's Burrard Inlet sawmill, also known as Moody's Mill, circa 1882. The sawmill is on the left and some employees' and managers' homes in the centre. *CVA OUT. P.96 N.32*

way or another in connection with this establishment . . . [there is] an extensive machine shop where repairs of the machinery are effected . . . The daily average output of lumber is about 60,000 feet and the aggregate amount cut and shipped from the 1st of January to the 5th of April, inclusive, was 4,118,481 feet.[13]

That year, 1876, mill management purchased the tug *Etta White*, one of the first steam tugs in British Columbia to have a propeller drive. She took over the *Isabel*'s former job of towing ships to and from the inlet and moving log booms.

On February 4, 1882, electric lights shone in Moodyville for the first time, reflecting across the waters of Burrard Inlet to Hastings Mill. At a cost of approximately $4,000, 10 lamps, or burners, equal to 2,000 candlepower were installed, all using direct current. They were the old carbon type on which an electric spark jumped 1.3 centimetres between the carbon sticks. Moodyville boasted the first onshore electric lights north of San Francisco. The innovation was so impressive that a delegation of the mayor and council from Victoria visited the mill to observe the lights in operation.[14]

The next few years were a period of successful growth for the Moodyville proprietors. The town was growing with the addition of the Terminus Hotel, started by Henry Hogan in 1874. A great deal of pressure must have been exerted on the mill managers to allow a pub on their land. The hotel was taken over by William Powers, a white-bearded gentleman, and his wife in the 1880s. They did their best to keep the hotel and bar respectable, but had difficulty controlling sailors who had been at sea for several months.[15] The building was also a headquarters for the steam ferry boats on the inlet.

The North Shore's first named streets lined the mill's shoreline. They were The Rookeries (very basic Chinese shanties) and Kanaka Row (homes built on pilings for the Kanaka workers). The *Daily World* reported on November 18, 1895 that a group of Chileans working at Moodyville had decided to build cabins on the foreshore on Dominion land to avoid a $5 tax imposed by the mill's management. They named it North Valparaiso.

The mill's ownership changed several times over the years and in 1891 an English company, the Lonsdale Estate, took it over. That year the business produced nearly 20 million board feet of lumber,[16] a great deal of it for

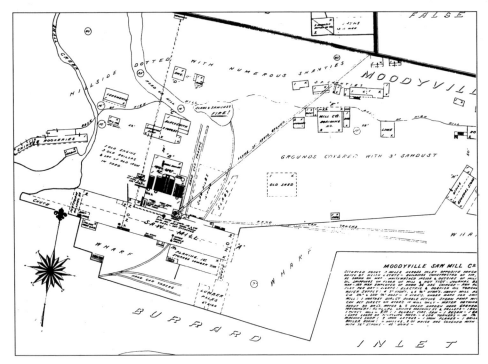

A map of the Moodyville sawmill showing The Rookeries (shacks, centre left), sawdust and wood slab piles, wharves and outbuildings. *Dakins Fire Insurance map, November 1889*

world export. Closed in 1901, the mill was sold the next year to John Hendry of Royal City Planing Mills.[17] In 1916 the mill burned down, and over the years modern development has eliminated all traces of an unforgettable era in Burrard Inlet history.

South Shore Pioneers

Before the mid-1880s, great walls of cedar and fir enclosed on three sides the clearing that comprised the town of Granville. The trees bordered Hastings Street on the south, Cambie Street on the west and Carrall Street to the east. The waters of Burrard Inlet lapped the edges of Water Street at high tide for four blocks along the shore. Undergrowth, stumps and logs littered the damp ground amid patches of luxuriant skunk cabbage. Just east of Carrall Street, at what is today Columbia Street, the waters at high tide during June and December flowed freely across the narrow tongue of land to actually join Burrard Inlet and False Creek.[18]

Many of the south shore residents were small-business proprietors. Along Water Street, stores, hotels and saloons abutted the water, often with pilings supporting floors that projected over the high-tide line. Their wharves reached out to attract customers. In 1875, of the 10 buildings along the shore four sold liquor. George Black, a Scot, had a try at the gold rush, then moved to Granville in 1871 and opened its first butcher shop, called the Granville Market, on the north side of Water Street. An early resident recalled:

> ...poor indeed would be the Scotch dance or picnic if Black, in Highland dress, were not there to give the affair a 'go'... I can see Black now in my mind's eye as, with a preliminary twist to his curled moustache, he would lean, one hand on his hip and the other resting on his knife, whose point was pressed into the block, telling some amusing story about something he had seen or heard of late.[19]

Black built his shop with convenience in mind. He slaughtered cattle and pigs on the rear deck and was able to lower their carcasses on a crane to his boat underneath. He and a helper rowed out to ships in the harbour to deliver orders or sell fresh cuts, which he sliced on the spot using the butcher's block on his boat. He allowed his hogs the freedom of the beach, where they could snort through the mud for shellfish and garbage. After many complaints from his neighbours about unattractive odours, he built an abattoir on False Creek. He kept a pet bear chained outside, but after it caused several problems he shipped it to Victoria on the steamship *Beaver*. When the bear got loose on board during the trip, several men

Granville circa 1884, showing the businesses along the shore before the Great Fire. *CVA DIST. P.30*

tried for a few hair-raising minutes to subdue it. Finally successful, they bound it securely and the boat continued its journey.

Ever the entrepreneur, George built the second hotel at Hastings, Brighton House, a two-storey building at the north end of the road from New Westminster. Two or three hectares of grass around it became popular as a cricket or baseball field. Often barn dances followed the games in the evening at a dance hall on the property.[20] In August 1884, Black held a

Brighton House, George Black's hotel near the shore at the north end of the road to New Westminster, circa 1888. *VPL 151*

ball for 170 people that the *Colonist* said was "one of the largest gatherings of youth and beauty that has ever been at Burrard Inlet."[21] George performed a solo Scottish dance in his Highland dress. He earned well his informal title "Laird of Hastings."

Black's neighbour to the east was Alex McCrimmon, whose Sunnyside Hotel at the corner of Water and Carrall Streets faced Gassy Jack Deighton's hotel, now known as the Deighton Hotel. McCrimmon had run a boot and shoe business at Granville, but realized that liquor drew more customers. The rear section of his hotel rested on piles over the water and a trapdoor in the floor allowed groceries, clothing and other articles to be raised from or lowered to canoes and boats underneath.[22] In 1873 McCrimmon built out into the inlet a large float that had ample space for thirsty boaters to tie up.

Waterfront at Granville in 1885, showing a long pier leading to the Sunnyside Hotel and the government float on left. *CVA WAT. P.39 N.20*

In 1874 William Jones and Joseph Mannion, a gentlemanly Irishman, purchased Ebenezer Brown's saloon on Water Street. Renovating and enlarging it as the Granville Hotel, they advertised it as one of the best hotels on the mainland. Mannion sold his interest in the hotel in 1886 and became one of the City of Vancouver's first aldermen.

Another of Granville's buildings was its first jail, built in 1871 on Water Street, with two cells. Constable Jonathan Miller's house was next door and Captain James Raymur, manager of Hastings Mill, was appointed magistrate. Miller was joined later by Constable Handy. Their policing duties were not too onerous, but one event made headlines.

On June 12, 1872, the marshy shoreline skirting the new town of Granville echoed with the shriek of the mill saws, the thumps and bangs of the sawn lumber and the raucous voices of the workers. The wharves were busy that afternoon, with canoes and boats departing and arriving and longshoremen loading lumber and spars onto a large sailing ship, when two small

Joseph Mannion operated the Granville Hotel in what would later become Vancouver. *British Columbia Directory, 1885* boats neared the shore. A keen-eyed worker noticed that their cargoes were anything but normal and notified Constables Miller and Handy. The police officers saw that the boats were filled with personal belongings evidently stolen from isolated settlers along the coast. They tried to arrest the two men in the boats, but the pair drew guns and headed out into the harbour.

The constables followed them, accompanied by Tompkins Brew, Burrard Inlet's revenue officer and constable. That night, in the darkness, they found the thieves on the beach at Jericho. The brigands, named Brown and Shipley, fired their rifles and Constable Miller returned shots with his revolver, injuring one of the men. The police retrieved both boats and their contents, but the rascals escaped.

Magistrate Raymur wrote a letter the next day to the government offices at New Westminster to report the incident, warning:

Give notice at once to the settlers at the North Arm [of the Fraser River] where they may go for provisions and to the Police at New Westminster. I have offered $50.00 for their capture which please justify my doing.

This incident caused great excitement and discussion among the residents on the inlet and evoked letters to the editors of the Victoria and New Westminster newspapers. It became well known as "the Battle of Jerico."[23]

Once the road from New Westminster and Hastings was pushed through to Granville in 1877, the arrival of the stage always brought the residents of the quiet town to life. In a cloud of dust the four horses galloped in and stopped with a flourish on Water Street between the Sunnyside and Deighton Hotels. Muriel Crakanthorp recounted to Major Matthews her mother's memories:

...the [nine] passengers would all get out, and be "sized up" by the assembled onlookers; everybody wanted to know who'd come in by the stage; ...the fare was one dollar, or two dollars return...the mail was thrown down, and hurried into the post office...Then the stage and horses would trot around to Trounce Alley [at the back of the Deighton Hotel]. The trip from New Westminster took about two hours, and the road was rough. Mother says the trip over was always an ordeal for her; she got "seasick"; lots of people did. Mother says Mrs. Lynn [sic] of Lynn

Creek, if she could not have the front seat with the driver she would walk to New Westminster and back rather than ride on the stage; she got so desperately seasick on the stage.

Lewis had that stage and...he had several drivers, and one was Mr. Green, with a long beard down to his middle, and he chewed tobacco, and he would talk, talk, talk, and the juice got on his beard; and the ladies were feeling squeamish.[24]

Outside the four-block-long clearing at Granville, people chose various sites for their homes. Between Hastings Mill and Hastings townsite a group of shacks housed a collection of disreputable characters who squatted on the land. They called it "Tar Flats."

Along the shore of what is now Stanley Park several men of much better character squatted with their families. Tompkins Brew, previously a government agent, and his aboriginal wife chose a location east of Deadman's Island. A longshoreman, Johnny Baker, lived with his wife at the present Nine O'Clock Gun site. Joseph (Silvia) Simmons built a house between Deadman's Island and Brockton Point and moved there with his aboriginal wife and their children after selling their grocery store/saloon in Granville. He made dogfish oil and sold it for 25 cents a gallon. He built a sloop; his daughter, Mrs. Walker, later recalled that as a little girl she helped him by holding the boards and handing him nails.[25]

During the 1820s the Hudson's Bay Company had begun to bring Kanakas to the Northwest Coast as servants. ("Kanaka" in the Hawaiian language means "person," or human being.) Some worked in the north of what is now BC at Fort St. James, and others were assigned to Fort Langley on the Fraser River. Later, as employment opportunities developed, many men moved to other locations and tended to settle near other Kanaka families. Most Kanaka men married aboriginal women, forming a bond with the Natives. The female children of Kanaka/aboriginal families usually married whites and became part of the white society.

Eihu, a Kanaka man, moved with his family to Hastings Mill after it opened. In 1869 they moved west toward Coal Harbour and were the first family to settle at the north end of what is now Denman Street, later the site of the Westin Bayshore hotel. Their cabin and outbuildings were the beginning of the "Kanaka Rancherie" and their fruit trees inspired its alternative name, "the Cherry Orchard." Gradually more Kanaka squatters built homes above the shore. Most of the men worked at Hastings Mill and their children followed a path beside the water to attend school there.

The Kanakas' biggest community in BC was on the Gulf Islands, but the second-largest was in Moodyville. By the 1890s, 10 or more Kanaka families lived at the North Shore mill site on the street known as Kanaka Row.[26]

Hastings Mill

"What is the meaning of this aggregation of filth? Aye, aye; and I'll make the beggars mind me. I will not permit a running sore to fasten itself on an industry entrusted to my care!"[27]

Thus Captain James Raymur, a polished man, established his policy as the new manager of Stamp's Mill on the south shore in 1869. Apparently Captain Stamp, who had left the company that year, had allowed an unsightly accumulation of waste material from the mill's operation to build up around the site. A group of aboriginals, Kanakas and roustabouts occupied shanties on the property with their dogs, cats, pigs and chickens. Raymur had a bunkhouse built for the single men and cottages for married men, and the Kanakas moved to Coal Harbour and their eventual Kanaka Rancherie.

Raymur didn't stop with an external cleanup. Very aware of the social developments at Moodyville, he soon established a library for his own employees and called it the New London Mechanics Institute, shortly afterward changing it to Hastings Institute.

Captain Raymur could not control the use of liquor at the mill to the same extent as the Moodyville owners because of his business's location so close to Gastown with its established popular drinking establishments. The bars attracted a very mixed crowd of men, many on the fringe of the law. On August 9, 1873, Raymur and two justices of the peace, Jerry Rogers and Coote Chambers, had printed in the *Mainland Guardian* a notice that stated their intention to oppose any request for a saloon liquor licence on the inlet that showed its owner planned to stay open after midnight or permit Sunday card playing.

In 1877, when the road between Hastings and Granville finally opened, hotels at New Westminster and Hastings became more accessible and were a distance away from Raymur's influence.

Born in Halifax and a loyal Canadian, Raymur encouraged and supported the community-strengthening Dominion Day celebrations that attracted crowds. Competitions in running, jumping, catching greased pigs and climbing greased poles preceded an outstanding free dinner provided by Raymur and other prominent citizens.

Although sawmill companies commonly established stores for the use of their employees, Hastings Mill Store—built strongly of red cedar and Douglas fir—endured and prospered far beyond the general life of such a facility. The storekeeper in 1870 was Richard Henry Alexander. In 1872 he became the mill accountant and postmaster of the new Granville Post Office located in the store.

The longer the store was in operation, the more varied its merchandise. Calvert Simson was the storekeeper for many years, and in 1950 he wrote for the Vancouver Archives a detailed description of the goods he had carried:

A general line of groceries, tobacco, cigars, pipes, men's suits at first brought out from England with the pants so high cut one hardly needed a vest, overalls, underwear made of flannel all wool, branded Mission, in blue and red colour, the red in big demand as a supposed cure for rheumatism, these were made in Victoria, also a fleecy cotton underwear with a nap, shirts, socks and a line of men's rough work shoes, both laced and elastic sides, made in Victoria, also some men's fine boots, men's hats and caps, some ladies wool piece goods, Indian shawls, cotton prints, grey and white cotton...A line of patent medicines was carried such as Thomas Electric Oil, pain killer, Peruna, Pains Celery Compound, these two latter being 75% alcohol were in much demand in the camps after a big drunk, Jamaica Ginger not allowed to be sold to Indians as Government claimed they used it to make liquor, St. Jacob's oil, Wizard Oil, scented hair oil, red rouge for Indian face colouring...In passing the storekeeper was called on to give first aid to any minor mill accidents. A line of tinware bought from a New Westminster tinsmith, English heavy, white, unbreakable crockery for camp use, a line of hardware such as rope, axes, single and double bit, saws, nails, files, axe handles, locks, hinges etc., oxbows, ox shoes, hickory goad sticks for the bull puncher who was very particular as to the quality.

...We always had a standing order for 50 tons of crushed barley for the oxen. An order sent November 19th, 1872 called for 2 gross of Preston and Merrills Yeast Powder, 6 cases Lard, 5 brls. Extra Golden Syrup, 10 x 5 gal. kegs Golden Syrup, 15 kegs Nails, 50 mats Yellow Manilla Sugar...Bundles, lanterns with double globes, (no cold blast lanterns in those days), at night nearly everyone carried one, the lighting system in Granville being about four posts with a glassed-in coal oil lamp on top of poles, on Water Street between Carrall and Abbot in front of Deighton, Sunnyside, Granville and Gold Hotels...Matches were the sulphur smelly kind put up in blocks in 5 gal. coal oil tins, matches were made in Victoria, canned Sockeye Salmon put up in one pound tall tins, the bellies salted were sold in kits 1/2 barrels and barrels, only the bellies were used, the other part thrown away, no other species of

Ox teams skid logs from the forest to the water at a logging camp near Granville, circa 1882. *VPL 19767*

salmon are canned, a lot of corned beef and pork in barrels was sent to the logging camps, also green salt sides of bacon to make pork and beans, fresh meat was sent to camps only when a tug went after a boom of logs, fresh pork was plentiful as each camp usually had a lot of hogs feeding on the swill. Ham and eggs were only supplied at Easter.

Loggers felling a Douglas fir near Kitsilano in 1885 stand on springboards that raise them above the wider tree base. *CVA TR.37*

... The B.C. currency in those days was 20, 10, 5 and 2-1/2 dollar gold and 50, 25 and 10 cent silver coins, bank notes were not in common use, and not favoured by the Indians ... The store did a big business with the camps and settlers up the coast, Indians and the mill men.

The mill help was paid so much a month and board, the single men eating in the cook house, the married men who boarded themselves received $10.00 per month in lieu of board; wages were low, hours an 11-1/2 hour day, but all there was to do was work, eat and sleep, Sundays off and three holidays a year, New Years, Christmas day and July 1st, with four bars in Gastown (Granville) to cater to the thirsty.[28]

The long eating house had a bell in the belfry on the roof that echoed regularly over the inlet at mealtimes. The mill also kept a small hog farm to help supply its needs. It was run by Ned Acton, known as "Hog Ned."

The store was nearly the only building left standing after the fire that destroyed the new City of Vancouver on June 13, 1886. The structure was moved in 1930 to its present location at the north end of Alma Street at Jericho Beach and operates as a museum, its shelves stocked with items from the late 1800s and early 1900s. Even the old post office is part of the store.

Raymur also encouraged the development of a school that opened on mill property in January 1873, in a frame building 5.5 by 12.2 metres, with 16 pupils. Twenty-one children attended Granville in 1874–75 and the school report noted:

Both here and across the harbour, the school population is very migratory, shifting from one milling establishment to the other, or moving entirely away to another place. This interferes with classification, renders abortive many of the teacher's plans, and seriously retards educational advancement.[29]

Raymur needed one more addition to raise Granville's social level—an Anglican church. Although Gastown had a Methodist church, it had been attended mainly by aboriginal people and Kanakas since 1873 and was unofficially known as "the Indian Church." In 1881 St. James Anglican Church opened on Hastings Mill land and the "respectable" group of residents at Moodyville and Hastings Mill attended.

When Captain Raymur died in July 1882, Richard Alexander took over as mill manager. He had been the accountant since 1872 and was an energetic, public-spirited person. A president of the Hastings Literary Institute (a forerunner of the Vancouver Public Library) and later a Vancouver alderman, he maintained his connection with the Hastings sawmill business until the end of his life in 1915.

On January 1, 1884, the *Daily British Colonist* reported that the mill's capacity was 75,000 feet per day. The appliances were modern and "every opportunity taken advantage of to introduce the latest wood working machinery." In 1889, pioneer lumberman John Hendry took over Hastings Mill and combined it with his mill in New Westminster. In 1891 Hastings Mill employees numbered 300 men, while Moodyville had 185 mill workers.[30] After later adding Moodyville mill, Hendry became the largest lumber manufacturer in BC. Hastings Mill continued in operation until 1928, when the land it occupied became too valuable to use for such a space-encompassing business. At that time it had 1,000 employees and an annual payroll of $2 million. A granite sculpture now marks the site.[31]

Six sailing ships load lumber at Hastings Mill in 1888. *CVA MI. P.21 N.57*

The North Arm

The North Arm of the inlet, later known as Indian Arm, was a quiet backwater that had been used since the 1870s by picnickers who enjoyed its accessibility. They made day trips by boat to picnic at Granite Falls and take in the scenery. The ladies baked special treats that everyone enjoyed as they sat at the shore near the falls. While the children played and the men explored, the women sat around in their long skirts, high-necked, long-sleeved blouses and straw hats, chatting and doing their "fancy work" (embroidery).[32]

Several handloggers were cutting trees and floating them to Moodyville or Hastings Mill. Two loggers, Steve Decker and John Hall, an Irishman, pre-empted land in the 1870s at Bedwell and Belcarra Bays on the east shore. Hall's pre-emption of 160 acres (64.7 hectares), where he lived with his aboriginal wife, encompassed more than half of the Belcarra peninsula. One day, after a drinking party, he shot and killed his mother-in-law for allegedly stealing some of his money. He was arrested and William Bole, a well-known defence lawyer, handled his case. After Hall was found guilty of manslaughter in 1882, lawyer Bole took over the title to Hall's land in payment of his fee and developed it as a summer resort for his family, naming it Belcarra, meaning "The Fair Land Upon Which the Sun Shines," from the Celtic words "baal" and "carra."[33]

Prospectors did find some ore in their probing of the high, rocky cliffs on the west shore. The *Port Moody Gazette* noted on March 22, 1884:

A gentleman named Morrison arrived from the North Arm on Sunday, bringing rich specimens of silver and copper ore. He was inclined to be reticent as to the location of his "find" but the impression is abroad that he has struck a veritable bonanza.

While Morrison's find did not pan out, others did. In his 1889 book *The Mineral Resources of British Columbia*, Mayor David Oppenheimer of Vancouver praised the output of two mines on the North Arm. The Lottie Mine, the property of John Rainey, had an 8.6-metre vein of ore; the surface rock assayed at $3 gold and $9.37 silver to the ton. At a nearby second mine, the No Surrender, assays from the surface ore showed gold worth $10.95 and silver $2.45 to the ton. Oppenheimer commented: "The deeper the shaft is sunk, the richer the percentage of gold to silver will become."[34] Although the cost of removing the ore prevented much development, the openings to the mines are still visible in the rock high up on the west side.

Around 1887, surveys were underway to enable the extraction of another natural resource from the North Arm, granite. In preparation for the quarrying of the rock at Granite Falls, cribbing was erected at the shore and shacks built at a nearby campsite. Some rock had already been shipped to Vancouver for use experimentally in building and found to be highly successful. A party of men hosting visitors from England travelled by steamer from Vancouver to visit and survey the site in the summer of 1887. Edward Roper, one of the British men, was impressed:

> A trail led from the landing place through woods of cedar, Douglas firs, hemlocks and maples, all of gigantic size, matted together with ferns of many kinds with mosses, lichens, hanging moss and trailing plants...We came to a fine fresh-water stream, which ran down roaring from the heights to join the sea.[35]

Port Moody and the Canadian Pacific Railway

During the 1870s Port Moody was an undeveloped, forested area at the eastern end of Burrard Inlet. Handloggers cleared trees near the shoreline, and the LeHarmon Logging Company sent its logs in booms to Moodyville sawmill. A tiny settlement developed when John Webster purchased a Crown grant on the east side of the North Road on Burrard Inlet. His dream was to develop a seaside resort and he built a hotel there along with cabins at the shore, naming the area Aliceville after one of his daughters. Although it was surveyed and subdivided in 1881, no trace remains today of the little settlement.

At the time there was no wagon road providing access to Port Moody, named for Colonel Richard Moody of the Royal Engineers. The new settlement could be reached only by boat. Bonson's Hotel at the end of North Road, on the inlet, provided rowboats for those heading for the town. Early in 1883 the steamer *Maude* began a passenger and freight service between Victoria and points on Burrard Inlet, including Port Moody.

British Columbia joined Canada on July 20, 1871, with the proviso that construction of a rail line to the west coast would commence within two years. While the lack of progress by 1873 caused threats in the west to cancel the agreement, the Canadian government did send out surveyors to search for possible routes and terminals from BC's interior to the coast. In 1878 three routes were suggested as possibilities—Bute Inlet via causeway to Vancouver Island, the mouth of the Skeena River to Prince Rupert, and Burrard Inlet. The residents of Victoria were devastated when the announcement was made that Port Moody on the inlet would be the official terminus for the Canadian Pacific Railway. Victoria businessmen and government officials had counted on the great influx of dollars that a railway terminus would engender.

The announcement caused a rush of land speculators, and surveyors arrived in Port Moody in 1881. When they landed they found that the shoreline was an unbroken wall of thick forest. In 1882 railway construction crews arrived and set up their accommodations. Often mountain sheep and bears were discovered attempting to steal food from the mess tents. The waterfront was a hive of noisy activity as the men began construction of an immense wharf with a frontage of 403.5 metres set on more than 20,000 pilings. An adjoining warehouse was 64 metres long and 14.6 metres wide.[36]

Gangs of men attacked the massive trees along the proposed rail line. Others followed and graded the road bed. In the spring of 1883 the *Duke of Abercorn* was the first of several ships to arrive at the wharf with a cargo of steel rails, plates, spikes and other equipment. The steamship *Victoria* delivered the first locomotive and tender on October 18. Three days later the engine, named the Lytton, steamed on a short section of track from the wharf and back, sounding the first railway whistle on Canada's west coast.[37]

The CPR's demand for lumber for construction of its buildings and wharves caused a mild boom in sawmills around Port Moody. Joseph Dockerill and one of his daughters, Nell, settled on the north shore of Port Moody at Pleasantside, where he built a sawmill and set piles along the shoreline as a booming ground. By the end of 1883 Port Moody Shingle Mill was making plans for expansion, adding machinery just to the west for a complete sawmill that had a capacity of 20,000 board feet per day. The Dominion Sawmill advertised its 50-horsepower engine with a daily capacity of 45,000 feet.[38]

Captain J.A. Clarke, after whom Clarke Street in Port Moody is named, constructed a large house on Hogan's Alley (west Murray Street). The government rented it from him for use as a courthouse while he ran his Elgin Hotel in Port Moody.[39] The Rocky Point Hotel advertised in the *Gazette* that the proprietors would hold a Grand Ball on New Year's Day 1884, with refreshments provided free of charge. The Caledonia Hotel near the shore

Port Moody shoreline in 1883, including the new CPR rail line. *CVA OUT. P.30*

welcomed guests at the terminus of the New Road (Clarke Road, also named for Captain Clarke).

A restaurant, store, butcher shop, post office, jail and CPR office crowded between the stumps on each side of the new railroad tracks, along with workers' shacks and tents. The first telegraph message had been sent between Port Moody and New Westminster before the end of the year. Patrick McDonald ran a ferry service between the end of the North Road and Port Moody, carrying passengers arriving on the stage from New Westminster.

The editor of the *Port Moody Gazette* expounded on the town's future:

We see the city upon its shores, in the future—and not remote future—the first, the grandest, the most populous and thriving city upon the Pacific slope of the American continent. We see its immediate shores lined with, in themselves, vast towns of struc-tures pertaining to the railway traffic of the place, and of enor-mous warehouses stocked with goods from all parts of the world.[40]

But if 1883 was Port Moody's boom year, 1884 was the bust. Rumours cir-culated that the government would be changing the site of the terminus to

Coal Harbour or English Bay. Editorials echoed the people's disbelief and anger. However, William Van Horne, CPR general manager, believed the Port Moody site was not large enough to provide sufficient space for the city that would develop. To reclaim enough land from the tidal flats would cost up to $4 million. He was convinced that the land area at Coal Harbour and English Bay would be ideal.[41] Speculators moved from Port Moody to Granville.

Vancouver

One of Van Horne's first suggestions was to change Granville's name to "Vancouver." He felt that name was far more appropriate for a city that would expand to a population of 100,000.

The land transaction arranged by the CPR was highly important for the whole of Vancouver. The provincial government signed a contract with the CPR on February 13, 1886, under which the company took possession of the entire length of Granville's waterfront, including the Granville Townsite Reserve, an additional 194.2 hectares that included the land from False Creek to Burrard Inlet, and a further large segment of land from False Creek almost to the Fraser River. The provincial government made this grant of a total 2,428.2 hectares to the CPR in return for the railway's extension of the line from Port Moody. As well, most private owners of property east and west of the grant donated to the CPR one-third of the area of their lots, anticipating a dramatic rise in their land values.

During the winter of 1885–86, men under contract to the railway cut, logged and burned until by the summer most of the forest on the Granville Townsite Reserve was levelled. Vancouver officially became a city on April 6, 1886; a council was elected, and soon-to-be-frustrated plans for dramatic growth began.

Sunday, June 13, 1886 was a sunny day, with a fresh breeze rippling the waters of the inlet bordering the new city. As usual the air was smoky from the dozens of fires set to clear branches, deadfalls and stumps from the logging sites surrounding the city. At about 2:00 p.m. the wind strengthened, spreading the sparks that were landing on tinder-dry wood. The wood sprang into flame. The fire raced across the land between False Creek and Burrard Inlet, from west to east, incinerating everything it touched.

Survivors shared their memories with Major Matthews:

W.H. Gallagher: The late Rev. Father Clinton arrived at [St. James] Church just as the fire reached the building and he rang the bell continuously to arise the public till . . . the church was about to collapse . . . There was a pathway about eight feet wide to the west side of the church to the water and hundreds of people . . . made for the Inlet. The tide was about half out. Finally Father Clinton [came to the water] and he had a young child in his arms and a boy of about six years on his back. There were hundreds of people standing in the water pretty well up to their waist at that point . . . The fire ran down the wooden sidewalk faster than I could run.

Emily Eldon: We were cut off by the fire; there was no escape, neither to the eastward nor to the westward. One thing alone remained: take to the water, and we were not long about it either.

On the shore were a number of people, including two lumberjacks, and [they] certainly were wonderful men, in their great gumboots up to their hips. Out of the loose lumber near at hand . . . they and others made a clumsy raft by placing beams and planks criss-cross one upon another, and onto this rickety pile of lumber—no nails or fastenings—15 men and two women scrambled as we pushed it into deeper water.

The fire was all around us and the flame was coming right over. Then at that moment a little steam pleasure-yacht from Moodyville saw our plight and by careful manoeuvering—she had to work and worm her way in to avoid the flames—reached us.

Andy Linton, boatbuilder: . . . my float had a new 18 foot boat on it and when the fire started we launched it . . . the people crushed and crowded onto my float and pushed off . . . out on my float the miners were taking shovels and scooping up water out of the inlet and throwing it on the boathouse . . .

W.F. Findley: . . . some people ran down on the Cambie Street Wharf. There they protected themselves as best they could, dashed or splashed water over themselves, the heat was terrific, some got into the water. There was a float down there and they waded out to it. The "Robert Kerr" sent her boats, and it was from this float that most of the women and children went; there must have been 150 people on the "Kerr" at the time...12 or 15 men remained behind; they were worn out carrying women and children to the float.

Alice Crakanthorp: We were at Moodyville...and I saw the terrific smoke coming from Gastown. And then I saw the steamers coming out—the "Robert Dunsmuir" and a little boat called the "New Westminster". They were half across (to Moodyville) with the refugees. It must have been about 3 o'clock when they landed at Moodyville. We went down to see them land; it was tragic to see the people come ashore; their shoes were charred. Jonathan Miller was carrying a big cash box in both hands in front of him. I think it must have been the post office papers because he had just been appointed postmaster at Vancouver, and his spectacles were lying on top of the cash box...He walked up solemn like; he always looked solemn. He turned to Mrs. Miller and said "Mother, I've saved my glasses."[42]

George Cary: That night I slept in Spratt's Ark and the wind blew through the floorboards; I was cold, very cold. Afterwards, of course, money was no use; it could not buy anything. I tried to get some blankets from those distributing relief supplies but there was none for me, they were all wanted for the women and children I suppose.[43]

W.H. Gallagher: For some time there had been a telephone from New Westminster to Onderdonk's at Port Moody, and by that means the news of the fire reached Port Moody and some ships lying there. Four sailors had volunteered immediately, started out, rowed all the way in a rowboat...and brought medical supplies...They were certainly weary after their long pull and no doubt very hungry too. At first the men distributing the food from the wagons said there was not a morsel left for the sailors but as they were emptying [in the dark] the crates and boxes of the food that had been sent in ... [they found] a little parcel; some thoughtful New Westminster woman had prepared some sandwiches, just fried eggs between bread, but with it was a little note which feelingly said she regretted it was very little, but was all she had. The sailor man who got the note turned and faced the east, raised his hand in an attitude of supplication, and offered the most beautiful prayer for New Westminster, and its people.[44]

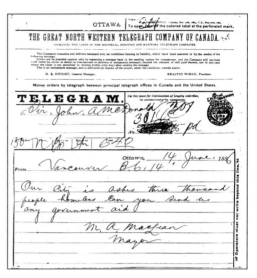

Telegram sent to Sir John A. Macdonald from the mayor of Vancouver on June 14, 1886, frantically requesting assistance after the Great Fire destroyed almost all of the new city's buildings. *NVMA*

Within 45 minutes Vancouver was nothing but a thick mass of smouldering embers. More than 600 structures were gone. All that survived were the Hastings Mill buildings, the Regina Hotel and the Bridge Hotel on False Creek. The next morning the Vancouver council erected its city hall—a tent with a hastily lettered "City Hall" sign. Planning meetings commenced immediately. Rebuilding was undertaken with such fervour that by the end of July businesses were operating and many homes were rebuilt.

Vancouver in 1887, looking north from the first Hotel Vancouver. *CVA DIST. P.62 N.47*

On July 4, 1886, 150 people arrived in Port Moody on the first passenger train to arrive from eastern Canada. The extension of rails along the inlet's shore to Vancouver was underway, but the first passenger train did not arrive there until the next year, on May 23, when celebratory crowds greeted the passengers. Ships and boats in the harbour flew colourful flags as the engine pulled in along the trestle, actually built in the inlet's water. Vancouver was connected by rail to the rest of Canada, and the CPR was busy with land sales and expansion.

False Creek

The CPR planned to build the final section of the rail line to terminate on English Bay at Kitsilano. This would eliminate the dangers of riptides at First Narrows for ships delivering cargoes to the trains. Plans included ocean docks to be built out from the Kitsilano shoreline at the mouth of False Creek, and railway yards with a roundhouse at Kitsilano Point.

The railway giant crashed head-on into a feisty Irishman, Sam Greer, who claimed to have owned the Kitsilano land for several years. The CPR disputed his claim and continued to lay tracks, which Greer pulled up at night. After he greeted the sheriff from New Westminster with a blast from his shotgun, the CPR's problem was solved: Sam Greer was sent to prison. For many years, land along the shore of Kitsilano was called "Greer's Beach."

The CPR extended its main line in 1886 to False Creek and built a wooden trestle over the creek to Kitsilano Point and then west one kilometre to the foot of the present Trafalgar Street. This effectively closed False Creek to sailboats and steamers that had been using the waterway to reach the expanding commercial enterprises along the shore—two lumber mills, a planing mill, a lime kiln, a brickyard and some wharves. Also, ships and boats would have difficulty using that route to deliver farm produce and other necessities such as coal, bricks and sand to the city unless smaller tugs and boats were used.[45]

The controversy continued between the city and the CPR for several years, with Van Horne even suggesting: "...I have always had a very decided opinion that it would be to the advantage of the City to fill up False Creek. If it is not filled, it will be a great nuisance indeed. I think eventually a sewer will be built right down the centre, and the rest filled up."[46]

Stanley Park

Resembling on the map the shape of a duck's head looking over its shoulder, the land comprising Stanley Park juts out into Burrard Inlet, forming the southern rocky barrier of First Narrows. Originally surveyed as a military reserve in 1859, the area was so popular with the citizens of the new City of Vancouver that the city council's first order of business was a request to the Dominion government "...praying that the whole of that part of Coal Harbour peninsula known as the Government Reserve be conveyed to the City of Vancouver for a Public Park."[47] By the time that approval was received in June 1887, the city had already surveyed a road around the park.

Site of prehistoric Indian midden near Lumberman's Arch in Stanley Park, 1888. Found in a deposit 2.5 metres deep, the shells were used as the surface for a road around the park. *CVA STPK. P.80 N.50*

At this time the western end of Coal Harbour dried to mud flats at low tide (now Lost Lagoon). At high tide a water route was passable for canoes from Coal Harbour west along a creek that reached the outer harbour at today's Second Beach. Canoeists could reach Siwash Rock, known until about 1881 as Nine Pin Rock, without having to fight the tides at First Narrows. Before the city constructed a wooden bridge to the park reserve, a huge fallen tree with roots and branches attached provided a primitive means of crossing the narrow opening at Coal Harbour. Picnickers balanced on the hefty trunk, then jumped from rock to rock until finally reaching the north side.

The park's official opening occurred on September 27, 1888, but it was formally dedicated the following year on October 29 by Lord Stanley of Preston, governor general of Canada, in whose honour it was named.

The first organization to use the shore of Coal Harbour was the Vancouver Boating Club, formed in 1886. The members built their first floating boathouse in 1887 and moored it at the west end of CPR Shed No. 1, at the foot of Burrard Street. Not long after the boathouse was built, the city took it over to use as a temporary hospital or "pest house" for smallpox cases. In 1888, with the horror of smallpox spreading through the squatters' homes in the park, Vancouver's health inspector ordered that all of their buildings be torn down and suitable recompense paid.

Despite worries of an epidemic, work went ahead on a driveway around the park. In 1888 workers with shovels and wheelbarrows excavated crushed and broken shells from the huge aboriginal midden at Whoi-Whoi and used them to surface the entire road, often turning up bones and skulls in the process.

The Vancouver Boating Club built a second boathouse in 1888 and moored it in the same place as the original. That year it also held the first of many regattas. Younger men formed the Burrard Rowing Club in 1890 and in 1899 the two groups amalgamated to form the Vancouver Rowing Club, still active. A few years later a new, large clubhouse with three storeys and a large assembly hall was built at Coal Harbour; it opened officially on September 9, 1911.[48]

Ships and Boats

As in any harbour in the early years, Burrard Inlet had a diverse collection of boats and ships, and unique individuals who ran them.

Sven Hans Hansen, known as "Hans the Boatman," was a memorable character to residents on the inlet. He accidentally shot off his right hand while duck hunting on False Creek. After a blacksmith forged an iron ring to replace his hand he was able to row a boat, and he delivered the mail from "End of the Road" at Hastings to Moodyville and back to Granville. With a good breeze he'd use a sail, and only very stormy weather prevented him from carrying out his appointed rounds. When larger boats took over the mail delivery Hansen went to work at Belcarra as a general handyman.[49]

Captain George Odin was the owner and skipper of the lowly steam scow the *Union*, which asthmatically transported freight from New Westminster to Burrard Inlet. His most colourful contribution to the inlet's history, however, was his second scow, also the *Union*, launched in 1874 and usually known by its nickname "the Sudden Jerk," describing its style of stopping. An old threshing-machine engine powered the two side-mounted paddlewheels forward. There was no reverse gear. If the captain blew the whistle, he caused such a loss in steam pressure that the engine died. If this didn't work, he could throw a sack into the gears, or hit the wharf pilings head-on. To back out of a moorage, the crew used a pike pole and oar to push the scow backwards until the engine could take over in forward

The *Union*, alias 'the Sudden Jerk,' on Burrard Inlet in 1873. The captain could throw an old sack into the gears to stop the vessel if other interesting methods didn't work. *VMM*

gear. As the noble craft aged, a rope attached to a buoy at one end and the engine at the other acted as a safety device in case the engine unexpectedly dropped through the hull.[50]

The demise of the *Union* was as colourful as its life. In 1878 the scow was transporting a cargo of hay down the Fraser River, heading for Moodyville, when the hay caught fire, probably due to sparks from the smokestack. The scow and hay burned gloriously and everyone on board jumped into the river and clung to the anchor chain. They were subsequently rescued, but "the Sudden Jerk" sank to its final rest.

On April 1, 1873, Captain James Van Bramer took over mail delivery on Burrard Inlet with his first boat, receiving $300 per annum from the postmaster general. In 1876 he had the *Leonora* built at Victoria as one of his mail and ferry boats, and also to be used for towing in the harbour. She had only a 2.7-metre beam and was quite small. He named her for his two daughters, Louisa and Nora.

During 1880, bustling Moodyville echoed to the sounds of hammers and saws for a new undertaking. Van Bramer, one of the former Moodyville partners and owner of the earlier ferries *Sea Foam* and *Chinaman*, had contracted for the construction there of a new craft for the Moodyville Ferry Company. The steamer *Senator* was 16 metres long, with one cabin amidships for the use of up to 12 female passengers, or for anyone on a wet, blustery day. The ship was named in honour of Senator Hugh Nelson, one of Van Bramer's former mill partners, and had her trial run on April 15, 1881.

The gregarious skipper, Captain Hugh Stalker, set a congenial atmosphere for the passengers, who often followed him ashore at Hastings Mill and continued their conversations at the bar in the Alhambra Hotel at Water and Carrall Streets. His willingness to turn the ferry around to pick up a late passenger also made him popular with tardy commuters. Fares were 10 cents for passengers, but livestock and wagons cost 50 cents each and were often towed behind on a scow. By 1888 passengers could leave Moodyville wharf at 7:00 a.m., 12:30, 2:15 and 4:00 p.m., and return from Vancouver at 8:00 and 10:00 a.m., 1:30, 3:00 and 5:00 p.m.[51] That year the *Senator* had the added assistance of the steam ferry *Eliza*, which kept a similar schedule.

Van Bramer continued the mail service until July 1, 1886, when the Burrard Inlet Steam Ferry and Towing Company took over.[52] The *Senator* spent many of her working days as the Moodyville ferry until 1900, then became a tug. She was rated as a derelict in 1925, towed to the southern end of Bowen Island and sunk to her grave in Manson's Deep.

With flags flying and bells ringing, the *Robert Kerr* was one of many ships that crowded the harbour to celebrate Vancouver's birth on April 6, 1886. A 58-metre fully rigged sailing ship built in Quebec in 1866 for Robert Kerr and Sons of Liverpool, her trading days between Britain and North America came to an abrupt end when she went aground in the San Juan Islands in September 1885. She was towed to Burrard Inlet for repairs, but when the insurance underwriters turned down the request for funding she was auctioned off to Captain William Soule, stevedore at Hastings Mill. He had her beached near the mill, repaired, and set out to anchor near the shore with a Captain Dyer on board as watchman.

The *Robert Kerr* was in the right place at the right time on June 13, 1886 when Vancouver was engulfed by fire. Dyer frantically lowered boats and was able to assist about 200 struggling refugees to climb aboard the ship, saving their lives.

Like all Vancouver residents, Captain Soule and his family had lost their house to the flames. They decided to move aboard the ship and were able to carry on a fairly normal life while awaiting completion of their new home. Mrs. Soule, in her long skirts, rowed to shore for household necessities and often entertained friends with afternoon tea in the captain's cabin. After moving his family into their new house some months later, Soule decided to raffle off the ship, planning to sell 80 tickets for $100 each. The raffle was never held; instead he sold the vessel to the Canadian Pacific Steamship Company, which put her into service as a coal tender for the company's ships.

The *Spratt's Ark* was another picturesque craft that had a few minutes of glory during the Great Vancouver Fire. Joseph Spratt, a partner in the Albion Iron Works in Victoria, in 1868 had invented a process for extracting the oil from herring. He built an "oilery" on Burrard Inlet, just east of the present foot of Burrard Street, and set up an oil-extraction business. In 1875 he had the 39-metre, square-built steam scow *Spratt's Ark* constructed to fish for herring, which were thick in the waters around Coal Harbour. The scow also became a cannery for the salmon retrieved with the other fish and was the core of Spratt's Burrard Inlet Fishing Company.

Whether because of the refuse dumped overboard from the *Ark* or the dynamite used to stun the fish, the herring population declined and the scow was moored at Spratt's wharf. During the Great Fire of 1886 some frantic survivors headed for the *Ark* and spent the night shivering on the bare deck boards, cold but safe.

Spratt's oilery had changed to fertilizer manufacturing that year, causing considerable negative comment from residents of the inlet. The smell that emanated from the plant was ". . . strong enough to stop every clock in town," according to the editor of the *Vancouver News*.[53] After the plant burned down in August 1886, Spratt's operation moved to the North Shore. The *Ark* was used for a time by Captain Charles Cates, as master, to transport stone from the granite quarry on Indian Arm. Then she became a bathing house on the Burrard Inlet shore.

Probably the most historic vessel to berth in the inlet was SS *Beaver*, the first steam-driven craft on North America's northwest coast. The Hudson's Bay Company had her constructed in Britain for use on the west coast as a floating fur-gathering depot, theorizing correctly that a steamship would be able to navigate shoals and small coastal inlets much more adeptly than sailing ships.

Launched in England on May 2, 1835, the *Beaver* was built of oak, 30.7 metres long with two paddlewheels, each 3.9 metres in diameter. After travelling to the west coast under sail, her steam plant was installed and the ship traded up and down the coast, visiting isolated settlements and aboriginal villages. Her single drawback appeared to be that she had only enough extra space to carry the 40 cords of firewood needed for one day's steaming. A team of woodcutters took as long to cut the wood as the furnace took to burn it.

Refitted as a survey ship in 1862 by the Royal Navy, then sold into local hands and operated as a tug in 1870, the *Beaver* carried cargo and towed vessels into Burrard Inlet and Nanaimo until she ran aground on a rock near First Narrows in 1883. She was successfully refloated, but remained out of service for four years. The 52-year-old craft was finally licensed for passengers in 1887 and for one year serviced logging camps scattered around the inlet.

On her final voyage, on the night of July 26, 1888, the ship again hit rocks near Prospect Point. The crew was able to wade ashore, but for four years the sturdy old *Beaver* lay on her side on the rocks, unprotected and open to all weather, a popular souvenir-hunting destination for sightseers and ship lovers. She sank on June 26, 1892, after a large wave from SS

One of the most famous wrecks in Burrard Inlet, the *Beaver*, lies on the rocks at Prospect Point in 1888. *VPL 798*

Yosemite dislodged the hull. The remnants are still there, in an officially protected site, some in less than six metres of water.[54]

Only two weeks after the first Canadian Pacific Railway train arrived in Port Moody, the first of the tea ships arrived on Burrard Inlet. The *Vancouver News* reported:

> The bark W.B. Flint passed up the Inlet on the way to Port Moody at 3 o'clock this afternoon. She was in tow of the tug Alexander. Her arrival created much talk and interest among the citizens, who inspected her closely by the aid of field glasses. The tug went at a rapid rate and the vessel soon disappeared from view.[55]

The 720-tonne American wooden sailing ship arrived at Port Moody with 17,430 half chests of tea after a 35-day voyage from Yokohama, Japan. It was the first of a veritable flood of tea from the Orient, destined for shipment east on the CPR.

The *W.B. Flint* was followed in September by the *Flora P. Stafford* of Nova Scotia and the British *Zoroya*, and in October by the German ship

Ships loading at the CPR trestle bridge at the foot of Howe Street in Vancouver, July 1887. *CVA WAT. P.21*

Bylgia, the San Francisco steamer *Queen of the Pacific* and the British sailing ship *Carrie Delop*. Stately sailing ships and smoky steamers from around the world delivered tea and other oriental products to Port Moody, and later Vancouver, the embarkation point for the railway that reached across Canada.

By 1890 Canadian Pacific Steamship Company's ships were a common sight at the CPR wharf in Vancouver, unloading tea, spices and silks from the Orient and filling with passengers heading for Hong Kong and Yokohama. Called "the China Steamers," the first were the *Parthia*, the *Abyssinia*, the *Port Victor* and the *Port Augustus*, all of about 2,275 tonnes but of very low power compared with more modern ships. The *Parthia* had a maximum speed of 12 knots, and often had to back up and try a second run through First Narrows if the tide was running full and strong. Nevertheless, the ships were very popular and often fully booked.

Other steamers carried passengers and freight from Vancouver to San Francisco, Seattle and Victoria. The effect of the new railway was resounding in a dramatic increase in overseas trade. Burrard Inlet shipping was reaching around the world.

CHAPTER 4

GROWTH AND DEVELOPMENT: 1890–1910

... the majestic fiord of the North Arm, hardly to be equalled in Norway, with its two grand waterfalls, its black and fabulous depths, its precipitous mountain walls, clad with forest to their lofty plateaux ... It is just as if a valley of the Selkirks had been filled half-way up with the deep sea ...

Douglas Slader, *On the Cars and Off*, London, 1895

Ｔhe CPR's connection to Vancouver had a profound impact on the number of ships entering the harbour and the amount of foreign trade goods arriving from across the Pacific Ocean. Liners picked up passengers from the railway and sailed off with them to the Orient. The Union Steamship Company initiated a profitable coastal service reaching as far north as Alaska and serving isolated communities.

The increase in shipping required improved navigational aids. Two more lighthouses opened on the inlet and a pilot service became available to ships entering and leaving. Boat builders, shingle mills and sawmills, docking facilities and other businesses vied for waterfront space. As growing numbers of workers and residents were attracted to the North Shore, West and North Vancouver ferries provided regular service.

Lighthouses

Walter Erwin and his wife had been faithfully operating the Point Atkinson Lighthouse for nine years when, in 1889, the Dominion government decided that in the interests of shipping safety a fog alarm should be installed at the rocky point. Until then the lightkeeper had responded to three sharp blasts of a ship's whistle in fog by hurrying outside with a hand-held horn, working a handle back and forth and generating a signal by means of twin bellows, repeating it until the ship's captain gave the signal to quit. The new fog alarm was constructed just west of the light tower; about 23 kilograms of steam pressure drove a rotating drum inside this "Scotch siren."

It was replaced in 1902 by a diaphone, a pulsating piston, more efficient and the latest technology. While the new alarm should have been more convenient for Erwin, in fact the opposite was true. His instructions were to maintain a weather watch at all times, day and night, even in clear weather. If fog, smoke, rain or snow appeared within 6.4 kilometres of the point, he had to activate the fog alarm. This involved more than flipping a switch. He had to keep the machinery in constant readiness, hauling coal and water for the boiler and sometimes cutting firewood if his supply of coal ran out. When lack of visibility threatened, he had to shovel the coal

Point Atkinson Lighthouse, circa 1910. The original lighthouse was built in 1874 and additions were made over the years. A hexagonal light tower was built in 1912.
CVA OUT. P1020

into the furnace and raise steam, then stay inside the building, enduring the deafening din from the horn, the hiss of steam and the noise of machinery. He could leave only if relieved by a competent assistant. In 1896 Erwin recorded 1,450 hours of the alarm in operation. Once every month he serviced the boiler by crawling inside, hammering any deposits off its walls and washing it out. It was a 24-hour-a-day job tending the light and the fog alarm and keeping the buildings and grounds in acceptable order, all for a salary of $700 per year and free rent.

As often happened to lightkeepers who lived so close to the sea, Erwin developed arthritis. His climbs up the stairs to service the light, the heavy burdens of coal, and the constant walking over uneven ground became almost unbearable as his condition deteriorated. After a fall from the tower ladder crippled him even more, he attempted to get approval from the government for a reasonable pension. For 26 years he had run the station without a day off. After three more years, he retired in May 1909 with a $33-a-month pension, succeeded by Thomas Grafton, who had acted as his assistant for 20 years. The mayor of Vancouver presented Erwin with the Imperial Service Medal in March 1911 for his outstanding service—a great honour, but of no financial benefit.[1]

While Walter Erwin was tending the light at Point Atkinson, two other lighthouses were erected on Burrard Inlet, at Brockton Point and Prospect Point.

Built in 1890, the Brockton Point light was of very simple construction. William D. "Davy" Jones was the first lightkeeper in charge of maintaining the coal-oil light and having the bell ring in foggy weather. The Marine Department in Ottawa accepted his offer to build his own house. He collected waste lumber floating in Burrard Inlet and constructed a simple shack that evidently satisfied his needs for a few years. On March 20, 1901, however, the British Columbia agent for the Canadian government wrote to Ottawa with a strong recommendation:

I inspected the Brockton Point Lighthouse, the fog-alarm and light were in very good working order and condition . . . but the upkeep of the dwelling has been neglected because it has been contemplated to build a decent looking house at the point that would be an ornament to the site, one of the loveliest spots in Stanley Park. I would most respectfully submit that something be done to this station before the visit of the Duke of Cornwall and York to Stanley Park [September 30, 1901]. The shack built by the Keeper, chiefly of drift lumber, picked up in Burrard Inlet is not worth any expenditure being wasted on it.[2]

This suggestion was carried out, and the shack was replaced by an attractive white frame bungalow with the fog bell in a tower on the roof and the light on a tall pole. A white picket fence and a flower garden surrounded the house.

Brockton Point Lighthouse, circa 1902. Note the fog bell on the porch at left. *CVA STPK. P.200 N.185*

The boat supplied to the keeper for rescues was well used, although the wooden landing was repeatedly being washed out by high winter waves and undermined by teredo worms. The agent's letter to Ottawa on March 4, 1907 reported that Jones had made 16 rescues. Davy Jones received a gold medal from the Canadian government on August 27, 1907 for his heroic feats.

Because of continuing groundings and sinkings at First Narrows, the Department of Marine and Fisheries in Ottawa had a second lighthouse constructed, located at the base of the cliff at Prospect Point. John Grove became the first lightkeeper on September 30, 1898. The base of the station was a square wooden building, white with red trim, set on a cement foundation. A fixed white light shone from a lantern on its roof, 8.5 metres above high water, and a bell hanging from the front gable sounded every 20 seconds during fog or heavy overcast. Only a few months after the opening, the government agent wrote to Ottawa on March 21, 1899, with recommendations concerning housing:

> [There are] two living rooms in the station, requiring a cabin be built and attached to the north part of the lighthouse at a cost not to exceed $300. This is very necessary to accommodate a keeper with a family [wife and two boys]. The water flows in and out of the cellar with the tide. [I want to] supply the keeper with 6 barrels of cement in order that he may repoint the joints on the outside and lay a concrete floor in the cellar for security of the foundation. The station is now supplied with a good boat...a boathouse should be built alongside of the rock on which the lighthouse stands...to include boat ways and a winch. J. Gaudin Agent.[3]

No action was forthcoming until finally, on April 8, 1904, after five years, the Grove family moved into their new cottage.

The Groves were well supplied with City of Vancouver water. They kept cows on just under one hectare of land provided for their use by the park commissioner. Grove's salary was $35 per month. The boathouse, built to the east of the station, housed a rescue craft that was put to good use. The boat ways, however, had to be repeatedly repaired due to wave and high-water damage.

In May 1910, a telephone link joined the Brockton Point and Prospect Point stations. Although the lightkeepers were in visual contact, emergencies were handled more rapidly by telephone. During that year a semaphore station also was set up near each lighthouse, using lights to signal information regarding ships entering and leaving the harbour. The availability of personnel to staff this service caused continuing problems.[4]

Ships and Boats

A few blocks west of Hastings Mill, two passengers stepped off the train at the end of the CPR line in Vancouver in 1888 and together initiated a plan that would transform water transportation from Vancouver for more than 70 years. William Van Horne, the CPR general manager, had travelled west with John Darling, a retired superintendent of the Union Steamship Company of New Zealand. During their visit to the city the men strolled along the shoreline, watching the activity on the wharves, assessing the quality and number of ships arriving and departing, and discussing the impact of the CPR on the need for improved water transportation for supplies and passengers. They heard about the new communities and logging camps on the coast, in Howe Sound and farther north, and recognized an opportunity for development of a profitable business enterprise.

During the next few months, Darling encouraged a group of local businessmen to purchase the operating assets of Captain Donald McPhaiden's Burrard Inlet Towing Company. McPhaiden had bought James Van Bramer's Moodyville Ferry Company when Van Bramer left British Columbia in 1886.[5] The steam tugs *Senator*, *Leonora* and *Skidegate* and eight scows made up the new fleet. On July 1, 1889, the Union Steam Ship Company of British Columbia (USS Co.) was provisionally formed, with McPhaiden's former company as its nucleus. The formal incorporation took place on November 16, 1889.

As plans developed for the purchase of steamers to build up the fleet, a wharf for their moorage became essential. The old City Wharf at the foot of Carrall Street stretched out over the mud flats north of the CPR rail line. The USS Co. management purchased the wharf from the city for $10,000 but had to battle the CPR, which claimed ownership of the land. A permanent lease to the USS Co. was finally agreed upon.

The first large ship tied up at the Union Wharf on May 14, 1890; it was the graceful *Cutch*, a 54.8-metre pleasure yacht built in 1884 for an Indian maharajah. He had died soon afterwards. The vessel was purchased for the USS Co. and sailed from Bombay in March 1890. After refitting, she could carry up to 150 passengers and more than 136.5 tonnes of freight. Her first assignment was to deliver CPR passengers and cargo from Vancouver to Nanaimo and return. The *Cutch* also became a popular weekend ferry for picnickers and campers heading for the beaches on Howe Sound, the Sechelt Peninsula, Point Grey and the Fraser River. The following year,

1891, the rebuilt *Skidegate* joined the fleet as a ferry. The USS Co. extended its service as far as Australia when it booked passengers on a four-masted sailing ship the *Leading Wind*.

Meanwhile, three steel ships had been prefabricated for the company in Glasgow. The hulls, boilers and engines arrived on SS *Grandholm* at the Union Wharf on August 13, 1891. An area for a shipyard was cleared of trees at Coal Harbour, and the crew of shipbuilders sent echoes across the inlet from their riveting and hammering. The *Comox* was the first vessel launched, with a capacity of 200 passengers, a dining and social room, a smoking room and eight comfortable cabins. She could also carry 136.5 tonnes of cargo. Next the 36.5-metre *Capilano* was launched in December, designed mainly for cargo handling. In 1892 the third vessel, the 38.7-metre *Coquitlam*, left the ways and took her share of cargo and passengers up the coast.

The *Skidegate* was taken out of service as a ferry in 1897, but the old reliable *Senator* continued to ferry passengers across the inlet to Moodyville until 1900, when the North Vancouver Ferry and Power Company launched its 22.2-metre ferry SS *North Vancouver*. The USS Co. decided to concentrate on its coastal service, but unexpectedly became involved in an entirely new endeavour.

In 1897 hopeful miners from around the world headed for the gateway town of Skagway, Alaska, and the new gold discoveries in the Klondike. On July 22, the *Capilano* was the first Canadian steamer to head for the Klondike. The vessel was crowded with dozens of passengers, plus 69 cows, 20 horses and mining necessities. In August the *Coquitlam* carried the first of her many contingents of prospective miners. The *News Advertiser* reported:

> The wharf presented a very busy appearance with several hundred people to bid bon voyage to the Vancouver people who were leaving for the gold fields...Her decks were piled high with freight and passengers' outfits...she had 70 cattle and four horses on board.[6]

As part of the USS fleet, the *Cutch* began a "Skagway Direct Service—No Stops" in June 1898. Service terminated when the yacht grounded in August 1900, 40 kilometres south of Juneau. She was eventually beached, repaired and sold by a group of Americans.

Although the USS Co. had encountered several setbacks in its first few years of operation, it eventually expanded and prospered and its wharf on Burrard Inlet was constantly bustling with activity—steamers landing, loading and departing, holidayers heading for summer resorts, and train passengers embarking for points north and west. In 1912 the increased demand on the wharf facilities encouraged management to widen the dock, enlarge the freight shed and modernize the machine shop. The Union ships were well on their way to a bright future.[7]

While the Union steamships were competently providing coastal service, the CPR launched its popular transoceanic service. Coloured streamers snapping in the breeze, and the Canadian Pacific's new red-and-white checkered house flag unfurled, the sleek *Empress of India* docked at the CPR wharf, greeted by band music and a cheering crowd that lined the street in spite of the rain. It was April 28, 1891, and the first of the CPR's Empress ships had arrived at Vancouver from Japan, carrying 131 first class passengers, 355 Chinese in steerage, and a crew of 306. The 1,810 tonnes of cargo were mainly rice, tea, silk and opium, with 25 mailbags on board.[8] The white hull was a traditional design, eye-catching with its clipper bows, bowsprit and figurehead.

After the CPR had arranged a financially lucrative contract for mail delivery in 1889, the company had commissioned three Empress liners from the Naval Construction and Armaments Company in England. Each had twin screws and speeds of up to 18 knots, promising to make their transpacific trips profitable for the company and enjoyable for the passengers and crews. The *Empress of Japan* and the *Empress of China* were in operation by the end of 1891.

Because of the speedy service from the Orient, Vancouver developed into one of the most important silk terminals in the world. The first Empress liners had special holds for the silk, with side ports that allowed rapid unloading. When a ship was docked at Vancouver, the skipper would roar "Silk talk!" through his megaphone and alert the dockside agents and chief stevedores. Silk bales wrapped in brown paper would be unloading on conveyors before the passengers began disembarking. The bales were marked as to their destination—often New York—then carted to the waiting "silk train."

These trains were specially designed for the greatest possible speed, so that the lucrative shipments could reach the east coast quickly. Their shorter cars allowed them to take curves more rapidly than the tradition-

One of the Empress ships loading at the CPR wharf in 1899. The ticket office is at left and baggage room at centre. *CVA WAT. P.50 N.34*

al type, and they had priority over anything else travelling the rails. Inside, varnished wood covered with paper lined the cars and they were made airtight and sealed to prevent moisture from getting in, making thievery difficult if not impossible. The precautions were worth the cost, as there could be 470 bales to a car, each worth about $800, making a 15-car train worth up to $6 million. These shipments continued until 1933.[9]

To provide coal for the Empress ships, the CPR purchased the old 58-metre *Robert Kerr* from Captain Soule of Hastings Mill and had her rigging and decks stripped out in 1891, transforming her into one of the numerous coal hulks towed along the inlet. A final and degrading assignment for stately old sailing ships, the hulks carried coal from Vancouver Island to supply the essential fuel for steamships and the railway. While still engaged in this humble but important capacity in 1911, the *Robert Kerr* hit a reef on March 4 and sank off Thetis Island in the Strait of Georgia.

The water was as black as the night when the little wooden tug *Iris* left the dock at 2:00 a.m. on November 25, 1904. A few lights reflected in the water. Brockton Point and Prospect Point Lighthouses were flashing their signals as Captain J.E. Fulton left the inner harbour and headed through First Narrows. He carried a crew of five and four passengers, but only he and one passenger were in the wheelhouse as the tug approached the Capilano River mouth. The propellers were fighting the boiling current, but suddenly the steering gear would not respond. Held in the grip of an especially strong surge, the craft landed with a grinding crunch on a gravel bar.

Those below who had just been settling in for sleep came pounding up to the deck as the tug slowly tipped to starboard. Water began to pour into the engine room. The crew threw the lifeboat into the water and all but the captain and second engineer scrambled aboard, the lifeboat being too small to carry them all. The men rowed frantically to a log boom tied up at the mouth of the Capilano, let off some men, then returned to pick up the two still on the *Iris*. Once on the log boom, the captain and his mate decided to wait there while the rest of the men rowed to the North Vancouver ferry wharf to get help.

Unknown to the crew, another drama was unfolding at the boom. As the tide was coming in it was forcing the logs under, and the two men were slowly sinking with them. In about one hour they were up to their waists in the roiling water. Their future looked bleak, but suddenly they spied the fish boat *New England* making its way through the narrows. The latter's crew heard the stranded men's calls for help and somehow were able to discern their half-submerged bodies in the reflected light. The pair were saved.

The sunken tug lay on the sandbar during that day, but had disappeared by the following morning. Some sections floated out into English Bay with the tide and John Grove, the Prospect Point lightkeeper, salvaged one piece and tied it up. By next day, all that was visible of the *Iris* at the mouth of the Capilano River was the broken point of a mast rising above the mud in which it was deeply embedded.[10]

The sunny afternoon of July 21, 1906 was perfect for a holiday on the water. The Union Steamship tug *Chehalis* left the Vancouver wharf with 14 passengers and crew and headed for North Vancouver to pick up one more person. A group of businessmen, their wives and some children were starting out on a three-week combined business and pleasure cruise to northern Vancouver Island. Captain James Howse steered the vessel into the strong tidal rip, heading west along the north side of the narrows.

At the same time, the graceful white CPR ship *Princess Victoria* was rounding Brockton Point, most of her 200 passengers on deck enjoying the harbour views. Nicknamed "the White Flier," the ship was gathering speed and heading into the narrows. Captain Griffin had to manoeuvre between a small launch on his port side and the *Chehalis* to starboard.

With a slight course change, the tug suddenly veered into the *Princess Victoria*'s path. There was a tremendous crash as the ship's bow smashed into the tug amidships. The doomed tug rolled under the water, but she resurfaced immediately and some passengers floated free. Within another minute she sank, stern-first.

Fred Rogers in his book *Shipwrecks of British Columbia* quotes U.O. Benwell, one of the tug's passengers, who saw the steamship's hull just before impact:

> Then came the crash, and I was hurled through the window as the tug rolled over and sank. It dragged me under, and when I regained the surface I noticed that I was covered with coal dust from the bunkers. I never saw my son and can only believe that he had been trapped below.[11]

Amid screams and shouts from the *Princess Victoria*'s passengers, a woman threw a lifebuoy to one man and a crewman tossed an orange crate to another. A small launch was able to save a third man. Davy Jones, the Brockton Point lightkeeper, put his boat into the water and saved the engineer, Mr. Dean.

Eight crew and passengers drowned. Their bodies and the *Chehalis*'s remains have never been found despite several searches.

The popular but weary ferry *Senator* was finally removed from service in 1900 when the new North Vancouver Ferry, a municipally operated company, took over operation of the service with the 22.25-metre-long SS *North Vancouver*. The service was more affordable and more prompt and the vessel could carry 200 passengers, but within two years it was obvious that a second ferry was necessary.

The North Vancouver municipal council could not afford to maintain the service and agreed in 1903 to lease its ferry to Vancouver solicitor Alfred St. George Hamersley's newly incorporated company, North Vancouver Ferry and Power Company (Ltd.). Plans were drawn up for a

The CPR ship *Princess Victoria* several years after her collision with the Union steamship *Chehalis*. *BC Archives I-31892*

new 39.9-metre ferry that supposedly would be able to carry 1,000 passengers and 12 to 14 teams of horses with wagons. She was built at Wallace Shipyards on False Creek. Named the *St. George* after Hamersley, she joined her sister ship in 1904. The two ferries docked at the foot of Carrall Street on the south shore and at the south end of Lonsdale Avenue at North Vancouver.

After a meeting of the North Vancouver Ferry and Power Company (Ltd.) shareholders on February 15, 1909, the North Vancouver *Express* newspaper published the directors' report:

> ...we carry about 1,500 passengers per day, in 19 trips, or an average of about 80 per trip; the *St. George* is licensed to carry 600 and the *North Vancouver* 200 per trip. We can comfortably handle all the traffic offering in three trips per day of the *St.*

North Vancouver's first ferry, SS *North Vancouver*, leaves Hastings Mill on the south shore and heads across the inlet, circa 1900. *NVMA 5451*

George...Your directors do not see much hope of being able to place business on a profit making basis in the near future, and if the people of North Vancouver will buy us out at any reasonable price, we would advise selling.

The City of North Vancouver had incorporated in May 1907, and took over the ferry system, naming it North Vancouver City Ferries Ltd. It authorized the construction of a third boat, and Wallace Shipyards Limited was selected to build the steel-hulled ferry for $93,000. She was launched from Wallace's North Vancouver yard in February 1911 and named the *North Vancouver Ferry No. 3*. SS *North Vancouver* was renamed the *North Vancouver Ferry No. 1* and the *St. George* became the *North Vancouver Ferry No. 2*. Their names were popularly shortened to "the Norvans."

A reliable ferry service made it possible for people living in Vancouver to buy cheaper land in North Vancouver and commute across the inlet.

Land sales in West Vancouver were not moving as well as expected because of the area's poor accessibility. After the Canadian government built a wharf on the south shore of West Vancouver at 17th Street, a group of businessmen including John Lawson and John Sinclair developed the West Vancouver Transportation Company. On November 8, 1909 the *West*

Vancouver No. 1 made her inaugural trip from the Hollyburn pier, through First Narrows and across Burrard Inlet to Vancouver. By July 1911, scheduled stops included Hollyburn, Vancouver, English Bay, the Great Northern Cannery in West Vancouver, and Caulfeild.

Although the ferry service itself was not making money, the company's real estate was selling well because of the increased interest in more easily accessible land. West Vancouver incorporated on February 28, 1912, and at its inaugural meeting on April 8 council decided to purchase the West Vancouver Transportation Company from the privately owned firm.

Not all of the craft on Burrard Inlet were involved in business enterprises. Small boats were a common sight, especially on weekends. In the late 1800s, boating enthusiasts formed several clubs including the Burrard Inlet Sailing Club (later the BC Yacht Racing Association), the Vancouver Boating Club, the Vancouver Rowing Club and, in 1903, the Vancouver Yacht Club. One of the first private steam launches was the *Nagasaki*, brought from Japan on a CPR liner in about 1890 for A.G. Fergusson, a CPR official. Sailing yachts were the most numerous, but boating was a popular pastime whether propelled by steam, sail or oars, and boaters often took part in races and regattas.[12]

Southeastern Coal Harbour, circa 1899. From left to right: Burrard Inlet Rowing Club, fishnet drying rack, shed and part of the old wharf from Spratt's Oilery, Vancouver Boating Club (one large, two small buildings). *CVA BU. P.194 N.119*

Deadman's Island

On a small island in Coal Harbour, accessible from Stanley Park by land at low tide, the trees had held the bodies of many dead aboriginal people over the years as the Squamish followed their traditions. This 2.22-hectare piece of land, which the Squamish had named Deadmans Island ("mans" as plural for "man"), had been the site of a "pesthouse" in 1888 during the smallpox epidemic. The people of Vancouver considered it part of their beloved Stanley Park. During the 1890s, squatters' shacks on pilings lined the shore and the city council's greatest concern about the island was how to remove those illegal homes.

Squatters' shacks line the shore of Deadman's Island in Coal Harbour before 1909. *VPL 2565*

In 1898 Theodore Turnbull Ludgate arrived in Vancouver from Chicago, where he had managed a sawmill. He purchased a home and began to make inquiries about appropriate land for a mill in the area. The people of Vancouver had no inkling that he would shortly initiate proceedings that would result in a prolonged struggle involving the Canadian and British Columbia governments and the Vancouver city council, a struggle that became known as "the Ludgate Affair."

Ludgate envisioned Deadman's Island as an ideal location for his lumber business, being on the harbour and close to the city. He quietly made arrangements with a local lawyer who assisted him in approaching the Department of Militia and Defence in Ottawa with a view to leasing the island. Ottawa issued an order-in-council on February 14, 1899, granting him a 25-year renewable lease on the island for a yearly rent of $500. Ludgate was ready to begin construction of the Vancouver Lumber Company.

City council did not learn of this arrangement with the Canadian government for two months. Council believed that the island was part of the naval reserve and, as such, part of the Stanley Park grant. Ludgate defended his plans by pointing out that he would employ up to 1,000 men, and there would be additional financial benefits to the city from ships landing at his wharf. He claimed that he would use only local timber that would be supplied by handloggers, thereby increasing their income.

Vocal factions divided the city for and against the plan. Many east-side working people saw great benefits, while homeowners in the "west end" saw the prospective smoky mill as a blight on their quiet residential area and a threat of fire from sparks. City council's meetings were crowded with residents who wanted to present their viewpoints and police were called in to keep order.

Mayor James Garden said that the plans had been veiled in secrecy and that the people of Vancouver should have been consulted before any lease was granted. He supported the feeling that this valuable property should be preserved for future generations.

The city could not tax Ludgate's leased land, because it belonged to the Dominion government, yet he stood to benefit from many services funded by civic taxes. The financial advantages in his deal were obviously worth fighting for, and fight he did. On April 23, 1899, he led 34 men in an invasion of the island and began to clear trees for the mill site. The police appeared and the mayor read the Riot Act. When the men continued to cut trees, they were all arrested, including Ludgate.

Petitions for provincial or federal title to the land were heard by the BC government, the Supreme Court of Canada and the English Privy Council, with differing judgements. All of this took time, and a decade passed.

Ludgate, meanwhile, embellished his original plans for a sawmill. The *Vancouver World* reported on March 27, 1909:

> ...the greatest development scheme that Vancouver has ever had...on the side of the island facing the inlet...there are to be three wharves...that will accommodate ocean steamers of practically any draught. At one end of these wharves there will be a graving dock capable of taking vessels of 200 feet length. On the wharf alongside there will be repair shops, where all the smaller vessels that now have to go to the island or Puget Sound, can be repaired...Next to the graving dock...a large wharf and warehouse with one of the largest elevators at the end [for wheat].[13]

Another attempt by Ludgate in 1909 to clear what had become known as "the Isle of Dreams" led to the arrest of two of his representatives, E.L. Kinman and F.L. Gartley, along with some of their workers. The group were removed from the island in handcuffs and held in jail cells. During the arrest two police officers were hit over the head with heavy clubs.[14] By this time most of the trees had been cut down. Kinman had also been threatening the squatters with expulsion. The Vancouver *Daily Province* quoted one of the island's residents on May 28, 1909: "What! put us out of our little homesteads on Deadman's Island after 12 years of quiet enjoyment. Well, not without a fight." Another battle was brewing.

Finally, in 1911, the Dominion's claim to the island was confirmed by the English Privy Council. The government cancelled Ludgate's lease and later transferred control to Vancouver city. Squatters' shacks continued to line the shore, and a tempestuous period of Vancouver's history came to a close.[15]

The North Arm

The isolated grandeur of Burrard Inlet's North Arm (later Indian Arm) led one early writer to predict that it was destined to become a rival to the famous watering places of Europe and North America. Lower

Mainland residents crowded the ferries leaving Brockton Point for Granite Falls, enjoying Sunday picnics and hiking. Many preferred the romantic moonlight cruises up the arm, content to quietly absorb the evening sights and sounds aboard ship. People were discovering potential sites for homes and cottages along the west side of the arm, accessible only by water.

Among the first were Hugh Myddleton Wood and his son Alexander, who obtained waterfront land just north of what is now Deep Cove and erected the first structures there. By 1907, 12 cottages had been constructed with their own wharves and beaches. Wood named the crescent of waterfront land Woodlands. Just north of Woodlands, Sunshine Creek was subdivided. Brighton Beach, at what had been John Rainey's Ranch, also enticed boaters with its wharf, esplanade and fruit trees. Lots at Point Beautiful had 8.5-kilometre views to the north and south.[16]

The most ambitious attraction was Indian River Park, 76 hectares at the arm's north end, on district lots 819 and 820, bordering the water, with the Indian River (previously called the Mesliloet) dividing them. Benjamin F. Dickens had arrived in Vancouver in 1898 from Belleville, Ontario. An advertising man, he and a partner purchased the *World* newspaper and he later joined the Royal Business Exchange as advertising manager and vice-president. His keen interest in promotion led him to purchase property at the head of the arm in 1906 from John Bain, a business associate. Dickens began development plans and surveys for a summer resort he named Indian River Park.

He explained: "I gave the streets North American Indian names such as Hiawatha, etc. That's how 'Wigwam Inn' came about."[17]

Dickens designed the site, drew up plans for a hotel and had more than 20 men working for him, landscaping and building. Lots did not sell as well as he had hoped, however, so when his finances ran low he sold a half interest in the project to a millionaire real-estate and stock broker, Baron Gustav Constantin Alvo von Alvensleben, son of a German count. According to land title records, on May 4, 1909, each man also purchased a half interest in the 56.6-hectare lot 1436, immediately to the southwest of the planned townsite, from Robert Clark for $3,000.

Alvensleben pushed plans for construction of a hotel on the new site. Built between 1909 and 1910, the 32-room Wigwam Inn was decorated with a German theme, reflecting Alvensleben's enthusiasm for a *Luftkurot* or "fresh air resort." The grounds were landscaped along the theme of a German beer garden, with stone-walled terraces and gazebos.

On June 10, 1910, the steamer *Baramba* pulled into the inn's dock with 600 passengers on board. Opening ceremonies were sumptuous and champagne flowed unstintingly. Singing German waiters, dressed in cutaway coats, served the guests. The inn attracted many well-known visitors, including John D. Rockefeller and John Jacob Astor in April 1911. The business appeared to be a success.

The Terminal Steamship Company provided year-round daily service from Vancouver, and twice-daily trips on SS *Britannia* during the camping season, to all points on the arm. A Union Steamship sternwheeler, the *Rothesay*, offered moonlight trips with "Fares for Gents 50 cents, Ladies 25 cents."

Across the water on the east side, near the north end, Captain Williams had been operating a granite quarry for several years at the base of Granite Falls. The Coast Quarries Company later bought him out. Many Vancouver buildings were constructed of the granite from the falls, including the post office and the old Vancouver courthouse.

Entrepreneurs attempted other business ventures. In 1906 a group of Vancouver businessmen started the BC Powder Company and built an explosives manufacturing plant on the west shore. A building stored nitroglycerine next to the packing house, storage magazine and office, the owners ignoring the potential danger of explosion. Because of the lack of road access and bad weather causing shipping delays, they experienced manufacturing and delivery problems and closed after about a year.

The most successful business enterprise on the arm was the first hydroelectric power plant in the Lower Mainland. Prior to 1903, a small steam plant in Vancouver had produced 1,500 kilowatts of power. With the growth in the city's population and businesses, a more powerful electrical generating plant became essential. In 1897 the British Columbia Electric Railway Company, with Johannes Buntzen as its general manager, incorporated the Vancouver Power Company as a subsidiary.

To generate power the company planned to use water from Coquitlam Lake in the mountains to the east of the North Arm. Crews dammed the end of the lake to raise the water level and built a 3.6-kilometre tunnel through the solid granite west to Lake Beautiful (also called Trout Lake and renamed Buntzen Lake in 1905). Penstocks carried the water 120 metres down the cliff face to the shore of the arm where Power Plant No. 1 was built. It was constructed of hewn granite, with the base 1.5 metres above high water. A wharf camp provided accommodation for workers. The first four power production units were installed in 1903–4 and electricity travelled over transmission lines south to Barnet, crossing Burrard Inlet on a single span 868.8 metres long.

Successful as the project was, the company recognized—even before completion—that a second power plant was needed due to Vancouver's rapid population growth. Because bedrock was too far below the surface around Power House No. 1 to permit its enlargement, they built a second plant about one-third of a kilometre south. Here they formed a solid foundation with the excavation of 22,937 cubic metres of rock for Power Plant No. 2, which was constructed of reinforced concrete. At three metres above sea level, a timber walkway led from the wharf camp at Plant No. 1 south to a new workers' camp built at Plant No. 2. By October 1914 the construction work on No. 2 was virtually complete. The Coquitlam-Buntzen Hydro-Electric Development generated 34,600 volts (later increased to 60,000) and four transmission lines crossed Burrard Inlet to

Construction workers living adjacent to Buntzen Power Plant No. 1 on Indian Arm, circa 1911. *Courtesy BC Hydro*

Barnet. The total cost of the project to 1914 was $7,983,456.[18] Improvements made in 1951 increased the kilowattage and permitted remote control from a power-dispatch office in Vancouver.

Today the lines terminate in east Burnaby, at the Barnard Substation. They provide electrical power to Ioco at Port Moody, Petro-Canada, Chevron and Shellburn oil facilities in Burnaby, as well as an additional capacity to the Horne Payne Substation in Burnaby.

The 1910 Shoreline

By 1910 the Vancouver shoreline was crowded with wharves and ships, but the beaches to the west from Point Grey to False Creek were mainly popular for recreation. Tents dotted the forest-bordered shore and picnickers enjoyed their days at the water. Dozens of salmon- and trout-spawning creeks fed into the inlet from Point Grey to Burnaby. A large tent colony of about 40 families occupied the land bounded by Alma Street, Jericho Country Club, 4th Avenue and the beach. Saving taxes and rent, the squatters had their own council, and roads and streets with numbered tents—Pipe Line Road, the Muddy Road, the Jericho Trail and the Waterfront and Skid Roads. The settlement began in 1909 with a dozen families and by 1912 numbered 300 people. They had metered city water piped in, their only consistent expense. Sanitary conditions were closely monitored and printed regulations ensured orderly conduct.

The *Vancouver World* of August 17, 1912, reported on the colony and interviewed W.J. Benson, a member of the group's committee:

> In the summer we practically live in the water, and during the winter we hold concerts, dances and card parties. We have practically a full orchestra amongst our number, and I can tell you we have spent some jolly nights here. I for one, and I know the majority say the same, could never live in a house again—this is what I call the ideal mode of living.[19]

But the city issued an order that month for the squatters' removal, as they were taking up valuable land and paying no rent or taxes.

A whaling station had operated at Jericho in the 1870s but in 1910 nearby residents and visitors were attracted by the multitudes of smelts. In

Major Matthews' book *Early Vancouver*, William Hunt recalled the smelt fishing:

> At one time the smelts used to come into [Kitsilano Beach] in millions. When we were camping, about an hour after high tide, somebody would be watching, and would halloo out "here they are," and all hands would turn out with all the dish pans they could get, and scoop them out onto the beach. At that time they were so thick that I have stood on the beach, in the edge of the water, and after getting all I wanted, would see how many I could pick up in each hand before they would go back in the wave. I have picked up seven or eight in each hand ... It was quite a sight to see them at night; just after the tide had turned; you could go down there at night, in the dark, and see them shooting around like balls of fire. They have a peculiar little rattle when their tails are wiggling...When it is calm, the water is full of phosphorus, and, as soon as they see you, they shoot off like balls of fire.[20]

Fishermen pull in salmon nets at Greer's Beach (later Kitsilano), circa 1893, when salmon were plentiful in English Bay. *CVA BE. P.142 N.92*

Fishing boats netted their catches in English Bay, and their lights at night spread out as an unforgettable fairyland for watchers from the shore. In 1931 W. Rorison recalled:

Each boat was necessitated by law to carry two lights; one on the fishing boat, the other on a float at the end of the net. We were still in the sail age—there were gas engines but few were used. The sails were stowed whilst fishing, and the hundreds, literally hundreds, of tiny lights flickering in the distance, the last light from the sun which had set, the smooth sea, made an enchanting summer's scene.[21]

Sail-powered salmon-fishing boats leave the English Bay Cannery and a tug moves the vessels to open water, circa 1905. *CVA SGN 10*

Several frame cottages and a long wooden wharf were all that remained at the English Bay Cannery site on the Kitsilano waterfront, just west of Bayswater Street. The company had incorporated in 1897 with the purpose of catching and processing all kinds of fish. It also made fish manure from offal and refuse. Often warm weather and a westerly breeze wafted

Cottages at left centre were used by workers at the English Bay Cannery at Kitsilano until 1906, when it was dismantled. This photo was taken at about that time; the cannery had opened on the wharf in 1897. *CVA BU. P.110 N.83*

offensive odours across the neighbourhood, provoking many complaints. The cannery was closed in 1906, and the long building that had covered almost the entire wharf was dismantled. A heap of red metal, waste scraps from cans, dropped through the floor, was uncovered at low tide, rising from the mud like a rusty island. The mound remained there for many years, gradually becoming encrusted with barnacles, mussels and seaweed.

Along the shore at Jericho a nine-hole golf course with club buildings had attracted golfers since 1905. The original Vancouver Golf Club, a nine-hole course, had operated there from 1892 to 1894. Close to the high-tide line, it had sand fairways but passable greens. After a ferocious winter storm drove logs and driftwood across the fairways, the golfers moved to Brockton Point, then to the Moodyville Rifle Range in North Vancouver. A new course built in 1905 at Jericho had dikes to hold back the tide.[22]

False Creek is actually a trough, shaped by erosion, water or glacial action, that used to extend 5.5 kilometres from the mouth inland to what is now Clark Drive. Low tide exposed muddy flats in the eastern half, but very high tides there overflowed into Burrard Inlet. After the CPR cleared 194.26 hectares on the creek's north shore in the late 1880s, industry flourished and took over the shoreline—shipyards, sawmills including

Dance hall, boathouse and campers at Greer's beach, circa 1905.
CVA BE. P.51 N.24

Greer's Beach (Kitsilano) in 1908. A popular campground at the north end of
Yew Street, it was dismantled that year because of improper sanitation.
CVA BE. P.24 N.16

planing and shingle mills, building-supply factories such as sash-and-door
manufacturers and even a prefabricated-home plant, brickyards and
cement works, foundries and machine shops. BC Electric's Light and
Railway Power House was located on the shore not far from the gasworks.

From Carrall Street to the creek's entrance the CPR's freight sheds, yards, workshops and roundhouse dominated the waterfront on False Creek's north shore.

According to the 1890 BC Directory, the Vancouver Saw and Planing Mills occupied 40 by 100 feet on the creek with all the latest machinery for turning out rough and dressed lumber. Thirty hands were employed, and expansion was imminent. The Flater Shingle Mill announced its production of 35,000 shingles daily.

Alfred "Andy" Wallace, ship and boat builder who had started in a small way on False Creek in 1894, advertised his expanded products in the 1901 directory:

> Tugs, Stern-Wheelers, Steam Yachts and Launches, Scows and Lighters, Ships' Wood and Metallic Life Boats, Columbia River Gravel and Clinker Fishing Boats, Pleasure Boats a specialty.

His 31-metre-long marine railway paralleled the west side of Granville Bridge. Wallace Shipyards was a well-known and respected firm, and in 1906 the boat builder became a true shipbuilder when Wallace opened a new, more spacious yard in North Vancouver. The company's repair work

False Creek industries around 1902 included the Robertson & Hackett sawmill at the foot of Granville Street (one of three on the creek) and Wallace Shipyards, to the left here. The small boats at right are Columbia River-class salmon-fishing boats built by Wallace, so popular that they replaced flat-bottomed skiffs. *CVA MI. P.68 N.54*

continued mostly at the False Creek yard until May 1910, when a fire damaged the plant. From that time on the business was concentrated at the North Vancouver yard.

The creek's south shore development proceeded more slowly because access by road was limited. In July 1891 the construction of the Cambie Street Bridge, following the opening of the Granville Bridge in 1889, provided better access. The Leamy and Kyle sawmill had operated on the south shore since 1886, but not until the 1890s did another business, a sawmill and shingle mill, open there. The shoreline remained mainly marsh and bushland. More convenient access encouraged development, and by 1910 the south shore supported more than 20 businesses—machine shops, lumber mills, building material suppliers and metal works. The eastern shoreline of the creek was mostly tidal flats, the home of countless waterfowl, and navigation was suitable only for small boats. One exception to the industrial development was C.C. Maddams' fruit and berry farm near the eastern end which supplied fresh produce.[23]

On the northern curve of English Bay beach, near the foot of Denman Street, Seraphim "Joe" Fortes contentedly spent his days, surrounded by children and adults, as Vancouver's first official lifeguard. Originally from the West Indies, he had arrived in Vancouver in 1885 on board a ship delivering freight to Burrard Inlet. He discovered the recreational potential for the sandy English Bay shore, and encouraged one of Vancouver's early

---

False Creek Coal Syndicate Limited

CAPITAL, = $20,000

DIVIDED INTO 20,000 FULLY PAID SHARES OF $1 EACH PAR VALUE STOCK FULLY PAID-UP AND NON-ASSESSABLE.
NO PERSONAL LIABILITY TO SHAREHOLDERS.

Only 5,500 shares not taken up. These are offered at par, payable 10 per cent. on application and 90 per cent. in one month. Shares not applied for previous to beginning of operations, may be withdrawn or issued at a premium.

DIRECTORS

J. H. Sanderson (of Prince Rupert Timber and Lumber Co., Ltd.), President.
Thomas Duke (of City Brokerage Co.), Vice-President.
James Borland, Plasterer.
Isaac B. Flater, Contractor.

Capt. G. H. French, Master Mariner.
J. N. Henderson, Druggist.
Alderman McSpadden (of Devine & McSpadden).
Colonel Albert Whyte (of West Shore and Northern Land Co., Ltd.).

Superintendent—John Bouskill.   Solicitors— Bowser, Reid & Wallbridge.
Bankers—Eastern Townships Bank.
Secretary and Offices—James L. Stewart, Room 8, 445 Granville St.

ABRIDGED PROSPECTUS

This Syndicate, formed under Section 56 of the Companies Act, 1897, and amending Acts, and more particularly to enter, prospect, search and work for Coal in False Creek, East of Westminster Avenue Bridge, under Provincial Coal and Petroleum Licence No. 2369, dated 16th December, 1907, embracing about 500 acres, issued to John Bouskill, of the City of Vancouver, B.C., and, in the event of operations being successful, to form a Company to acquire all right, title and interest in and to the said Licence in terms of agreement entered into with John Bouskill, Albert Whyte and James L. Stewart, who are jointly interested in said Licence.

It is a well known fact that Coal exists in the City of Vancouver. Borings have been made on several occasions in different parts of the City and neighbourhood, but no trace has been found that this has been done in False Creek where this Company purpose beginning operations, the Expert being confident that a five-foot seam of Coal will be discovered within 500 feet of the surface. Should a five-foot seam of coal be found it will be equivalent to 5,000 tons per acre, or 2,500,000 tons in 500 acres, and a conservative estimate of the value of this is $1.00 per ton.

Forms of application and other information may be obtained from the Directors, Solicitors, Bankers and Secretary of the Syndicate, also City Brokerage Co. and Devine & McSpadden, Vancouver, B.C.

Promotion for shares in 'coal syndicate' on False Creek predicts a five-foot seam of coal within 500 feet of the surface. *Westward Ho!* magazine, May 1908

Joe Fortes, circa 1910. He was a popular lifeguard at English Bay during the early 1900s. *CVA 371-2694*

mayors to have a road opened through the trees and underbrush from the new city to the bay.

The kindly Fortes taught hundreds of children to swim, and officially rescued 26 people from drowning, although the actual number was probably much higher. In 1910 he was living in a small cottage near the shore, in Stanley Park, and he continued to live there until he died of mumps and pneumonia on February 4, 1922. His funeral was one of the largest ever held in Vancouver. As the organist played "Old Black Joe," his coffin was carried from Holy Rosary Cathedral. His memorial stands in Alexandra Park, on Beach Avenue.

From the 1890s English Bay beach was popular as a swimming area. Until the city parks board took over its management in 1905, the shoreline housed a motley collection of buildings. The city gradually bought up all of the waterfront property, a process that lasted until 1981. In 1907 a long pier with a dance hall attracted visitors.[24]

Two trestles cross False Creek, looking northwest from Oak Street and 8th Avenue, circa 1892. *VPL 506*

The shoreline of Stanley Park was still mostly in its natural state in 1910, except for the Prospect Point and Brockton Point Lighthouses. The Nine O'Clock Gun had become a third permanent structure in 1894 because Davy Jones, the Brockton Point lightkeeper, was very disturbed about one of his assigned duties. He had to set off a charge of dynamite near the lighthouse every evening at nine o'clock, according to his chronometer, as a signal to captains of ships in the harbour. As they were dependent on an accurate knowledge of the times of the tides, they set their chronometers to coincide with the flash from the detonation—not the sound, which carried in the air more slowly. The lightkeeper later explained his concerns:

We used to have a long pole sticking out over the water. Just about where the new lighthouse stands now... like an exaggerated fishing rod... Instead it was fitted with a telegraph wire. [It] ran along it and hung down for a few feet over the water. It was my questionable privilege to bait this line every day with a stick of dynamite fitted with a detonator. At nine o'clock in the evening off she went... If the button at the other end of the wire had been touched, or a short circuit, or any one of a dozen possible accidents had happened anywhere along the line while I was working at it, my promising career would have been cut short.[25]

Jones thought he should devise a less dangerous method and began to petition the government for a cannon to replace the rod and dynamite. In 1894 a 1.98-metre brass muzzle-loading cannon was installed on a wooden base

The Nine O'Clock Gun, circa 1935. It was installed on the Coal Harbour shoreline of Stanley Park in 1894. *Leonard Frank photo*

within a wooden shed, very close to its present location at Halleluja Point. Built in 1816, the gun was delivered from Nanaimo, where it had been part of the city's defensive armaments during the American-Canadian boundary disputes in the mid-1800s.

The lightkeeper set the charge of about a half kilogram of black powder in the gun, and at nine o'clock every evening the telegraph operator at the CPR office in Vancouver would tap a key, closing the circuit and causing the gun to fire. The time was co-ordinated every morning using a chronometer in accordance with a signal from the Dominion Meteorological Bureau in Montreal.[26] Originally "the Time Gun," the name was changed to "the Nine O'Clock Gun." It remains in operation, in a new enclosure, and sends out its electrically fired nine o'clock booms, sometimes heard as far away in the Lower Mainland as the town of Mission.[27]

On Coal Harbour's southern shoreline a shingle mill and Charles Robertson's shipbuilding business faced across the bay to the Royal Vancouver Yacht Club headquarters.

Australian hardwood pilings supported the CPR Piers A and B just east of Coal Harbour. Stretching along 3.2 kilometres of shoreline and out into the inlet from the company's docks, the wharves accommodated the Empress liners and those travelling to and from Australia. The CPR Princess coastal steamers also tied up there. Docking space was already crowded only two years after construction, and plans were underway for the construction of two more piers in 1911. A corral on the eastern end provided a storage area for cattle while they waited to be freighted up the coast.

Moving from west to east along the inlet, the adjoining dock belonged to R.V. Winch and Company Ltd., commission merchants and shipping agents, situated at 739 Hastings Street West. Next, the Union Steamship

Squatters' shacks in 1898 on the west shore of Deadman's Island, which could be reached by a footbridge from Stanley Park. *CVA STPK P.125*

The Evans, Coleman & Evans wharf at the north end of Columbia Street, circa 1904. The company imported a wide variety of materials. Note the CPR rail line in foreground. *CVA WAT. P.97 #2 N.85 #2*

wharf with a large shed near the foot of Carrall Street was almost constantly occupied by at least one of its seven steamers heading up the coast with freight, or taking passengers for weekend picnicking trips or to resorts. Beside it, the Johnson Wharf Company's 180.5-metre shed and large new wharf led out into the inlet from the foot of Columbia Street. Just east of Johnson's, two long piers jutted out from Evans, Coleman & Evans, a pioneer shipping company. It advertised in the 1910 British Columbia Directory as shipping, coal and commission merchants, and railway builders, providing cannery supplies as well as fire and marine insurance, with offices and wharves at the foot of Columbia. Beside the Evans piers, the North Vancouver City Ferries Ltd. dock was the south shore's embarkation point for North Vancouver.

Next came a roughly planked, narrow pier that served as home base for an assortment of fishing boats and boat builders, crowded together in a rare stretch of undeveloped shoreline. It would soon become the official steamship dock for the Grand Trunk Pacific Steamships. John and William H. Hind Brothers' tugboat slip abutted the City Wharf next in line at the foot of Gore Avenue, where the brothers ran their business as steamship agents. A little farther east, the New England Fish Company's cold-storage building and wharf received fresh fish that were then sold wholesale. Beside that, Hastings Mill wharf was the oldest business on the south shore waterfront, in operation since 1865.

A typical day at the Hastings Mill wharf began at 6:00 a.m. A long line of men slouched beside a four-masted sailing ship moored at the dock, waves slapping against her hull. As the sun burned off the early morning mist, Captain Soule, the stevedore in charge, crossed the heavy planks and moved along the line, selecting longshoremen for the day's loading. The 20-man crew took up their positions. Although their work clothes were almost identical—pants, long-sleeved shirts, wide suspenders and fedoras—their sun-browned faces and rugged bodies reflected an ethnic diversity from around the world, many having been merchant seamen who had jumped ship.

The morning's peace erupted into the rattle of action—lumber thudding down wooden chutes from the mill level to the wharf, men's shouts as they hand-hauled the lumber through the ship's side ports into the holds, whistle signals from a worker on the dock directing the loading, the creak of ropes and pulleys, and the constant overlay of the saws' whine from the mill. As the day wore on, the smell of salt water was overpowered by the

Five sailing ships load lumber at Hastings Mill, circa 1890. Note the hatch openings in the bows. *CVA MI. P.47 N.38*

pungent aroma of cedar and fir. At high tide the ship's top deck reached the wharf level and some of the men converged on a stack of huge timbers, 12, 14 and 16 inches square and too long to manoeuvre into the holds. Making a roadway with planks crossed by wooden rollers, they skidded the cumbersome beams onto the ship's deck, manhandling them into position along its length, on each side of the masts.[28] By 4:00 p.m. the loading was completed and the men moved off, some heading for home, some to the bar in the Alhambra Hotel to down a glass of ale.

To the east the BC Sugar Refinery, incorporated in 1890, was the first industry in Vancouver not related to forestry or fishing. It is still in business today. Five shingle and lumber mills edged the shore on each side of the BC Marine Railway Company Ltd. wharf at the foot of Victoria Drive. One of them, the Hastings Shingle Manufacturing Company Ltd., incorporated in 1901, had a capacity of 1.25 million shingles a day and was said to be the largest shingle mill in the world. The BC Marine Railway company completed the 6.5 kilometres of shipping services east from Coal Harbour, taking up most of the Vancouver waterfront.[29]

The men of the shoreline were an assorted collection of characters with chequered pasts. *British Columbia Magazine* in March 1911 described a group just hanging around in the sun one afternoon on the Hastings Mill wharf:

> There were Giki, the Japanese, and Nook, the Siwash, whose tribes dovetailed in the far-off past; Jann Singh, the Punjabi; Fung Kow, the Pekinese; Rocambiar, the Ear-ringed French seaman; Olaf, the son of Olaf, the hay-colored Souwegian, "ban sailorman"; Hans Blamm, the Dutch fo'mast hand; Dirk Bolt, the English bo'-sun with the blue and red tattooing on his carbonadoed hide; and Jake Dogg, the harbor pirate, all of that breed of men the world nails to its crosses.[30]

Many of them called home the small cabins that were built on floats scattered along the shore, squeezed between piers and ships, from Coal Harbour to the sugar refinery. Some of the men were waterfront tramps, picturesque harbour hoboes, tobacco-chewing indolents, or men too old to work but still attracted by life on the water. Some earned a living but preferred their freedom from taxes, rent and enclosed spaces. As the article continued, "They knew the harbour and its ships as a suburbanite knows the houses on his own street."

East of the Second Narrows, on the south shore, Burnaby had become a municipality in 1892, but the only road along the shore was the Barnet, opened in 1903 from North Road to the North Pacific Lumber Company on the shore. The sawmill was one of Burnaby's first industrial developments. A railway station on the CPR line served the business. In 1910, after a disastrous fire the year before, the buildings of a new mill crowded the shoreline and the beginnings of a company town were evident.[31]

At Port Moody, the end of the inlet, log booms destined for the mills nudged ships being loaded with lumber from the Canadian Pacific Lumber Company, which also had a planing mill and dry kilns at the foot of Douglas Street, and from the Emerson Lumber Company Limited near Rocky Point. The Robert McNair Shingle Company Limited mill had begun operations in 1908 on the north shore, and was a busy family-operated business.

The old steamer *Delta* chugged back and forth daily from Port Moody to Vancouver, delivering workers and shoppers to and from the city.

The Indian Arm shoreline, still called the North Arm in 1910, was dotted with 60 to 70 summer homes, most with wooden landings or floats, and

Emerson Cedar Mill, circa 1908. It was built on the south shore of Port Moody in 1905 and employed 125 men. Later Emerson Lumber Company Limited, the business remains in operation as Flavelle Sawmill Co. Ltd. *Port Moody Station Museum*

three major businesses, the British Columbia Electric Railway Company's Power Plant, a quarry at Granite Falls, and across the head of the arm Wigwam Inn in its first year of operation.

The population of the whole of North Vancouver at this time numbered about 6,000. The City of North Vancouver encompassed an area of 1,618.7 hectares, and its electrical system attracted businesses to the North Shore.

Aboriginal reserves numbers 2 and 3 were part of the wooded shoreline between Roche Point and the Seymour River. Between there and North Vancouver city, Cutter Island and the Seymour River and Lynn Creek estuaries attracted many boaters and picnickers who made day trips or set up tents along the shore for a few days' holiday. Along this part of the shore, west of Lynn Creek, were the buildings of the old Moodyville lumber mill.

The new North Vancouver Lumber Company, previously Emerson's sawmill, had a large saw and planing mill between St. George's Avenue and Lonsdale. Its wharf and log slide to the water were busy with boats, tugs with log booms, and ships loading cargoes of sawn lumber.

This "Cary Fir" allegedly was felled on the North Shore of the inlet in 1895 by local logger George Cary, shown here on ladder. The tale of the giant tree began as a hoax supported by this photo in 1922. *VPL 1236*

Wallace Shipyards Limited abutted the west side of the lumber mill, between Esplanade and the inlet. Andy Wallace had opened this new yard in 1906, while still maintaining some operations at his False Creek plant. The opportunity for a larger space—120 metres of waterfront—and the added benefit of electricity attracted him. A long wharf fronted his busy machine shop, and a 1,500-tonne marine railway led to his shipbuilding shed. Wallace Shipyards had become a very important part of British Columbia's marine services and provided numerous jobs. Besides repairing ships of almost any size, the company built four large barges here between 1906 and 1910 as well as the *North Vancouver Ferry No. 3*, a 44.2-metre vessel. The site remained a centre of shipbuilding and repairs for many years.

At the foot of Lonsdale Avenue, the concrete North Vancouver ferry wharf attracted several small businesses that lined the road on both sides. A building-supply warehouse and a hay, flour and feed building could be seen to the east side of the wharf. Pete Larson's popular three-storey Hotel North Vancouver on west Esplanade was within easy walking distance for commuters. Rates were $2 per day or $10 per week, with special rates for families and steady boarders.

About 90 metres west of the ferry dock, Captain Charles Cates' wharf and his warehouse and freight shed, 37 metres long, extended into the water. To the west of that was W.W. Gilmour and Company, building yachts, launches and boats. From there west, between the shore and Esplanade, a public park and bandstand occupied land that is still popular today for recreation. A narrow, 80.5-metre-long floating wharf led out from shore to a boathouse. At the Mission Reserve, tall twin spires marked the site of St. Paul's Church, which the Squamish people had renovated the previous year, replacing the single steeple.

At this time an island divided the mouth of the Capilano River into two streams. The water to the east entered the inlet several hundred metres from the river's present course. Squamish Reserve No. 5 paralleled both sides of the river.

St. Paul's Indian Catholic Church at the Mission Reserve in North Vancouver. The Pacific Great Eastern railway line crossed the water on a raised bed, directly below the church. This area is now a road and parking lot. *Irene Alexander Collection, from a 1948 painting by Robert Alexander*

From the Capilano River westward the soon-to-be-formed District of West Vancouver reached to Howe Sound. The first attempt to establish a town in the area was made by a Vancouver civil engineering firm, Herman and Burwell. In about 1890 it developed a formal plan for a coal town, to be named Newcastle, on district lots 554 and 555, just west of 3rd Street and south of Keith Road. A 20-centimetre bore was drilled into the ground, but the plans were eventually abandoned.[32]

A few homes and shacks could be seen from the water in 1910, and in the summer many people camped along the shore in tents. The McNair-Fraser Timber Company's log booming ground on four waterfront lots and the Hollyburn ferry wharf at the foot of the present 17th Street were just east of John Lawson's home, a two-storey structure that had been built in the 1870s and occupied into the 1880s by Navvy Jack Thomas and his family. In this area a large fire had killed most of the trees, and the lower hillside was mainly a forest of grey skeletons. The land was very open here, with a view along the shore for several hundred metres. To the west, evergreens hid the few houses. Signs of George Marr's handlogging operation were visible at Dundarave, his booming ground just west of 25th Street.

The Great Northern Cannery in 1908 at Sandy Cove, which became the 4100 block of Marine Drive in West Vancouver. *WVMA 268 WV RAH*

At Sandy Cove, The Northern Canning Company Limited was operating a fish canning plant that had been built around 1900 for The Great Northern Cannery Company Limited. Sailing ships tied up at the wharf, some having brought tin from England that Chinese workers made into cans. Other ships, later in the season, loaded cases of salmon for delivery to other cities. Small houses formed a company town for workers beside the cannery buildings.[33]

On the rocky point of Pilot Bay (now Pilot Cove), the next cove to the west, a one-storey white house provided accommodation for the Burrard Inlet pilots. A long veranda faced west, and a flag flew from a tall staff during daylight hours to indicate to sea captains that a pilot was available. A coal-oil light at night signalled ships requiring a pilot's assistance. A boathouse, constructed mainly of driftwood, occupied a cleft in the rocks and a small log boom and dock protected its entrance.

The original New Westminster District Pilotage Authority had been established in 1879 in response to the urgent need for professional assistance to ships' captains traversing the hazards of the First Narrows. Three captains were employed as the first pilots: James Christensen, Donald Urquhart and Billy Ettershank (who named Ettershank Cove on the West Vancouver shoreline). They were expected to provide their own boats, which could be open or decked, and which had a black hull and the owner's name painted on the stern. The contact between a pilot and a ship's captain was termed a "speak."

During this busy period the pilots tied up at Skunk Cove or travelled around the inlet while watching for ships. In 1890 the graceful 15-metre *Claymore* was launched and became the official pilot vessel, also anchored at Skunk Cove. The men lived on board during their week's tour of duty and earned $150 per month.

During the last half of the 1890s a pilot house was constructed, where the men could live while on duty. At times a Chinese cook provided meals, and a boatman was always responsible for rowing pilots out into the inlet to "speak" ships and for picking up relief pilots. Family members could visit, although female visitors were discouraged.

Because the pilot house provided accommodation, the *Claymore* was sold in 1903 and became the flagship *Slani* for the Royal Vancouver Yacht Club. The boatman now used a gasoline launch and a tender, the *Pilot*. His position over the years was filled by men whose names are familiar on the North Shore—Captain Charles Cates, William Grafton and his son Thomas (later Point Atkinson lightkeeper) and Captain Frank Kettle.

The pilot station at Pilot Bay (now Pilot Cove in West Vancouver), circa 1900. It provided accommodation for Burrard Inlet ships' pilots and its red-and-white flag indicated to captains that pilots were available. *WVMA 315, WV RAH*

By 1910 six pilots worked for the Vancouver Pilotage District, formed in 1904. When it was dissolved in 1920, becoming part of the amalgamated British Columbia pilotage districts, the pilots left the house at Skunk Cove, and Captain Kettle and his wife, Mary Jane, took up residence there until his death in 1947. The house, donated to the West Vancouver parks board, was intentionally burned to the ground in the 1950s, leaving only traces of the concrete foundation.[34]

The businesses around Burrard Inlet's shoreline were predictors of future development. Many were small and would be replaced by larger enterprises, but the trend toward future commercial and residential areas was evident even in 1910.

A WORLD PORT: 1910–35

*The harbour represents Vancouver's greatest single asset and is an
essential link in the railroad and shipping lines of Canada. It may be
regarded as one of the most valuable of national resources, of vital
importance alike in peace and war.*

—"A Plan for the City of Vancouver," Vancouver City Council, 1928

Although World War I caused a slowdown in the development of
Burrard Inlet as a major international port, the postwar period
saw tremendous growth in the number of vessels loading and
unloading and the amount of freight, especially wheat from the Canadian
West. The opening of the Panama Canal in 1914 increased deep-sea docking facilities, a decrease in Canadian railway freight rates and the construction of grain elevators on the harbour attracted foreign trade.
Impressively large piers built along the Vancouver shoreline allowed several dozen vessels to load and unload at once.

Shipbuilding increased and large businesses such as Imperial Oil
opened facilities at the waterfront. A third lighthouse was added to aid
navigation at First Narrows, which was dredged to permit safer passage. In
1925 Second Narrows Bridge became the first structure crossing the inlet.
By 1935 Burrard Inlet was a world-class port.

The Port

In 1913 the Canadian government passed an act of Parliament that incorporated the Vancouver Harbour Commission, a board of three elected
members. They were empowered to regulate and control, by bylaw, navi-

gation and all works and operations within the harbour. The legislation also gave them the authority to administer and develop the port and to impose rates, fees and dues for revenue purposes.[1]

After the opening of the Panama Canal, and the end of World War I in 1918, the volume of trade mushroomed. In 1909, 71 vessels of foreign registry had entered the port; in 1926 that figure rose to 1,029. Exports expanded from one million tonnes in 1921 to approximately 3.5 million tonnes in 1926. Imports rose from about 2.35 million tonnes in 1921 to 4.7 million in 1926. During 1924, 814,878 passengers landed, rising to 1,022,000 in 1926.[2]

One pressing problem facing the commissioners was the entrance to the inner harbour. The Capilano River deposited tonnes of sand and gravel every year at its mouth, narrowing and filling the entrance at First Narrows. In fact, geologists have speculated that without human intervention in removing the buildup and building a dam on the river Burrard Inlet could have turned into Burrard "Lake."[3]

As a response to increasing pressure from shipping interests, the Dominion government in 1910 ordered a dredge for Vancouver: SS *Mastodon*. All day, every day, the continuous sound of clank-clank-clank echoed around the harbour. It became a part of daily life to residents and workers. The endless chain of steel buckets and the sluices on the dredge slowly cleared away the accumulation of sand and gravel from the mouth of the Capilano River. Two tall, thin smokestacks near the bow sent up twin clouds of smoke, marking the dredge's sedentary moorage, while ships and boats, free to travel, sent their wakes splashing against her hull on their passage through the narrows. Huge scows received their loads from the *Mastodon*'s buckets and were towed to the outer harbour to dump their burdens.

Dredging at First Narrows in 1911 deepened the entrance on the north side, but vessels continued to ground on the edge of the unmarked bank. *Harbour and Shipping Magazine* reported in July, 1921:

Local mariners have christened the edge of the dredge-cut, in the First Narrows, Burrard Inlet, where so many vessels have "touched" owing to the absence of a beacon, "Calamity Point". Three more casualties were reported during the last month, and yet nothing is done.[4]

A shoal just west of Calamity Point was named Gumboot Shoal because in earlier days a post with a gumboot on it had marked the shallow water.

The Harbour Commissioners also were being pressured to remove the dangerous Parthia Shoal west of Brockton Point, named for the CPR steamer *Parthia* that had grounded there in 1890, and Burnaby Shoal southeast of the point, named for Robert Burnaby. The *Mastodon* was positioned beside the priority hazard, Parthia Shoal, in 1913 and she dug away the gravel to a depth of 9.1 metres. In the summer of 1923 the Department of Marine and Fisheries ordered that the sandbanks at the harbour entrance be cut back an additional 150 metres and the waters off Brockton Point be deepened.[5]

In spite of these ongoing problems, ship docking in the harbour continued to increase, rising to 1,284 vessels in 1929. Grain became a highly important cargo. The first grain export from Vancouver had been oats, shipped in sacks to Africa in 1899 for the horses in the Boer War. Between 1910 and 1912 some wheat and oats were exported. The opening of the Panama Canal gave Vancouver a strategic shipping position, saving 25.1 days on a trip from Vancouver to Liverpool and lowering freight rates.

A wooden sounding board east of the log-booming ground on the east shore of the Capilano River, circa 1914. A steamboat captain sounded his whistle to judge his distance from shore in fog or darkness. He counted the number of seconds for the echo to return, divided them by two (as it travelled both ways) and, knowing that sound travels 1,000 feet per second, judged his distance from the board. *VMM, Vancouver Harbour file*

All grain until this time had been delivered by rail to Atlantic ports; many people expressed doubt that it could ever be successfully carried from Vancouver through the Panama Canal to Britain and Europe, because they thought it would spoil in the tropical heat. In 1917 the decision was made to make a trial shipment. Longshoremen loaded 800,000 bushels of wheat into five steel steamers that had been under construction in BC for the Imperial Munitions Board in England. Chemists from the Grain Research Laboratory were on each ship and daily tested the grain's temperature and moisture. The cargo arrived in England in excellent condition, proving that shipments from Burrard Inlet were valid and practical.

Not until 1921 did the first bulk shipment of grain leave Vancouver for the United Kingdom. SS *Effingham* sailed on January 7 with 2,080.84 tonnes of wheat.[6] Only one grain elevator was available at Vancouver. It belonged to the Harbour Commissioners, and had a storage capacity of 250,000 bushels.

The story of this elevator involved one of Vancouver's most colourful and controversial politicians. Although several people have promoted the development of Vancouver's waterfront over the years, Henry Herbert "Harry" Stevens deserves special consideration as a port visionary. As a Vancouver alderman from 1910 to 1911 he served on the Harbour Improvement Committee, then won election to Parliament in 1911 and held his seat for the next 29 years. During that time he actively promoted the harbour's development. Recognizing the importance to Vancouver of the Panama Canal, he was responsible for having the first grain elevator built on Burrard Inlet—Dominion No. 1, in 1914. Because of World War I and the consequent lack of ships to transport grain, the storage facility sat idle for several years. Locals dubbed it "Stevens' Folly," but the explosion of the postwar grain trade proved that his promotion of grain imports to Vancouver was wise foresight.

Stevens secured some of the city's first shipbuilding contracts. As early as 1912 he encouraged the appointment of Dominion government engineer A.D. Swan to survey the waterfront. Stevens later supported the recommendations that the Harbour Commission be put in place and that harbour improvements could be considered public works. Granville Island development was part of his plan for a world-class harbour. As a Conservative member of Parliament for Vancouver he served as minister of trade and commerce in 1921 and of customs and excise in 1926.[7]

The construction of tall grey elevators along the shore increased rapidly until, in 1933, altogether seven provided storage capacity for 7,843,000 bushels; three were owned by the Harbour Commissioners, which leased No. 2 at the south foot of Heatley Avenue to Alberta Wheat Pool and No. 3 at the foot of Vernon Drive to United Grain Growers. Four were privately owned by Alberta Wheat Pool at the foot of Cassiar Street, Vancouver Terminal Company Limited at the foot of Vernon Drive, Midland Pacific at the south end of St. Andrews in North Vancouver and Columbia Grain Elevator Company Limited on Wall Street in Vancouver. By 1932, 105,006,925 bushels of grain delivered from the Prairies by rail and shipped from Vancouver made up 70 percent of the total port exports.

Gerry McGeer also contributed to the port's development. He was twice elected mayor of Vancouver, and served as a Liberal member of the BC legislature and the Canadian Parliament, but during a period in the 1920s when he was not holding office McGeer for several years represented BC at the hearings of the national Board of Railway Commissioners. The BC government was determined to have freight rates lowered; the railways were charging more for transporting goods from the Prairies to BC than for hauling the same freight to eastern Canada. Using his skill as a debater and his determined tenacity, McGeer maintained pressure on the commissioners until acceptable rates were set, thus substantially increasing the flow of goods through the port.[8]

This was Burrard Inlet's so-called "grain export stage," when additional deep-sea piers were added, totalling 24 in 1931 and accommodating 62 vessels at one time. Sixty million dollars were spent on other port facilities from 1923 to the 1930s: 796-metre-long Ballantyne Pier in 1923, Canadian Pacific's 765-metre-long Pier BC in 1927, the Canadian National Timber Pier in 1930, the Great Northern Railway Pier, the Terminal Dock and Warehouse and the Harbour Commissioners' Terminal Railway.

Exports of lumber, lead and zinc, canned salmon, fish meal, fertilizer and fish oils all increased during the 1920s.[9] The Harbour Commissioners' report for 1934 showed 51,757,614 bushels of grain exported.

The abundant fish from BC coastal waters added to the exports. In 1934 nearly 25,000 tonnes of fresh and frozen fish, salt salmon and herring, salmon roe and cured seafood left the port for 23 countries. Canneries exported more than one million cases of salmon and pilchard.

The number of arrivals of all types of vessels rose, with 11,672,726 net tonnes of deep-sea and coastal ships entering in 1934 and 405,000 pas-

A cargo of silk is unloaded from SS *Achilles* at Vancouver in 1927, prior to being rushed east on a silk train. *VPL 2838*

sengers departing. Burrard Inlet was well on its way to fulfilling its destiny as a great world port.

Industries

With world economies recovering after the war, the market for petroleum oil, gasoline, kerosene and coal oil was rapidly increasing, but the product had to be shipped by rail across Canada to British Columbia. The first West Coast refinery, the British Columbia Refining Company Ltd., incorporated on September 9, 1908, opened at Port Moody on the south shore of Burrard Inlet at the location of the former CPR station. In 1910 part of the plant was destroyed by fire, but it was again in full operation by February 1912.

That year the Imperial Oil Company opened a large storage facility, Impoco, on the Burnaby shore at Berry Point. The company also purchased adjacent land for its first West Coast oil refinery, with plans to process crude oil from Peru. Because of differences of opinion with the Burnaby council, the company instead selected land in 1914 at the present Ioco site on the inlet's north shore at Port Moody. The location was ideal with its constant supply of fresh water to use for processing, a deep-water anchorage and, because plans for another refinery in that location had fallen through, an acceptable purchase price. Production at the Ioco facility started in January 1915 with a capacity of 1,000 barrels a day. Gasoline, diesel fuel, different types of oil and kerosene were sent out by ship, railway and truck across BC.

Many employees commuted to the site by ferry, such as the *New Delta*, from Vancouver and Burnaby or the motor launch *Sonrisa* from Port Moody, but between 1915 and 1919 the company began construction of workers' homes at Ioco. In 1920 a permanent townsite just to the east of the refinery started to grow until, by 1923, 68 homes housed workers and their families, who also benefitted from a school, churches, stores, post office and sports facilities.

When Imperial Oil made a major oil find at Leduc, Alberta in 1947, the company was released from the pressure of having to depend on uncertain offshore oil sources. Trans Mountain Pipe Line Co. Ltd. brought oil from the Alberta fields to Ioco, and the Imperial Oil refinery became the first on the Canadian west coast to use solely Canadian crude oil. In April 1952 the company announced a $12-million Ioco expansion. Production skyrocketed to 22,500 barrels a day in September 1953 with modern equipment that replaced the original refinery. Over the years production continued to expand and reached 40,000 barrels a day in 1980.

As roads into the area developed, families moved away from the town-site. Gradually homes were demolished or moved to new locations. Fourteen houses remained in 1998. The plant closed as a refinery on July 31, 1995, and became strictly a storage area for finished products such as heavy fuel oil. The plant had become too small to be productive, and three huge refineries in Alberta could supply BC's needs. The oil tanks and buildings still dominate the shoreline and add a mystical quality to the area at night with the bright beams of large lights reflecting across the water.[10]

Lumber mills had been an expanding industry for many years. In 1913 the Vancouver Lumber Company opened offices at the old Cates wharf at the foot of Rogers Avenue in North Vancouver, and in about 1915 took over the Red Fir Mill at Roche Point near the entrance to the North Arm, renaming the business Vancouver Cedar Mills Limited. It was commonly known as "the Cedar Side." The company's advertisement in the British Columbia Directory of 1916 announced its growing business:

Vancouver Lumber Co. Limited
Vancouver Cedar Mills Limited
Manufacturers of Pacific Coast Timber Products
False Creek Mills daily Capacity 200,000 feet Lumber
Roche Point Cedar Mills, 100,000 feet Lumber, 700,000 shingles
Fir, Red Cedar, Spruce, Hemlock
Shingles, Bevel Siding, Lath
Wholesale and Retail

In 1916 the Canadian Robert Dollar Company constructed the Dollar Mill at Roche Point just north of the Vancouver Cedar Mill. Robert Dollar, the American owner of the British Steamship Line, had moved its operation from San Francisco to Vancouver. He wrote in his memoirs that with business flourishing he decided to build his own "modern, up-to-date saw mill... [and] buy our own saw logs but soon found out that we must buy... our own forests and get out our own logs."[11] Using its own vessels, the company loaded lumber at the large dock on the North Arm for shipment around the world.

Vancouver Cedar Mills Limited, at Dollarton on Indian Arm, was known as 'the Cedar Side' and advertised a daily capacity of 700,000 shingles in 1916. *VPL 2462*

Ships load at the Dollar Mill wharf near Roche Point on Indian Arm in 1923. *NVMA 6904*

Capilano Timber Company's 70-tonne Chimax locomotive, 1918. It was used for hauling logs. *UBC Capilano Timber Company Collection*

The business was very successful, but it was difficult for workers to reach due to lack of roads, a bridge or ferry service. As a result the company constructed a townsite. Dollar wrote:

> Each house has a garden and a rent of $15.00 a month includes water, electricity and wood. A post office with a daily mail service has been established which is called Dollarton.[12]

During the 1920s a narrow road was put through to Dollarton, and workers could take a seven-passenger jitney from the foot of Lonsdale Avenue to the mill. Both mills closed in 1929 at the onset of the Great Depression. The Vancouver Cedar Mill never reopened, but the Dollar Mill started up again in 1932 and operated until 1943, when it was sold.

Along Burrard Inlet from Port Moody into False Creek sawmills dotted the shoreline, exporting millions of shingles and tonnes of lumber. It was a profitable business employing hundreds of men. A continuing problem to shipping, however, was the presence of log booms being towed through

First Narrows to the lumber mills on the inlet. The strong tides made it impossible for towboats to control their booms, often forcing approaching ships to stop or change course. The high number of minor and near accidents resulted in so many complaints that Vancouver city council recommended in 1928 that lumber mills should be discouraged on Burrard Inlet, their logical location being on the Fraser River, but established mills remained.

The BC Shipping Act of 1916 was intended to attract venture capital for construction of shipyards and ships to carry freight on ocean routes, not coast or inland water trade. The loans and subsidies promised did encourage growth in shipbuilding during the war, but after 1918 the yards gradually ran out of work. From 1921 to 1940 BC yards built no more oceangoing vessels.

Wallace Shipbuilding of North Vancouver, which in 1921 became Burrard Dry Dock, received the prized CPR contract to build the first post-World War I passenger ship. The *Princess Louise* was part of the CPR's Princess fleet on the coast service and the first of the Princess ships to be constructed in Canada.

The 4,097-tonne *Princess Louise* was launched on August 29, 1921 and the fine Wallace craftsmanship was reflected in her 125-seat dining room, ornate halls and staircases. Accommodation included 210 beds and 26 single berths. The more expensive staterooms had adjoining baths and cabins had hot and cold running water. The sea trials were impressive. The ship handled beautifully, a tribute to Wallace's shipbuilders. For the next 40 years the vessel was kept in almost continuous service.[13]

With the reduction in ship construction, some yards closed and several concentrated on repairs. J.J. Coughlan and Son, the False Creek yard that had been building steel ships, had plans drawn up for a large dry dock on the south shore of Burrard Inlet at Vancouver in 1920. The company had two years in which to raise capital in order to receive a government subsidy, but was unsuccessful. In 1921 the Wallace company agreed to pay for all expenses already incurred if the subsidy could be transferred to a new firm, Burrard Dry Dock Company Ltd., and the site located at or near its North Vancouver yards. The deal went through and by March 1924 four pontoons were in place with a lifting capacity of 15,241 tonnes. The official opening of the completed 11 pontoons took place on August 1, 1925, making it the first large dry dock on Burrard Inlet.

J.K. McKenzie, with his young son, stands on a barge at his waterfront business, circa 1935. McKenzie Barge and Derrick Limited was set up in North Vancouver around 1930. *MBMW*

Large industries on the inner harbour were very obvious, but dozens of small businesses tucked into the shoreline also contributed to the economy. Coal Harbour's marine industries crowded together, making a continuous row of wooden buildings and docks along West Georgia Street from Cardero to Stanley Park. Shipyards, brass and propeller works, sheet metal, blacksmithing, electric, diesel and machinery companies hummed and rattled all day with the sounds of motors, band saws, lathes, metal on metal, hammers and men's voices. About 10 shipyards worked on all types of vessels, from a North Vancouver ferry to small pleasure boats: Hoffar Motor Boat Company (later Hoffar-Beeching), Burrard, Benson, Menchion, Black Ball and Andy Linton are a few that the Coal Harbour Oldtimers, a group of those who worked there from the 1920s to the 1950s, still remember with nostalgia.

Henry and Jimmie Hoffar also built airships at their shipyard. Their first aeronautical contract was to fit floats to a Curtis Jenny owned by Billy Stark, Vancouver's first licensed pilot. In 1916 they began work on their first seaplane and on July 16, 1917, Jimmie took the "hydroplane" up for

A typical early tug, the *Sea Lion*, built at Coal Harbour in 1905 and here tied up at the Evans, Coleman & Evans wharf, circa 1906. Its siren was a musical scale that played "How dry I am, How dry I am, Nobody knows, How dry I am." *CVA BO. P.563*

the first flight above downtown Vancouver.[14] Boeing Aircraft of Seattle bought out the Hoffar-Beeching shipyard in 1929. While still producing boats, the new owners constructed an aircraft plant at the rear and built four wooden flying boats during 1930 and 1931, then five mail planes. These biplanes carried four passengers and a pilot. The fuselage was of tubular steel and the wings' wooden supports were covered with linen. In the plant's wing department, women were responsible for sewing the wing linen. The company also took in air force flying boats and small land planes for repairs.

The noisy waterfront and ramshackle buildings are gone now, replaced with an attractive park, boat slips, condominiums and the Westin Bayshore hotel. The Oldtimers still meet regularly.

Fishing had always been an important industry on the BC coast, and the fish dock on the south shore of Burrard Inlet was a central distributing location. *Harbour and Shipping Magazine* highlighted a new fisherman's wharf in 1932:

> The Vancouver Harbour Commission's fish dock at the foot of Campbell Avenue, which was completed last year, and has been

The Boeing aircraft assembly plant at Coal Harbour in 1932.

Campbell Avenue fish docks in Vancouver, 1931. *VPL 2761*

occupied by the wholesale fish markets formerly located at the foot of Gore Avenue, is quite a busy place, fifteen of the market places provided having been taken up, and only one still remaining vacant. Facilities provided include an ammonia refrigeration system, for the insulated fish cooling rooms, an ice storage building, and smoke house. There is an inner basin with light cranes for unloading fish and an outer basin with an 800 foot float providing a large amount of berthing accommodation for fishing craft, many of the seine boats and other fishing craft tieing up there during the off season as well as those making a more temporary stay to take on supplies. It is not uncommon to see thirty or forty craft of various sizes around the fish dock.[15]

Halibut was a common fish, with 62,420 kilograms unloaded in April that year and prices ranging from five to 14 cents a pound. Red cod from the Strait of Georgia, salmon from the west coast of Vancouver Island, sole and herring from the waters off Point Grey, shrimp and smelts from Burrard Inlet, crabs from Boundary Bay, as well as octopus, squid and skate made up the selection of seafood at the docks.

Men Along the Shore

The busy harbour services were expanding as more products were imported from and exported to a worldwide market. Vitally important to the efficient operation of the port were the longshoremen. In 1975 a group of retired members of the International Longshoremen's and Warehousemen's Union published *"Man Along the Shore!"*, a book made up of interviews with old-timers who recalled their experiences around the docks as far back as the early 1900s, before modern machinery, practices and ships improved working conditions. Some of the men's stories open a window into their working lives:

> J.S. Woodsworth: A hundred men stand on the street in front of the Auxiliary Hall on Cordova Street. It is 8 o'clock on a foggy morning in October [1918]. They are waiting for a possible job. The longshoremen proper have the preference . . . They have been waiting since 7 o'clock. They will wait all morning. Some of them will be back in the afternoon. Some will wait on the chance of a

Squamish Native longshoremen at Moodyville wharf, circa 1890, with lumber ships in background and Chinese laundryman at centre front with what historian Major Matthews captioned a "bundle of 'washee.'" *CVA MI. P.2 N.26*

night job. They waited all day yesterday in the rain. Day after day they have been waiting for the past week.

George Webster: When I worked at the Hastings Mill there were still sailing ships coming in.

How did they handle their lumber? A lot of it was very heavy lumber; fletchers [six-inch lumber any length or width] and squares and that sort of thing. Oh some of it was long...Any big long stuff we took in from the stern. There was an opening in the stern.

Paddy McDonagh: When I was down there they were of course still loading sailing ships with lumber at Hastings Mill. And at that time they had donkey engines on scows. The ships had stern ports and everything was hauled in with the donkey through or over the stern. Of course at that time the Indians from the North Shore did all that work...

In those days we used to do quite a bit of work at Dollarton, in the late teens and early '20s. The transportation they had then was dump trucks. They would take us up in these dump trucks, rain, hail or shine. One day we were going down into Dollarton and the brakes failed on the truck that I was in and it ran into a ditch. They did away with dump trucks then and used to take us up in boats. That was a blessing because we had to stand in the trucks unless you were lucky enough to get a seat.

J.S. Woodsworth: But is his work itself interesting? He shoves his truck [dolly] to the sling. The loaders put on four cases...He "breaks", throwing his truck into balance, then across the shed he wheels his load. The pilers stand ready to receive it. He throws up the handles and by a deft movement withdraws the blade of the truck, leaving the four cases one on top of the other ready for the pilers. Then back he slowly wheels his truck to the sling...His load is ready. Across the shed again, a trucker ahead of him and a trucker behind him going through the same motions. Back and forward—loaders to pilers—pilers to loaders. The pile of salmon cases grows slowly—it is twenty cases wide, twelve high, and before night will be twenty deep... "Twenty minutes more", says

Longshoremen unload cargo at a Vancouver dock, circa 1912. *VPL 13668*

a fellow trucker as he passes. He need not say more. Twenty minutes till noon and freedom.

Alex Will: We used to get the occasional job and it would be at one of the places that was a real dread. The Columbia Elevator. They had no dryers in those days and we would be sitting in the grain, shoveling, and very often 10 or 11 o'clock at night from early morning. Your knees would be real cold because you could hear coming down the spouts, not only the sound of grain but the sound of ice, clicking against the sides of the spout and very often you would raise your knee a bit and remove a chunk of ice. The boys had all sorts of burlap sacking wrapped around their bodies and there would be the click, click, click of shovels going...no matter how hard you worked one side [of the ship] was bound to get a bit of a list on it...the siderunner would get into a panic. "Hey, shovel harder, boys, the ship is getting a list."

Frank McKenzie: A lot of those grain boys died from that wheat. You know, the dust. I knew quite a few who passed away. Used to use handkerchiefs around their mouths and nose.

Harry Walters: At the Sugar Refinery in those days they had dollies on tracks and the loads were landed on these dollies which ran by gravity from the ship to the refinery and the empty dollies would be returned to the ship by gravity. The sacks of sugar would weigh 250 pounds. Two men to a sack. The sacks used to stick together and the men below had spuds [wooden peavey handles with one end wedge-shaped] to pry them apart. That was a tough job. No let up...There were a lot of men who couldn't stand up to that kind of work. The sugar was the tough job on the beach. It was worse than lead and lead was tough too...

I used to hate going down to Evans Coleman and Evans to unload sulphur. I remember one time that we were on sulphur. I was coming up with a load from underneath the coaming and the bucket hit the edge of the coaming and the sparks flew and everything blew up. The smoke was so thick and cloudy that the guys down below couldn't find the ladder. It seemed a long time before they all got out of the hatch.

Ray Mason: One time we had a salt ship come in . . . from the Turk Island in the West Indies and we had to use compressors to bore holes in the salt and use a short charge of dynamite to break it up. It was just an absolute solid mass.

Ernie Jowett: I have mentioned that I have seen many changes but my eyes popped when I saw my first fork lift working. We used to have to pile 60 foot steel using bars and peavies and that was real hard work. But the fork lift made the job easy.

Several unions represented the workers over the years. The 1929 constitution and bylaws of the Vancouver and District Waterfront Workers Association included clauses to "promote harmony between the members and their employers." Wages in 1931 were 83 cents per hour for dock work with $1.25 for overtime, and 87 cents per hour for ship work with $1.30 overtime.[16]

Considering the difficult working conditions, it is not surprising that two major longshoremen's strikes hit the waterfront between the two world wars. On October 8, 1923, 1,400 members of the International Longshoremen's Association went on strike for higher wages. Instead of negotiating, employers locked out the workers and brought in strikebreakers who were housed, under guard for their protection, in ships at the waterfront. After the employers organized the strikebreakers into a new union, the Vancouver and District Waterfront Workers Association, incorporated with no right to strike, the strikers voted on December 7 to return to work. The employers gave permission for only some of the workers to go back, and many of the rest never returned to work at the docks.[17]

The longshoremen's union reached a new agreement in 1934 with the Shipping Federation. Workers would receive 30 cents per hour for ship work and 76 cents per hour for work on the dock. Although the contract was approved, the men were still unhappy with working conditions and wages. When a labour dispute erupted in Powell River, the Vancouver longshoremen refused to handle the port's paper exports. The Shipping Federation declared a lockout and again formed its own union and refused to negotiate.

The long-simmering dissatisfaction exploded into a major protest and on June 18, 1935, approximately 1,000 longshoremen marched to Ballantyne Pier. Dozens of police were waiting. When the men refused orders to disperse, officers fired tear gas at the crowd. During the altercation at least 28 men were injured and two dozen were arrested. The "Battle of Ballantyne Pier" was remembered as a dark day in the port's history, engendering long-lasting bitterness.[18]

Impact of World War I

Although World War I raged far away in Europe, its shock waves reverberated around Burrard Inlet. Plans for construction of Second Narrows Bridge were shelved. The promising beginning of a strong grain trade evaporated, and Vancouver's first grain elevator lay idle. All available ships were being used for food and war supply shipments. For the same reason the lumber industry was suffering. Sawmill yards were full to overflowing with cut wood. Foreign markets were eager for BC lumber, but vessels to transport it were not available.

Shipbuilding was one industry that did benefit. Wallace Shipyards in North Vancouver built six wooden Mabel Brown-type auxiliary powered schooners (named after the first of the six ships launched). Each of the five-masted 68.5-metre-long vessels could carry 1.5 million board feet of lumber. In January 1917 the *Mabel Brown* carried a cargo of lumber to Australia. Wallace also built the first steel steamer in BC, the *War Dog*. Launched in May 1917, the 3048-tonne vessel was immediately taken over by the Imperial Munitions Board.

More steamers were constructed by Wallace and three other Burrard Inlet firms—J.J. Coughlan and Son of False Creek, Western Canada Shipyards of Vancouver and Lyall Shipbuilding in North Vancouver.[19] These were part of BC's overall ship contributions to the war effort, an important factor in an Allied victory.

Because of the war, the British Columbia government perceived a threat from the sea directed at the Burrard Inlet harbour. On August 10, 1914, HMS *Shearwater* delivered two four-inch-calibre guns to Stanley Park. They were mounted 31 metres above the water at Siwash Point, commanding a good view of English Bay and the entrance to First Narrows. Two tents housed the gun crew and a lookout was posted high in one of the trees. All was in readiness by August 18 when the guns were test-fired. On September 2 two 60-pounder field guns were delivered from Ontario on a rush order; they were set up on the northwest side of Point Grey overlooking the harbour entrance.

These guns were in position less than a month, and the guns at Siwash Point were unstaffed by June 1915. Fortunately, neither gun emplacement was needed.[20]

Meanwhile, on the shore of the inlet at Barnet a top-secret wartime project was taking place. Inside a large compound protected by barbed wire and patrolled by military guards, searchlights illuminated a clandestine ship-building site where 460 men were working continuously on shifts 24 hours a day. Supposedly building oil barges, a company was secretly constructing five submarines for the Russian navy.

In the United States the Seattle Construction and Drydock Company under the management of James Paterson had built three submarines for the US navy in 1912 and 1913, and sold two others to the government of British Columbia in 1914. In 1915 Paterson's company received an order from the Electric Boat Company in Connecticut for five more submarines ordered by the Russian government for use in the Baltic Sea against the Germans and in the Black Sea against the Turks. European shipyards were too busy to accept the order, so the Russians had approached the American shipbuilders.

As the United States was bound by the American Neutrality Regulations, a clarification was needed before submarines could legally be constructed for a belligerent country. The decision was made that they could be built in Canada with materials shipped from the United States, as long as further fabrication took place before launching. Construction materials would be considered commercial products and not war-vessel components.

In 1915 Paterson formed the British Pacific Construction and Engineering Company, incorporated in British Columbia with offices in Vancouver. He leased 250 metres of waterfront property at Barnet and immediately had the area fenced and buildings constructed. The Canadian government was not informed of the plans.

The contract called for the construction of five steel hulls. The American Electric Boat Company was to deliver by rail to Barnet all necessary materials, down to the rivets. The submarines were 45.8 metres long and 4.8 metres wide, with 300-horsepower electric motors capable of propelling the craft at a submerged speed of 14 knots. By March 1916 all five hulls and engine parts had been constructed, knocked down and shipped in crates to Vladivostok, and the site at Barnet was dismantled.

One of several submarines being built for Russia in 1917 near the Burnaby shoreline.
UBC Special Collections, J.V. Paterson Collection

In 1917 Paterson received a second order for another six submarines for Russia. He leased a site on the railway land near the CP Steamship docks on Burrard Inlet's south shore, just east of Coal Harbour. Work was progressing rapidly when the Russians cancelled their order at the end of July; they had decided to withdraw from the war. Nevertheless the hulls were completed, crated for storage[21] and eventually purchased by the US navy, which had them shipped to the Puget Sound Navy Yard at Bremerton, Washington. The Burrard Inlet plant was dismantled and equipment returned to the United States.

Ships and Boats

The year World War I began, Gurdit Singh Sarhali, a Sikh from India, chartered the 100.3-metre *Komagata Maru* in Hong Kong and set sail for Vancouver with 376 East Indian men on board. Stories of the prosperity enjoyed by Indian nationals in Canada had travelled to their home country and many men were eager to emigrate. Gurdit Singh knew about Canada's restrictions on Asian immigration but hoped to challenge the law successfully, then establish a steamship line that would carry passengers from India to Vancouver and lumber from Canada to India.

The old tramp steamer entered Burrard Inlet on May 23, 1914, paint peeling on its funnels and deckhouses, red rusty patches along its hull. Harbour authorities did not allow it to dock, saying they had to determine the legal status of the immigrants. The Vancouver public had strong feelings against Asian immigration, dating from riots in 1887 and 1907 when working men protested against the hiring of Orientals at low wages in place of white men. While the ship stayed at anchor in the middle of the harbour, 24-hour-a-day patrols monitored the area to ensure no one jumped ship and to prevent weapons from being smuggled aboard. Only Captain Yamamoto and one of his men and Gurdit Singh and his secretary were allowed to land. They attended a meeting and returned to the ship.

Twenty passengers claimed to have their home already in British Columbia, saying they had been on a temporary visit to India. Their claims were checked and they were released. A physician found that 90 passengers were suffering from disease and some were ordered deported. On July 6 the Court of Appeal ruled that, according to section 23 of the Immigration Act, the prospective immigrants could not be admitted to Canada.

In the meantime, money was due on the ship's charter and on its cargo of coal, supposed to have been unloaded in Vancouver. The money was raised by local East Indians and the bills paid, but the ship remained at anchor with the passengers becoming more and more unruly. They were desperate; many had used their life savings to finance the passage. Supplies of food and drink on board were running low. Immigration authorities provided the Sikhs with some essentials and offered to provision the ship for a journey home.

Although by this time Captain Yamamoto was more than willing to head back to Japan, he was virtually a captive on his own ship. The passengers would not allow him to fire up the boilers. He made a formal appeal to the police to assist him in regaining control, and what followed became known as "the Battle of the *Komagata Maru*."

On the night of July 18, 160 police officers and special immigration officers approached the *Komagata Maru* aboard the ocean-going tug *Sea Lion* in response to the captain's official request for assistance. Militia members waited on shore for emergencies. The boarding party, under orders not to use guns, was at a disadvantage from the beginning as the deck of the tug was 4.6 metres lower than that of the ship. As the tug came alongside, the passengers bombarded the police with coal, bricks and pieces of scrap iron. The Sikhs attacked with clubs made of driftwood and long bamboo spears pointed with knives. Many of the lawmen were injured, including Chief of Police Malcolm McLennan. The deck of the *Sea Lion* was a bloody shambles. As the tug withdrew to shore, cheers and shouts rang out from the *Komagata Maru*, the men jubilant that they had overpowered a professional force.

The time had come for major decision making. The 91.4-metre cruiser *Rainbow*, one of the first two belonging to the Royal Canadian Navy and based in Esquimalt on Vancouver Island, was refitted and manned. On July 21 it entered Burrard Inlet and anchored near the *Komagata Maru*, with two 15.2-centimetre and six 10.1-centimetre guns visible and ready for action. Khaki-dressed troops held rifles at the ready. Vancouver citizens crowded the shore, waterfront streets and harbour rooftops, awaiting events.

Under great tension, members of the government made one final offer: if the passengers on the *Komagata Maru* gave the captain back control of the ship, the provincial government would write to the prime minister to ask that the claims for repayment of money to the members of the East

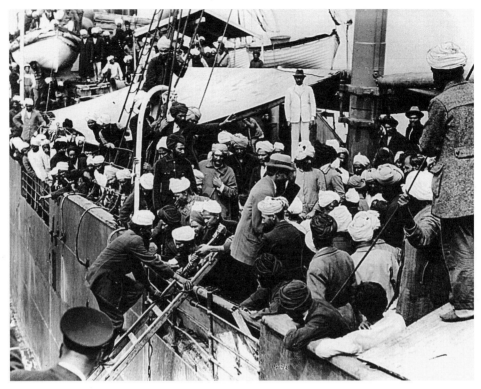

The *Komagata Maru* brought 376 Sikhs from Asia to Vancouver on May 23, 1914. Canadian immigration authorities refused permission for the ship to dock and a notorious saga began. *VPL 6232*

Indian community who had donated funds to pay for the ship's charter and coal would be "thoroughly looked into by an impartial commissioner."

The passengers and representatives of the East Indians in Vancouver held many consultations throughout the next day. At about 5:00 p.m. the news arrived that they had accepted the agreement and the ship would leave. Government representatives arranged provisions for the return voyage. Supplies included 800 sacks of flour, 272.1 kilograms of curry powder, 2,721.6 kilograms of sugar and 227.3 litres of molasses. The *Komagata Maru* chugged out of the harbour on the morning of July 23, headed for Yokohama.[22]

The commission set up to rule on the claim for recompense to the East Indian community in Vancouver for their financial outlay decided that they had no grounds for asking for reimbursement because "most of them had been actuated by dishonest and seditious motives."[23]

The Vancouver South Asian community was divided and angry over the entire incident, and a series of shootings followed as revenge against police informants. William Hopkinson, an immigration inspector, was assassinated, and Mewa Singh was executed for his murder.[24] A stone lion was installed in 1989 at Portal Park in Vancouver on the 75th anniversary of the incident.

During the prewar period a new service was added to the Vancouver Police Department. The land-based officers were not effective in dealing with ever-increasing opium smuggling. Merchant ships delivered the drug close to Vancouver, and crew members threw it overboard attached to coconut matting. Local dealers in small, fast boats retrieved the packages and took them ashore. In 1911 Police Chief Rufus Chamberlin requested that the Board of Police Commissioners purchase a police boat that could be used to fight the smugglers.

The board agreed and the first police boat, *V.P.D. No. 1*, was built at the Hoffar Motor Boat Company yard on Coal Harbour. She was about 11 metres long, with speed of more than 21 kilometres an hour, and housed an electric lighting plant. She proved very useful in many types of crime investigations. In 1921 the *William McRae*, staffed by 2 officers, replaced *V.P.D. No. 1*. She assisted federal authorities in some of their investigations, located drowning victims and carried out regular patrol work. In about 1936 the *Teco II* was added, the first police craft with a two-way radio. The police boats have been upgraded over the years.[25]

The West Vancouver ferry *No. 1 Seafoam* was a common sight in the harbour in 1911. Often it towed a barge containing the personal effects of families moving to West Vancouver, now more popular because of the ferry access. The *Seafoam* left the Vancouver terminal at Columbia Street, headed across the inlet to the Hollyburn pier at 17th Street and then made for the Great Northern cannery, Skunk Cove and English Bay.

The West Vancouver ferry service was not without its problems. At English Bay passengers had to offload into lifeboats to reach shore, as the dock facilities made disembarking difficult. This stop was cancelled later in the year; the tides at First Narrows were a challenge even for this sturdy boat. On August 4, 1912, the *Seafoam* went aground on the rocks near Prospect Point, fortunately with no serious damage.

That year West Vancouver Municipality Ferry Service purchased the ferry business from John Lawson and his associates for $6,000 and had a

The West Vancouver ferry *Hollyburn*, docking at Ambleside in June 1936. *WVMA 1987-066*

new wharf built at the foot of 14th Street. Additional ferries joined the *Seafoam*: the *Doncella*, the *Sonrisa*, which continued to provide service until 1936, the *No. 5* in 1915, the *No. 6* in 1925, the *Bonnabelle* in 1935 and the *Hollyburn* in 1936.

Sailings were usually uneventful, but a few were memorable. In 1915 the *Sonrisa* had to rescue two men trapped on a sinking airplane. In 1934, the *No. 5* grounded in fog on the Stanley Park shore. In February 1935, SS *Princess Alice* crashed into the *No. 5*, drowning one of the ferry's passengers. The West Vancouver ferry service was discontinued on February 8, 1947, when the *No. 6* made its last run.

Towboating became an important and expanding business prior to World War I. The first large steel tug, the *Dreadful*, constructed in England, joined the fleet in 1913. That year Captain Charles Cates formed C.H. Cates Towing, a business that became famous on Burrard Inlet. His sturdy tugs specialized in docking and moving ships around the harbour, but also were involved in assisting at emergencies on the water, salvaging and helping to fight fires. In 1921 C.H. Cates & Sons Limited was incorporated, with offices in North Vancouver at the foot of Lonsdale Avenue.

The hull of the first Cates tug, the *Charles H. Cates*, is lowered into the water at North Vancouver in 1923. Those that followed also were named for the owner, but were numbered as well. *NVMA 787*

In 1923 the power that drove the tugs increased immensely with the introduction of diesel engines. The *Radio*, built by Cates at his False Creek shipyard, and *Seawave* were the first two local diesel tugs. This new, speedier type of boat operated efficiently with a smaller crew and could tow log booms and barges without having to stop repeatedly for recoaling. Most towboats were operating with diesel fuel by the end of the 1920s.

Captain Charles Henry Cates, circa 1930.
He founded C.H. Cates & Sons Limited, a
major tugboat company whose name is
still seen on the inlet. *CVA PORT. P.741*

The Canadian Pacific Steamship *Princess Sophia* was berthed at Skagway, Alaska, on Wednesday, October 23, 1918, loaded with 360 passengers heading south for the winter. After a hilarious farewell party, the ship departed at 10:10 p.m. Less than four hours later it struck Vanderbilt Reef in the Lynn Canal and went aground in a blizzard. Rescue attempts were impossible in the high seas and low visibility. Late in the afternoon of Friday, October 25, high tide and waves apparently washed the *Princess Sophia* off the rocks, and all passengers and crew perished.

During the following weeks, bodies were picked up on the shores and taken to Juneau or Skagway, where they were identified if possible and embalmed. The CP steamer *Princess Alice* was sent to pick up the remains and deliver them back to Vancouver, Victoria and Seattle; the funeral ship left Juneau on November 8 with 159 bodies in coffins.

Dubbed "the Ship of Sorrow" by the *Vancouver Sun*, the *Princess Alice* with her silent cargo slowly approached the black-crepe-decked CP wharf and docked at 11:00 p.m. on November 11. A few grieving relatives waited on the wharf, although most had left for home as the ship had not been expected to arrive until after midnight. A few blocks away, jubilant, noisy crowds filled downtown Vancouver streets to celebrate the end of World War I.

At seven o'clock the next morning the crew began the removal of caskets to a temporary morgue on the dock, where relations could confirm identification. Flag at half mast, the *Alice* then motored quietly away from the dock, crossed the inner harbour and left Burrard Inlet for Victoria and Seattle to deliver more bodies to loved ones.[26]

Not all ships and boats passing through the harbour were conducting legal business. When the United States enacted Prohibition in 1920, outlawing the sale of alcoholic beverages, a thriving but clandestine "Rum Row" along Vancouver's shore was made up of about 60 small vessels, launches and schooners. For several years they transported cases of bourbon, rye, gin and rum down the Washington and Oregon coasts, attempting to evade the US revenue department cutters and hijackers, and surviving storms and rocky shorelines. Cases of cargo were usually moved, one by one, from one vessel to another as darkness, swells, wind and waves made footing dangerous. One boat reportedly could carry up to $1 million worth of illicit booze.

The *Malahat*, a Victoria-built auxiliary schooner, became known as the "Queen of Rum Row"; often it would carry 60,000 cases of liquor. Captain Robert Pamphlet of North Vancouver, a teetotaller, was one of the experienced skippers. On February 6, 1925, his ship, the *Pescawha*, loaded with 1,000 cases of whiskey, made headlines when it was involved in a deep-sea rescue off the mouth of the Columbia River.[27]

Many Vancouver residents fondly recall the romantic Moonlight Cruises to Bowen Island in Howe Sound, and excursions to resorts on the southern BC coast. The *Lady Alexandra* was the Union Steamship Company's "excursion queen" and carried more than one million holidayers for picnics and overnight stays between 1924 and 1953. The *"Lady Alex"* was

The rum-runner *Truicella* on Burrard Inlet, circa 1925.

converted to a floating restaurant in 1959, moored in Coal Harbour, then towed to California, where she operated as a nightclub for several years.

The following memories were recounted at age 91 by Donat McMahon, a gentleman who has loved the sea all his life:

To one, now an old-timer, who grew up on the upper slopes of North Vancouver with a commanding view, the sights and the sounds of the harbour made a deep impression, leaving lifelong memories. Sounds from the harbour could be heard day and night, and when atmospheric conditions were favourable would be particularly sharp and clear. This was the age of steam—steam ships, steam locomotives, steam rollers for road work, steam donkeys in the woods, and thus steam whistles, which had a distinctiveness of their own.

By the sound of the whistles one could picture what was taking place out on the harbour. A long, a short, a long, a short whistle would indicate a CPSS Princess arrival, while one long, two short and one long would be that of a Union Steamship about to berth at her dock. Then one long followed by two short whistles would be a tug with a tow announcing her presence to the signal station at Prospect Point as she proceeded outbound through the First Narrows. Three short whistles meant that a ship was going astern while backing away from its berth into the harbour. By the sound of the North Vancouver ferries' whistles one followed their movements, while the high-pitched air whistles of the West Vancouver ferries marked them from all other craft. All vessels entering or leaving the harbour were required to give one long blast on their whistle, notifying the signal station at Prospect Point of their approach.

Sometimes, of an early morning, the frequency of ships' whistles would be an indication that the harbour was blanketed in thick fog, not unusual at certain times of the year. The North Vancouver ferries' short toots as they made their way across the harbour, and the sounds of the CP night boat from Victoria, and an hour later the one from Seattle, could be heard as they felt their way cautiously into the harbour and to their berths. Small craft and the West Vancouver ferries also tooted frequently.

Factory whistles marking the start and end of shifts—and there were a number of plants about the harbour—together with the sounds from the big shipyard in North Vancouver were also indications of life on the harbour. I well remember on a clear night hearing the sound of the CPR's Transcontinental freight train, the Seaboard Limited, which pulled out from the depot yards every night at precisely 10 o'clock, puff-puffing as it got its load moving. Suddenly, with a bit too much power by the engineer, the wheels would lose traction and spin with a "chuff-chuff-chuff" until brought under control again. Its long wailing whistle echoed across the harbour, another mark of the age of steam. Soon steam would make way for another power source, the diesel internal combustion engine that would revolutionize the railroad industry and lead to mile-long freight trains and much larger deep-sea ships of a very different form.[28]

The Union steamship *Lady Alexandra* entering First Narrows in 1924. First Narrows Lighthouse is at upper right. *CVA P.287 N.120 #2*

Rowboats, sailboats, canoes and small outboard-powered craft were popular transportation for families living near the Burnaby shoreline. They could rent rowboats at Barnet for 75 cents, but several water lovers had their own boathouses at the shore.

Summer days enticed the sailors out for a quiet trip up Indian Arm, fishing along the way. Some stopped at Belcarra Park or Deep Cove for a picnic, others went to the end of the arm and dropped their lines at the mouth of Indian River. An abandoned orchard on Port Moody's north shore attracted apple pickers.

Some young people enjoyed rowing or paddling across to the aboriginal reserve in North Vancouver, swapping tobacco for fish and filling sacks with clams from the beach. Whatever the attraction, small boats were a common sight at the eastern end of the inlet.[29]

Lighthouses

The year 1910 was one of change at Point Atkinson. Thomas D. Grafton was confirmed as the new lightkeeper on April 1; at 46 years old, he had been Walter Erwin's assistant for the preceding 20 years. Construction began on a new 34-metre hexagonal cement tower with six buttresses. When completed in 1912 it attracted admiring sightseers. A new duplex for the keeper, his wife Emma and their family and an assistant lightkeeper added some modern conveniences but still there was no electricity.

The new pressure vapour light operated on coal oil. The prismatic reflector revolved on a bed of mercury by means of weights, using the same principle as a grandfather clock. The keeper had to wind the works every 2.5 hours to ensure it kept up its one revolution every 10 seconds. In a small building below the tower, the horn on the fog alarm sounded once every 53 seconds in overcast or foggy conditions.[30]

The Graftons' life was more comfortable and social than the previous lightkeepers'. Tom hacked out a trail to Caulfeild so they could visit neighbours along the shore. His entries in the official log are generally routine, with a few exceptions:

February 1, 1911: Started S.E. wind & cloudy light fog Put fire on in fog alarm cleared off then S.E. wind & cloudy & rain until midnight.

August 12, 1911: Several times had to start fog alarm because of thickness of smoke from Point Grey.

October 1, 1912:...11-10 pm light turning must have stopped some time after assistant was to have called me at midnight I woke up 1-5am [1:05 a.m.?] found that light was stopped run up to tower started light revolving then looked for man found him asleep in fog alarm woke him up and told him that that would not do sleeping in his watch when he told me to go to hell & blackguarded me with foul talk I told him to get out of the fog alarm and as soon as it got daylight to leave the station he left 630 am for Caulfeilds to catch boat for town.

December 27, 1912:...Gasoline Launch broke down drifting on to rocks on Point men calling for help Launched boat but before we could get to them the Launch struck the shore throwing the two men in the water rescued the two men but could not do anything with Launch as the wind was very strong & a heavy sea running sea put the Launch high and dry men went to Vancouver leaving Launch ashore.

Life at the lighthouse continued in its daily routines until January 12, 1933, when different handwriting in the log reported:

Started light E. wind. S. shore in sight till 4 a.m. Then hazy on S. shore till noon. Light W. air till 6 pm Hazy in Bay at 9:50 pm started alarm 11:00 p.m. compressor belt broke throwing keeper into flywheel. Doctor summoned from West Van arriving at 11:45 p.m. Alarm ran till midnight. Calm, hazy in Bay and off Point Grey.

Keeper Tom Grafton returned to work six months later. He enjoyed fishing, but his use of dynamite to stun herring for bait was the end of him. In the log entry of October 6, 1933, his son Lawrence wrote:

Started calm with light haze in bay. Pt. Grey showing all morning dimly. Lightkeeper was killed instantly sometime before 6 a.m. from a dynamite blast which exploded accidently in his hand. The body was recovered at 7:15 a.m. by his youngest son, drifting in the submerged boat about 200 yards off the point. Light W. wind during the day. Then calm with light fog drifting out bay from 9:30 p.m. till midnight. S. shore lights in sight till midnight. Partly cloudy.[31]

Lawrence, born at Point Atkinson, took over as lightkeeper temporarily until the appointment was officially given to Ernie Dawe in 1935.

The large amount of sand and gravel washed down the Capilano River had built up on the north side of First Narrows to such an extent that an increasing number of ships were grounding, especially in bad weather. The Prospect Point Lighthouse and fog alarm were efficiently providing warning for the south side, but the Dominion government decided to construct a fog bell on the north side at the mouth of Capilano River. Alex Rood was appointed as fog alarm keeper on August 8, 1911. A letter from the government agent to the deputy minister of the Marine and Fisheries Department stated his qualification for the job: "[He] is the only white man living in the locality of the bell on the north side of Vancouver Narrows . . . there are a number of Indians there."

His work appeared to be satisfactory until complaints from steamship captains evoked a telegram from T. Robertson of Marine and Fisheries in Victoria on January 28, 1913:

Your bell reported not working by steamers passing last night from twelve to two. This state will not be tolerated. You must have alarm working when required. Reply by wire as to reason.

Letter from Rood to Robertson the same day:

Sir the bell alarm won't work. You had better send any [sic] expert to fix it there are something wrong with the clock work it is [unclear] and had bet[t]er be at[t]ended to at once. A. Rood Keeper of station nort[h] sid[e] of first Narrows Vancouver.

On March 11 the government fired Rood for inefficiency.[32]

On May 17, 1913, the First Narrows Lighthouse was operational and a new fog alarm began its duties on June 1. George Alfred Harris, a certified engineer, became the first lightkeeper on July 4, 1913, earning $1,320 per annum. He had worked at the Anvil Island Brick Company in Howe Sound before obtaining his new position. He stayed at the cramped station alone for several months with only a little coal oil stove to cook on, a tiny table and a rocking chair. His small mattress had to be pulled up to the ceiling during the day to leave space for him to carry out his duties.

In 1914 he finally was able to bring his wife Elizabeth and their son and daughter to the newly constructed keeper's house just behind the station. The buildings sat on pilings at the mouth of the Capilano River in a line with West Vancouver's Burrard Inlet low-water shoreline. At all but the lowest tide they were surrounded by water, forming an artificial island.

Harris's 18-year-old daughter, Dorothy, liked to help out with the light and fog alarms. In later years she recalled that the brass lamp was kept polished like a mirror. The plate glass around the outside of the tower had to be cleaned daily because of salt buildup from the sea. She was equally adept in a canoe, rowboat or motor boat, and rescued several boaters in trouble at the narrows.[33]

On March 16, 1925, George Harris died at the First Narrows Lighthouse. His body was lowered to a boat and rowed to shore. Elizabeth took over his duties until Alfred Dickenson was appointed keeper in December. Alfred and his wife were there only three years when he began a series of applications for transfer to a "more modern" light station, but refused those offered. The station's cross beams and supports were being

The First Narrows Lighthouse at the mouth of the Capilano River, 1916. It opened in May 1913 and a fog alarm was added the next month. The keeper lived there alone until a house was built and his family joined him in 1914. *VPL 8316*

weakened by teredo worms and urgent repairs were necessary, but the government would not put money into renovations. The Dickensons were concerned about their safety.

John Grove at Prospect Point and Davy Jones at Brockton Point continued to run their stations with the additional responsibility of supervising two assistants each. These men were responsible for operating a semaphore station near each location; at Prospect Point it was sited at the top of the cliff. They had to signal ships arriving at and leaving the inner harbour and give them details about other vessels in the vicinity. Davy Jones had the added responsibility of maintaining the beacon and fog bell on Burnaby Shoal southeast of Brockton Point.

The keepers had to maintain a complete record of all vessels arriving and departing, although in November 1913 the government advised them to report only the large vessels, including scows and log booms, because traffic in the harbour had become so heavy. Keeping shipping records, daily logs, cleaning and operating the lights and fog signals, and rewinding the weights for the fog alarms every 30 minutes when they were in operation were only a portion of their daily jobs. Boathouses, their ways, and the

The new Brockton Point Lighthouse under construction, circa 1914.
BC Archives A-00184

Prospect Point Lighthouse at First Narrows in the 1930s, with boathouse and boatways on the east side and the *Empress of Japan* passing. Stairs led up the cliff to the signal station. *CVA BO.P.10*

family homes were constantly in need of repair. The supervision of their assistants in the semaphore stations could be time consuming. At times letters came from the government with complaints from ships' captains that the semaphore lights weren't working when they should have been, and the lightkeepers had to find reliable replacement staff at fairly low wages.

They had to deal with less important complaints, as well. On July 5, 1911, the Board of Park Commissioners wrote to Grove to complain that lemonade was being sold to park visitors from the semaphore station. Grove replied that because his assistants had to carry their water for nearly half a kilometre, they felt that they were using it in a worthwhile way by profiting from their hard work. He was ordered to have them discontinue the sales.

The management of the semaphore station at Prospect Point was transferred to the Vancouver Harbour Commissioners on November 1, 1922. It upgraded the station with an arrangement of balls and cones, megaphones and telephone that signalled to ships entering the narrows to tell them what vessels or tows were ahead of them.

The light station was finally electrified in January 1926 and John Grove retired on August 1. He and his wife received permission to continue occupying the house. He died in March 1935, and his wife moved out two months later. In September the Board of Park Commissioners notified the Department of Marine in Victoria that it was going to burn down the house.

One of Davy Jones's responsibilities was removed when the government closed the Brockton Point semaphore station on May 15, 1918. Jones retired on November 1, 1924 and was awarded the Imperial Service Medal. E.E. Beck took over temporarily until John Walsh became the permanent keeper on February 28, 1925.

Around 1931 Walsh became responsible for maintaining the Calamity Point beacon and fog bell on the north shore near the place where the water pipelines entered Burrard Inlet from the north. That year his house was moved away from the shoreline and a continuing disagreement began among Walsh, the Department of Marine in Victoria and the parks board over who was to cut the large area of grass, plant flowers, weed, and keep the grounds "beautiful" as befitted Stanley Park. This continued until Walsh retired on July 1, 1936, with a pension of $445.56 per annum. The Vancouver Harbour Commission took over responsibility for the station.[34]

Second Narrows Bridge

Once dubbed "the Bridge of Sighs," the Second Narrows Bridge has endured a long history of failed plans, procrastination, delays, financial problems, damage and destruction.

The original bridge was built to provide rail and vehicle access to the North Shore to attract potential homeowners and businesses. The first company to receive a charter to build a railway on the North Shore was the Burrard Inlet Railway and Ferry Company, incorporated in 1891. The charter was allowed to lapse. The next year the Burrard Inlet Tunnel and Bridge Company was established with plans for a tunnel under First Narrows and a bridge over Second Narrows. These would provide access for railway lines, a street railway and pedestrian traffic. Again the charter lapsed. In 1899 the Vancouver, Westminster and Yukon Railway Company was established and received a bridge subsidy of $22,000 from the Dominion government. Problems in obtaining further subsidies caused delays.[35]

In 1910, the Burrard Inlet Tunnel and Bridge Company was reinstated by a group of property owners who issued shares in the business. The City of Vancouver purchased $200,000 worth, and the City and District of North Vancouver subscribed $100,000 and $150,000 respectively. Construction appeared imminent, until the additional bridge height required by the Canadian government increased the cost. Although further federal and provincial subsidies were promised in 1912 and 1913, the projected cost escalated to $2,225,000 exclusive of the approaches. To reduce expenses, the plans were changed to include construction of a smaller bascule-type span (raised by a counterweight) rather than a swing bridge. A call for tenders in January 1914 resulted in six bids, but the declaration of war in August 1914 put all plans on hold.

Although pressure continued for the bridge construction (the price of waterfrontage on the North Shore was 25 percent of the prevailing value of Vancouver harbour frontage), serious interest did not surface again until 1922. Government subsidies and shares were arranged and a contract was signed between the Northern Construction Company Ltd. and J.W. Stewart, and the Bridge Company, on July 25, 1923. To keep costs down, the 56.38-metre bascule span was built at the south end, in water shallower than at the centre of the narrows. This drew numerous complaints from shipping companies and predictions of danger to passing ships.

The bridge's total length, two kilometres, stretched from the south shore to a point immediately west of Seymour Creek in North Vancouver. A railway line crossed the centre of the single-deck bridge, with a one-way 3.05-metre road on each side of it and a sidewalk along the roadway on the east side. In the centre, the clearance between high-tide level and the bridge's lowest truss was only 6.76 metres. The approximate cost was $1.8 million and the shareholders were the District and City of North Vancouver, the District of West Vancouver and the City of Vancouver.[36]

For the first time, a bridge spanned Burrard Inlet. The Vancouver *Daily Province* announced the official opening on page 1 on November 7, 1925:

> Amid the shrill blasts of steamer whistles, and the clamor of automobile horns, Hon. W.H. Sutherland, minister of public works for British Columbia, at 2:30 p.m. severed the pale blue ribbon stretched from rail to rail of the Second Narrows bridge, officially opening the span which links the north shore with the south.
>
> Thousands of people from Greater Vancouver witnessed the opening ceremony from the bluff overlooking the bridge on the Vancouver shore, and a tremendous cheer went up as the ribbon was cut and the parade, led by the automobiles bearing Dr. Sutherland, Mr. D.C. Coleman, Vice President of the C.P.R., members of the Provincial Parliament, the City Council and the three north shore councils, crossed the span to the north shore followed by a caravan of motor cars stretching for several blocks.

The first span across Burrard Inlet, the Second Narrows Bridge, was completed in 1925. It provided a rail line, a road for cars and a pedestrian sidewalk. *NVMA 6986*

The crowds enjoyed free entertainment in North and West Vancouver.

Less than two years later, on March 10, 1927, the freighter *Urana* hit the centre of the new bridge, causing $77,000 worth of damage. The next year the *Norwich City* collided with and damaged the bridge. Between 1925 and 1930, 16 accidents jolted the structure, from minor contacts to major crashes costing thousands of dollars. Opponents of the span's design sent critical letters to the newspapers, and tried to influence the government to take action toward revising the span.

On the morning of Friday, September 19, 1930, an empty 5,080-tonne steel log barge, the *Pacific Gatherer* (formerly the *William Dollar*), was being towed under the bridge on a rising tide. In the grip of a strong current she drifted underneath the centre span, where she became lodged against the underside. Repeated attempts by the crews of several towboats failed to move her. The men watched in horror as the tide raised the buoyant barge, forcing her inexorably against the girders. As bolts sprang, concrete broke away and tortured metal shrieked. The pressure finally dislodged the 711-tonne span from the piers. With a tremendous heave it lurched eastward, slithered off the piers, and with a titanic splash dropped into the 24 metres of water below.

The barge was towed to an anchorage in Bedwell Bay in Indian Arm. The Pacific Salvage Company and Burrard Dry Dock were hired to raise the remains of the centre span from the bottom of the inlet. Divers worked in the frigid water to place cables under the span. With scows on both sides attached to the cables at low tide, the wrecked structure rose from the bottom as the rising tide lifted the scows. Tugs then towed the burden to Burrard Dry Dock. The span was set on the floating dry dock and surveyed for possible reclamation. As a decision was not made quickly, workers moved it onto piles and a framework just west of the ferry dock, where it stayed for some time. When the Canadian government finally deemed it unsafe for reuse, it was cut up for scrap and sold to Japan.[37]

The North Shore would be without a bridge for nearly four years because of financial and legal problems. Income from tolls had amounted to about $800 per day; in contrast, the cost of barges to transport cars and freight across the inlet in the absence of a bridge cost the Harbour Commissioners about $6,000 a month.

There was agreement that a reconstructed bridge should include changes to the original plans, and an earlier suggestion resurfaced. In 1931 the Cote Commission had suggested construction of a lockless canal four kilometres long, 60.9 metres wide, and deep enough for ocean-going ships, which would cut through North Vancouver land parallel to the shore. The mouths of Seymour and Lynn Creeks would be diverted to the canal's western end. The Second Narrows Bridge would then be reconstructed as a fixed span with a railway and highway crossing and a swing span over the canal. Earth dredged from the canal site would be dumped on the tidal flats and used for the development of industrial sites. Although a few proponents of the scheme continued its promotion, it was not popular.

After the Bridge Company went into receivership in 1932, the Vancouver Harbour Commissioners bought the business and conveyed it to the Crown in 1933. With financial problems finally resolved, construction began right away. Tenders were called for a new lift span, 85.9 metres long and close to the centre of the channel, though the bascule remained in place near the south shore because of the prohibitive cost of removing it. The official opening took place on June 18, 1934, under the auspices of the Vancouver Harbour Commissioners.

ANNOUNCING THE OFFICIAL

REOPENING

JUN 1 6 1934   OF THE

Second Narrows Bridge

MONDAY, JUNE 18

AT 2 P.M.

To All Passenger and Vehicular Traffic

●

TOLLS

Only Official Tickets Issued by Vancouver Harbour Commissioners
Will Be Accepted

Single Trip

PERSONS,
each .... $ .05

AUTOMOBILES,
including driver .... .15

**Commutation Tickets May Be Purchased
In Books as follows:**

PEDESTRIANS AND PASSENGERS,
books of 40 tickets $1.00

AUTOMOBILES,
books of 40 tickets 3.00

AUTOMOBILES,
books of 20 tickets 1.75

Tolls for Trucks, Motorcycles, etc., Upon Application

●

VANCOUVER HARBOUR COMMISSIONERS

Announcement of the reopening of the Second Narrows Bridge after damage closed it for four years. Vancouver Sun, *June 16, 1934*

False Creek

False Creek was only two-thirds its original size by 1916. The eastern flats had been filled in and the reclaimed land used for Great Northern Railway and Canadian Northern Pacific Railway terminals. That year, 13.8 hectares of mud flats were built up with material dredged from the channel and made into Granville Island. The two kilometres of railway tracks

Vulcan Iron Works Ltd. in 1918, one of the original factories on Granville Island.
VPL 20429

running across the centre of the island made the site very popular with businesses, and by 1923 all lots had been leased to industry.

For years industrial waste routinely was dumped into the creek. Smoke from the 11 sawmills bordering about half of the shoreline and effluent from BC Electric Company's gasworks engulfed the island in a noxious haze. Sixteen outfalls of raw sewage from nearby residential communities added their noisome odours to the oily, foul-smelling water. False Creek was not the place to be at low tide in warm weather. Rat Portage Lumber Company's name aptly described the neighbourhood's four-legged residents. Noise from the CPR's yards and shops on the north side added to the daily mechanical din.

Public pressure resulted in construction of a line to transport some of the sewage underwater, where it would be expelled out in English Bay. The

Sawmill and log booms on the south shore of False Creek, 1912.
Stuart Thomson photo, CVA 99-325

number of sawmills was gradually reduced—fires took their toll, and during the 1930s financial failures forced closures.[38]

The hard monetary times encouraged squatters to set up residence along the shore. A cluster of floathouses, what we now would call "live-aboards," hugged the south shore near Burrard Bridge. In her book *Destination Cortez Island*, June Cameron recalls local characters who lived there when her family moored their boat in False Creek in the 1930s:

> Among those who made the dock a permanent home was a man
> called Rudy Kipling, who was a writer and was related to Rudyard
> his famous India-born namesake. There was another local resident
> in the tough years of the Depression... This old fellow lived in a
> cave just above the high-water mark, in among the discarded lum-
> ber, sawdust and mud on the bank at Rat Portage. He used a
> stained piece of canvas as a partial wall to keep the wind and rain
> under some control, and he had a bed of sawdust and old clothes

at the back. He cooked in the bottom half of a steel barrel and managed to survive by selling the crabs he caught out in English Bay. All of Vancouver's sewers emptied into adjacent waters, so the crabs had reason to be there. Nobody, including himself, seemed concerned about his awful living conditions.[39]

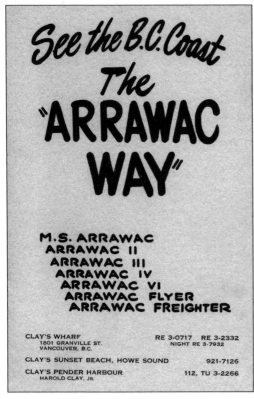

Brochure for the *Arrawac* line.

In 1932, in the midst of this unappealing waterfront, Harold Clay set up one of the first marinas in British Columbia, just west of the Granville Bridge on the south shore. Clay's Wharf survived until the 1970s. Boat owners who moored there can clearly recall Harold, clad in a greasy overall, towing boats around the marina with a rope attached to the stern of his rowboat, his dog sitting up on the bow seat. His carefully varnished and painted motor launch *Arrawac* was a neat, clean contrast to its surroundings.

English Bay

Vancouver city council maintained the English Bay area, from Kitsilano to Point Grey, as an industry-free location. In about 1910 the name of the district from the mouth of False Creek west to Jericho was changed from Greer's Beach to Kitsilano, a variation of the name of Chief Khahtsahlanogh of the Squamish people.[40]

In 1913 the mouth of False Creek was dredged to deepen the channel for shipping; the sand was used as fill in the low land beside the beach, a favourite spot for bullfrogs. Early residents of Kitsilano called the nightly chorus "the Canadian Band." Even after the swampy land was filled, the frogs continued their summer evening performances that at times almost amounted to a roar.

A squatter's summer residence on the shore at Point Grey in 1920 uses a derelict barge as a foundation, with two tents joined for living quarters. *Dorothy Dobson Collection*

On January 1, 1920, Peter Pantages, a Vancouver cafe owner, initiated the Polar Bear Club. Members swam at the English Bay bathing beach on New Year's Day to demonstrate to the world that Vancouver weather permitted swimming all year round. Pantages himself swam in English Bay three times a day. The tradition continues, attracting hundreds of swimmers and spectators yearly.

As an indirect result of the Great War, English Bay became the site of a seaplane base. Airmen who had served in World War I returned home to Canada and many wanted to continue flying, but no Canadian legislation existed to govern and establish rules and regulations. After a great deal of pressure from the enthusiastic airmen, the Canadian government enacted the Air Board Act on April 29, 1919, and a seven-member board was placed in charge of regulating and managing all aspects of Canadian aviation.

That autumn the board selected a Vancouver location for the first west-coast Air Board flying station, at Jericho Beach on English Bay, abutting the Jericho Golf and Country Club. The site was especially appealing to the board because the BC government provided it free of charge. The

English Bay Bathing Pavilion, circa 1930. *CVA BE. P.18 N.101*

usually peaceful beach at the end of Point Grey Road resounded with the hubbub of construction during the spring and summer of 1920. Clearing the sand of driftwood, a crew prepared a cement foundation and a wooden slipway into the water. A pier and floathouse paralleled the ramp out into English Bay. A hangar was constructed of timber framing, with canvas curtains on each side. Administration of the base would be carried out from a set of wooden buildings.

Britain had donated more than 100 World War I planes to Canada, and the United States provided 12 Curtis H5-2L flying boats. Jericho received its share. In 1921, the first season of forest patrols, the service helped to prevent forest fires and monitor the spread of tree disease. Planes also followed ships inbound from the Orient, enabling customs officers to monitor suspicious packages dropped overboard, usually containing drugs. Aerial photography, the transportation of fish fry and delivery of work parties to remote areas were a few of the diverse assignments carried out.

Although the airmen were flying refurbished aircraft, the number of accidents was limited. One tragic exception was a crash off Point Grey on September 11, 1922, when two of the three crew members perished.

Jericho became a seaplane training base after the Royal Canadian Air Force Operations Squadron No. 1 was formed on April 1, 1925. The trainees were also introduced to the use of carrier pigeons when aircraft wireless was not available.

Despite cutbacks during the Great Depression, the base continued to operate successfully during the 1930s. When signs of a new war in Europe increased and Japanese involvement threatened, five more BC flying boat stations were added.[41]

The first construction at the Point Grey site of the University of British Columbia began in 1914 with the library and science buildings. Their completion was delayed by World War I and by government procrastination until, in 1925, the Point Grey campus opened.

The rock for the structures' granite facings was quarried on an island north of Vancouver and brought by tug and barge to the beach below the university site. The workers built a pier for unloading the granite, and a cable railway hauled it up the steep cliffs. The westerly winds off the Strait of Georgia were a hazard to the unloading operations, so five or six old warships were sunk in an arc offshore to provide a breakwater. These submerged hulls, along with a small number of other sunken ships, supposedly gave the popular sunbathing area Wreck Beach its name.[42]

At the time, the cliffs at UBC were covered by conifers and maples. In later years erosion became a serious problem. In January 1935 an enormous amount of water from extended rainfall and snow built up east of the university's main library. Crews released the accumulated water into Campus Canyon, which intersected the Point Grey cliffs on their north side. As a result 76,000 cubic metres of sand were washed out, creating a huge gully extending inland to the present Law Building on campus. The cliff erosion, mainly as a result of changes in groundwater seepage, continues despite many attempts to prevent it.[43]

Water Mains

One of the growing pains the expanding Vancouver population was experiencing was an inefficient water supply. The first water main, 30.1 centimetres in diameter, had been laid underwater across First Narrows in 1889, carrying drinking water from the Capilano River watershed to Vancouver taps. Six mains were completed at First Narrows by 1912, but even at that time Vancouver needed extra water, and in December 1908 two more lines were laid under Second Narrows, carrying water from the Seymour River for the first time.[44]

Over the years, the mains lying on the floor of First Narrows were damaged several times by passing ships and often the pipe joints leaked. When the government began dredging sand and gravel washed down from the Capilano River at the harbour entrance, mains had to be raised to allow the machinery to operate.

After many years of planning, construction of a pressure tunnel 121 metres under the bedrock of First Narrows began in August 1931. The tunnel was 946.7 metres long, with an inside diameter of 2.28 metres. By the time it was completed, at a cost of $1 million, 18,000 barrels of cement had been used to fill the space between the 2.13-metre-diameter pipe and the rock surfaces of the tunnel.

When the water began to flow in June 1933 the tunnel had the potential to deliver more than 909 million litres per day, but before that amount could be realized a dam high up the Capilano River would be required as a reservoir.[45] The Cleveland Dam was built in 1954.

Indian Arm

Captain George Richards of the British Admiralty surveyed and named several geographical features of the North Arm of the inlet in 1858–59. It was officially changed to Indian Arm in 1921 because the Vancouver Harbour Commissioners felt it needed a distinctive name, rather than merely a descriptive one.

The Indian River, at the head of the arm, had its commonly accepted name confirmed the same year, replacing several map references to it as the Mesliloet River. "Mesliloet" had been the river's, and arm's, aboriginal name, meaning "as far as the water goes" in the Tsleil-Waututh language. Captain Richards also named Roche Point after Lieutenant Richard Roche of the British navy, and Deep Cove for the great depth of water out in the bay. Deep Cove village was known from 1927 to 1940 as Deep Water Post Office.[46]

Several sightseeing and picnic boats had carried passengers up Indian Arm since the 1890s. As more people purchased waterfront property, improved access was essential because no roads had been built into the area. In the spring of 1912 the Second Narrows Ferry Company instituted a passenger service from Vancouver, making four trips a day, for 10 cents per passenger, to five points of call on the arm.[47] This new service was in response to

Regatta at Deep Cove, North Arm, circa 1915. *ZL*

residents' discontent with the previously existing service. An editorial in the *BC Saturday Sunset* on June 15, 1912, complained:

> A sternwheeler, the "Skeena", wanders about the North Arm on a secret schedule known only to the company. No one outside the sacred precincts of their offices has ever been able to discover the system of guesses by which the "Skeena" is run . . . The companion of the "Skeena", the "Defiance", is guaranteed to defy the earliest rising traveler to catch her before she leaves port. After she leaves anything can catch her.[48]

In January 1908 MV *Bellara*, owned by the New Brighton Ferry Company, had begun to serve the arm as a Travelling Post Office (TPO). Captain James A. Cates was the official postmaster from January 1908 until February 3, 1910. Captain Hugh Stalker was the ferry's owner-operator with assistance from Captain J. (Paddy) Gilmore until World War I broke out. F.W. Foster took over as postmaster from Captain Cates in March 1910 and served in that capacity until September 1913. In January 1914 Captain Herbert S. Hilton became postmaster and also took over the com-

Boaters circa 1910 on Indian Arm, a popular location for regattas and picnics. *ZL*

pany. He changed its name to Harbour Shipping Company Ltd. and advertised his services as being daily mail, passenger and freight boat service.
He leased Wigwam Inn from owner Edward J. Young, a millionaire lumberman of Madison, Wisconsin.

Although a general belief has existed that this TPO was the first in the
British Empire, in fact it was not even the first in British Columbia. Several
steamers acting as post offices, with their own postmarks, travelled BC
waters from the 1880s on.[49]

In 1920 a new business, Harbour Navigation Company, was incorporated with $100,000 capital and issued 1,000 shares. The company's first
annual report, submitted on July 19, listed John Douglas Stalker, William
Booth Skinner and James Henry MacGill, all of Vancouver, as directors.

The company acquired several craft to serve Indian Arm. The *Lo-
olbee*, a yacht previously owned by the R.P. McLennan family of
Vancouver, provided ferry service (the craft had been named for three of
the McLennan children—Logan, Olga and Beth). A new boat, the *Lake
Buntzen*, and the *Enilada*, a yacht formerly owned by land promoters on
the west coast of Vancouver Island, also made the run into the arm. In
1924 the company had a new diesel-powered ferry built, the 30.5-metre

Harbour Princess, with room for 250 passengers; it remained in operation until 1987.

Captain J. Douglas Stalker was the postmaster and Harbour Navigation Company manager. The ferry service operated six days a week in summer and two days a week in winter, making scheduled stops at Belcarra, Woodlands, Sunshine, Brighton Beach, Thwaytes Landing, Buntzen Bay, Jubilee, Weldwood logging camp and Wigwam Inn. A white four-gallon (18-litre) gasoline can raised to the top of a pole signalled the boats to chug in to the float at other points for unscheduled stops.[50]

From June 2, 1925 to December 31, 1929, Harbour Navigation leased Wigwam Inn and the surrounding land for the use of its holidaying passengers. On April 21, 1927, the company also bought land at Belcarra Park and developed it with a dance pavilion, 10 cabins, picnic grounds and a small store.

Three years later the company purchased MV *Scenic*, a boat that served Burrard Inlet for more than 70 years. Constructed in 1908 as the *Falcon* at Anacortes, Washington, she was 20.7 metres long and 4.2 metres wide, with a 100-horsepower gasoline engine. After serving for a few years as a navy gunboat near Port Townsend, she was purchased by William Brewster of the Port Moody Ferry Company in 1916 and served between the foot of Columbia Street in Vancouver, Port Moody and Ioco until about 1920. Harbour Navigation purchased her in about 1930, had her rebuilt, then put her into service as the third Burrard Inlet Travelling Post Office on Indian Arm. Captain Stalker remained postmaster, but other skippers took her out on runs, delivering the mail from an open window in the wheelhouse.

One of the most popular skippers during the 1930s and 1940s was Captain Andy Anderson, a white-moustached Yorkshireman known as "Cap'n Andy." Children and adults alike looked forward to his arrival.

Meanwhile, ownership was changing at Wigwam Inn. One of the original owners, Benjamin F. Dickens, recounted in 1937 the eventual sale of his interest in the land:

Finally [Alvo von] Alvensleben and I separated our interests. The hotel license had to be in my name, and I did not like that; my dear old mother would have turned in her grave if she had known I had a license to sell liquors. [He sold his share of the hotel site,

The popular Wigwam Inn, circa 1912, shortly after it was built. The Fraser River stern-wheeler *Skeena* made daily passenger trips into the inlet during the summer. *CVA LGN 546*

district lot 1436, to Alvensleben on August 12, 1910.] So, I took the townsite and he took the rest, that is I took the registered townsite only, being part of D.L. 819 and 820. Afterwards I got in touch with Edward J. Young of Madison, Wis., and sold my interest, lock, stock, and barrel—about 1917.[51]

When war with Germany broke out in 1914, Alvensleben was visiting his family there and was not allowed to return to Canada. He went to Seattle, where he was interned as an enemy alien after the United States entered the war in 1917. Wigwam Inn, part of the Indian River Park Company, was taken over by the Custodian of Enemy Property.

Edward Young, who had already purchased the townsite section from Benjamin Dickens, also bought Wigwam Inn in March 1917 from the trust

Pilings at the north end of Indian Arm in 1927, installed in preparation for a large sawmill to be built on the Indian River. The business never materialized. *MC*

company holding the property. For some time he had been president of the Vancouver Lumber Company in North Vancouver, and in 1927 began construction of a sawmill on a lot that was part of Dickens's original townsite at the east side of Indian River. The business was eventually abandoned, with only wooden pilings left standing offshore.

Abandoned Dreams

Along the shores of Burrard Inlet major improvements took place over the years, but many other proposals were never realized.

Since 1887 Vancouver city council had been requesting that the Canadian government grant it ownership of all False Creek land east of Westminster Avenue (now Main Street) so that the shoreline could be filled in and used for new businesses. In 1901 the Dominion government approved a grant to the city of all the False Creek bed east of Carrall Street. The immediate need for development plans resulted in several proposals. Perhaps the most ambitious was the "Proposed Improvement to False Creek Docks East of Westminster Avenue," put forward in December 1905.

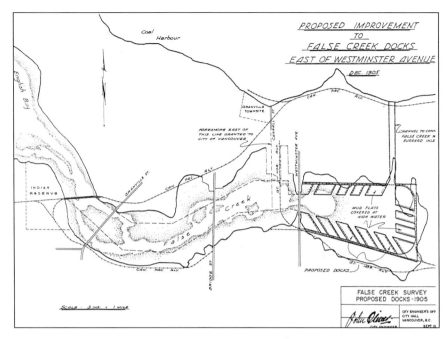

A 1905 proposal to build docks at the eastern end of False Creek and a canal into the harbour. *Vancouver City Engineer's Office*

The plan called for the basin to be dredged to a suitable depth for medium-sized coastal ships. Fourteen finger piers around the south, east and north shorelines would have the advantage of rail service. A canal would cut through from the northeast corner to the shore of Burrard Inlet, so that ships could enter and leave the main harbour without having to pass through the potentially dangerous tidal waters at First Narrows. The plan was so popular that a bridge built to join the north and south sides of Westminster Avenue in 1908 was equipped with a drawbridge section to enable ships to pass through to the docks and canal when the plan was implemented.

The Great Northern Railway made a proposal to city council in 1909 to build a rail terminal on 24.7 hectares around the eastern shore, a horseshoe-shaped area of tidal flats. Although the city's plan for the docks was still viable, it was dropped in favour of the railway's proposal to develop a central railway terminal on landfill in the eastern portion of False Creek.[52]

With the opening of the Panama Canal in 1914, planners predicted a significant increase in shipping entering Burrard Inlet. Because the development of the city waterfront would be so costly, at least two plans were offered between 1917 and 1919 as a cheaper alternative, both suggesting the development of ocean docks extending into English Bay at Kitsilano near the mouth of False Creek, with railway yards, industrial buildings and a lighthouse. The cost of land was much lower there than along the city waterfront.

The Canadian government authorized the Vancouver Harbour Commissioners in 1919 to spend $5 million on port improvements. Although the commission was initially in favour of the Kitsilano plan, a change in government and in commissioners led to the building of Ballantyne Pier on the city's harbourfront instead. Kitsilano proposals were shelved.

The Vancouver Terminals Company presented its own plan in 1912 for increased harbour and industrial facilities. Its "Spanish Banks Harbour Development" proposal involved the reclamation of 275.2 hectares of Spanish Bank land on the outer harbour, reaching from Alma Street to slightly beyond Point Grey. The cost would be approximately $75 million and would include 60.7 hectares of dock space. The advantages cited for

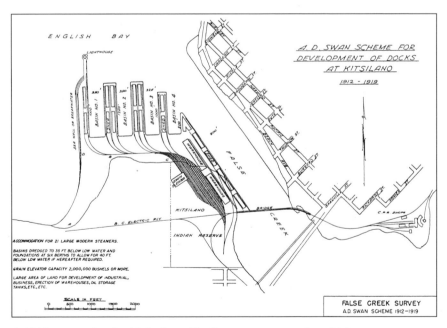

A 1917 proposal to build docks at Kitsilano to accommodate 21 large steamers, a grain elevator, warehouses, storage tanks and more. *Vancouver City Engineer's Office*

this development, as an alternative to the inner harbour, was the easier accessibility by water and land, especially rail. Tides and fog would cause minimal interference to ships docking. However, the project was expected to lower residential housing values, and to interfere with the public beach. Because it was also very expensive, the plan was left to gather dust.[53]

Farther east, a world-class dockyard and ship-repair plant was in the early stages of development in 1910, to be located at Roche Point in North Vancouver, at the mouth of the North Arm. Long a dream of Captain Nicholas Thompson, a prominent Vancouver businessman, the dockyard would extend 304.8 metres along the north shore of Burrard Inlet and 152.4 metres back into the densely wooded land. It would be part of a planned industrial town to be named Roslyn. The Vancouver Drydock and Shipbuilding Company had raised capital in England for the project and planned to purchase the land from the Imperial Car Company, which was proposing a railway sleeping-car works.

That year the Canadian Parliament passed the Dry Docks Subsidies Act to encourage shipbuilding in Canada, an encouraging move for the dockyard planners. The Roche Point proposal progressed to the stage of a formal agreement with the Canadian government, but it did not receive the required subsidy and plans were dropped. In 1916 an attempt to revive the proposal fell through because the subsidy again was not granted.[54]

In 1912 a creative group of engineers proposed one of the most daring plans on record for the inlet. Instead of a bridge at Second Narrows, they suggested a dam be built across the narrows, a project no more costly than a bridge, thus turning the North Arm into a fresh-water lake. The dam would be constructed of two bulkheads, with wharves bordering each side. Two locks would provide access to the upper lake, one for large and one for small vessels. To prevent silt from flowing out of Seymour Creek and filling the channel, the mouth of that stream would be moved half a kilometre to the west.

Proponents of the dam were convinced that its construction would overcome several defects of the existing harbour. The velocity of the tide at First Narrows would be reduced, making entrance and exit safer for ships and boats. Vessels would be able to moor in the fresh-water lake and lose the barnacles and mussels on their hulls. Docks and log booms would be free of the ravages of teredo worms. The top of the dam, 9.2 to 15.3 metres wide, would include a road for tramways and a railway, and graving docks

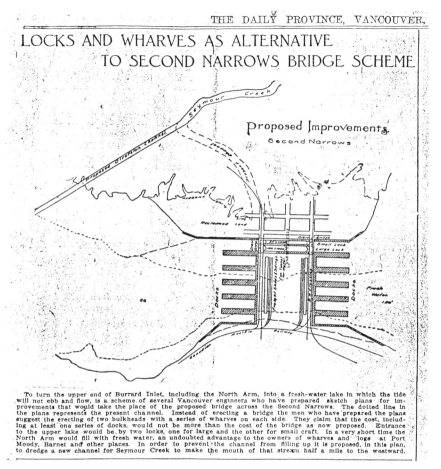

LOCKS AND WHARVES AS ALTERNATIVE TO SECOND NARROWS BRIDGE SCHEME

Proposed Improvements.
Second Narrows

To turn the upper end of Burrard Inlet, including the North Arm, into a fresh-water lake in which the tide will not ebb and flow, is a scheme of several Vancouver engineers who have prepared sketch plans for improvements that would take the place of the proposed bridge across the Second Narrows. The dotted line in the plans represents the present channel. Instead of erecting a bridge the men who have prepared the plans suggest the erecting of two bulkheads with a series of wharves on each side. They claim that the cost, including at least one series of docks, would not be more than the cost of the bridge as now proposed. Entrance to the upper lake would be, by two locks, one for large and the other for small craft. In a very short time the North Arm would fill with fresh water, an undoubted advantage to the owners of wharves and logs at Port Moody, Barnet and other places. In order to prevent the channel from filling up it is proposed, in this plan, to dredge a new channel for Seymour Creek to make the mouth of that stream half a mile to the westward.

An engineer's plan to build a dam with locks and wharves across Second Narrows instead of a bridge, which would have turned the North Arm into a freshwater lake. Daily Province, *January 22, 1912*

would provide shipping services. The level of the inner harbour would be higher, thus eliminating the need for the high pilings necessary for the existing wharves because of the large difference between high and low tides. With the freedom for large ships to enter the North Arm, the area would undoubtedly be developed by manufacturing enterprises without the high taxes of city land.[55]

In spite of the apparent advantages of a dam, the government did not approve the plan. Although the scheme resurfaced in 1931 after damage to the Second Narrows Bridge, it became another abandoned dream.

CHAPTER 6

THE WAR AND BEYOND: 1935–60

For the defence of Vancouver, the Forts on both sides of the Straits of Juan de Fuca and the Fort at Yorke Island act as barriers to an attack on [the city]... The role of the Forts in Vancouver is to repel any hostile vessel in the waters adjacent and to assist in repelling any troops attempting to land on shore.

—Fire Commander's Orders, October 1942[1]

While the Allies were fighting in Europe during World War II, industry on Burrard Inlet made a significant contribution to the war effort. The amount of shipbuilding exploded and became one of the dominant West Coast industries, strongly contributing to the Allies' sea victory. The Lions Gate Bridge was completed and its navigational aids became an essential part of directing the increasing traffic in the harbour.

Residents felt the cold chill of the war close to home when the Canadian government set up military bases with antiaircraft guns and searchlights at points around the outer harbour, and the flying boat station at Jericho Beach became a pilot training centre and offices for the Department of National Defence.

Lions Gate Bridge

First Narrows is the gateway to Burrard Inlet's inner harbour. Turbulent with tidal action, it has been the scene of many shipping accidents and some disasters. Although a fairly narrow stretch of water, it was a barrier between the north and south shores, discouraging North Shore settlement—especially in West Vancouver—and expansion of industry. Since 1892, when the Burrard Inlet Tunnel and Bridge Company had proposed a tunnel under First Narrows, plans for other crossings had been suggested. In 1912 the *Vancouver World* reported:

> The citizens of the West Vancouver district are at the present time deeply interested in the project of the Burrard Inlet Tunnel and Bridge Company [a new company] to build a tube under the First Narrows.[2]

This type of proposal has been echoed several times over the years, even to the present day.

Public opinion was divided over bridge proposals for many years, and one strong factor against a bridge centred on the need for an access road through Stanley Park. On June 25, 1927, the City of Vancouver held a plebiscite requesting approval for the construction of a road through the park. The people voted it down. A letter to the editor of the *Province* said that if the road was built the park would resemble a cherished oil painting slashed in two and hung with one half on either side of the mantelpiece.

Suggestions for a bridge over First Narrows finally received serious consideration in the early 1930s. Business interests were looking for waterfront land on the North Shore but, more importantly to a future bridge, the undeveloped mountainside land in West Vancouver was potentially a prized investment for businessmen with capital.

Alfred J.T. "Fred" Taylor, a British Columbia engineer and entrepreneur, was able to interest British investors in purchasing West Vancouver real estate. The cornerstone of his plan was to buy while prices and wages were low. In 1928 he formed British Pacific Securities, and a bridge across First Narrows was essential in promoting the land development. In 1930 Taylor and one of his major British investors, William Stephen Eyre, a wealthy retired banker, visited West Vancouver, then headed to Ottawa to discuss with the federal government their proposal to build such a bridge. They received encouragement from Prime Minister R.B. Bennett.

Following its collapse in 1930, the Second Narrows Bridge was closed until 1934, a situation that encouraged stronger public interest in a span across First Narrows. In 1931 Taylor and his group purchased two existing bridge-construction charters that had been granted in 1926 to the First Narrows Bridge Company Limited. Joined by money from the Guinness brewing family in Britain, the company had enough capital to build a bridge and to purchase more than 1,618.7 hectares of West Vancouver land for $75,000. The investors formed a subsidiary company, British Pacific Properties Limited, with West Vancouver land development its sole purpose.

Plans for the bridge surged ahead. The leading bridge designers in Canada, Monsarrat and Pratley of Montreal, were in charge. The British Columbia government approved construction in April 1933 and the North Shore municipalities followed suit in August. Vancouver city council held back on its permission, probably influenced by pressure from the CPR, which feared that improving access to North Shore real estate would devalue its own unsold land in Vancouver. A frustrated Fred Taylor agreed to pay for a plebiscite. On December 13, 1933, 70.8 percent of Vancouver voters approved the bridge construction.

The last major hurdle was permission from the Canadian government. Despite his earlier apparent support for the project, Prime Minister Bennett now found unspecified reasons to hold up the project. A compromise was finally reached. On April 29, 1936, the federal government passed an order-in-council agreeing to the project. Although the name Jubilee Bridge was popular in Vancouver, which was celebrating its 50th anniversary, the structure was named Lions Gate Bridge in 1937, after the twin peaks, the Lions, in the mountains behind the North Shore.

Taylor, meanwhile, was able to secure a strong commitment from the Guinness family toward the West Vancouver "Highlands" development. Another group of British capitalists provided enough additional backing to allow the bridge to become a reality.

On March 31, 1937, work began on road clearing through Stanley Park. Teams of horses hauled the logs away and the smoke from brush fires spread out to the narrows. On April 9 bridge construction began on the south shore at Prospect Point. The seabed was dynamited and caissons sunk into position on the north and south sides. A North Shore viaduct, 669 metres long, raised the roadbed to a suitable height. Towers rose 111 metres into the air. Catwalk cables were stretched like lifelines between the towers.

For their installation the narrows closed for one hour to water traffic at 4:50 a.m. on May 2, 1938, the only closure during the entire construction process. Catwalks were then attached. The main cable bundles contained 61 individual strands, each 3.65 centimetres in diameter. The steel roadbed was formed of 174 sections, each weighing 1,597 tonnes. On August 16 the men poured 7.6 centimetres of concrete over a "Tee grid" system. Workers painted the cables red, the other steelwork green, and the underside of the bridge brown.

Pedestrian traffic across the Lions Gate Bridge began on November 12, 1938 and the span was open to two lanes of cars two days later. Tolls were five cents for pedestrians, bicycle riders and vehicle passengers, and 25 cents for autos and drivers.

Two couchant lions were installed at the south portal in January 1939, each weighing 6.6 tonnes; each head alone weighs 2.03 tonnes. Fred Taylor placed a few personal items inside one of the lions, which were designed and built by Vancouver sculptor Charles Marega. He was the first professional sculptor to work in BC and taught for several years at

Construction of the Lions Gate Bridge began in 1937 and the span was officially opened in 1939. This view shows the first section built out to one of twin towers. *WVMA 1992-126-001*

the Vancouver School of Art, forerunner of the Emily Carr Institute of Art & Design. He died suddenly at the school on March 27, 1939, after one of his classes.

The bridge officially opened on May 26, 1939 and has become a worldwide symbol of Vancouver.[3]

Eileen Scott began working in the Lions Gate Bridge office in 1947 as a secretary, in the building on the north side that is now used by the bridge police. At that time 40 toll collectors (shift workers), three sergeants and

Background: Lions Gate Bridge during construction, as seen from Stanley Park. *Leonard Frank photo, NVMA 3622*

Opposite bottom: Lions Gate Bridge cables are prepared for connection, 1938. *NVMA 5293*

Left: Construction workers on the bridge cables, 1938. *NVMA 5296*

Below: Workers on the bridge deck, 1938. *NVMA 5294*

Toll booths at the north end of the Lions Gate Bridge, March 1951.
Eileen Scott Collection

a Mr. Fiddler, the head man, reported there. Eileen recalled the more rural atmosphere:

> A Mr. Weiker lived down by the Capilano River. His bay horse, Babe, would get lonely in the orchard so she'd jump the fence and wander up to see the collectors, and I guess they had carrots for her. She'd be standing there with her head in the booth door and a car would come along, and she would just wander out of the way, then come back again. Sometimes I'd ride her, up Taylor Way, before it was paved, and take her over to Stanley Park. I didn't have to worry about cars. When I used to ride up, the bridge collectors would try to charge me five cents for each leg and five cents for the tail.
>
> The manager, Lord Peregrine Willoughby, had his office in the Vancouver Marine Building. He was very English. He insisted that the men working for the bridge company had to be war veterans. One of the control sergeants, Gus Kreiger, had a hook for a hand. He'd had his arm blown off. Another man, Gerry Martin, had crashed in the tail of a plane and had injuries all over his body.
>
> There was a little house, a signal station, on top of the bridge. The men who worked there climbed up on a ladder to reach it. Did

you hear the story about a poor man who was caught in the rip tide and the lookout yelled down with his loudspeaker, "Are you in trouble?" The man looked all around and he couldn't see a thing, and he called, "Yes, God, I'm in trouble." So they sent a boat to rescue him."

Eileen had studied at the Vancouver School of Art, where Charles Marega was one of her teachers. She remembered: "He always wore a snowy white shirt and a black suit. He was a real gentleman. I was in his class the day he suddenly died."[4]

Eventually, bridge traffic became so heavy that in 1952 the two lanes were changed to three. The BC government purchased all the bridge shares for $5,959,060 in January 1955, under the name of the British Columbia Highways and Bridges Authority. By 1957 more than 10 million cars per year were travelling over the span. The government was able to recoup its expenditure and ended the tolls on April 1, 1963.

Lions Gate Bridge, circa 1940, with the *Princess Marguerite* heading west. The CPR Princess ships served the BC coast for many years. *NVMA 3623*

Rumours of the possibility of a third crossing of the narrows have continued to the present. Tunnel, new bridge or expansion of the present Lions Gate Bridge? The question was unresolved in the year 2001.

The Impact of World War II

Canada declared war against Germany on September 10, 1939. Three weeks earlier three Vancouver military units had mobilized at Ottawa's orders; their mandate was to cover vulnerable points with gun emplacements and searchlights. The old World War I emplacement at Stanley Park above Siwash Rock, the north shore of First Narrows (dubbed Narrows North by the military) and the heights of Point Grey became sites of frantic activity.

The Royal Canadian Engineers laboured through rainy days and flood-lit nights at Point Grey to build huts for the militia (these residences were located where the Museum of Anthropology at UBC now stands). Two six-inch guns arrived by barge and were hauled up the cliffs. Temporary emplacements were reinforced with sandbags, and shells were stored with only tarpaulins for protection. Permanent reinforced concrete emplacements were finally completed a year later. Underground tunnels were then used as magazines, also available as possible air raid shelters.

The first defences at Narrows North were two "12-pounder" guns set up on the gravel spit at the Capilano River mouth. A three-storey concrete gantry was built a little farther north, just west of the Lions Gate Bridge, and the guns were relocated to its roof on October 6. Eight manually controlled searchlights were available to assist the gunners in the dark. As some alarms had been raised by floating logs and canoes, new, stronger searchlights were installed by December 1941. Their beams were able to shine near water level to enable the watchers to discriminate between periscopes and flotsam or jetsam. The men lived in wooden barracks at the site. The militia also established four heavy antiaircraft guns on the west side of the river at what is now Ambleside Park.

Crews set up a base at Point Atkinson where the Port War Signal Station was responsible for the control of all water traffic arriving at and departing from the port of Vancouver. The station included "examination" guns, searchlights, and military quarters at the rear of the light station— eight buildings housing the officer's mess, kitchen, guardhouse, ablutions hut and sleeping barracks. Every ship entering the harbour was required

A six-pounder Hotchkiss used as an examination gun at Point Grey in 1941. *Middlemass Collection*

to identify herself. If the captain ignored the request, the battery would fire a shot two degrees ahead of the vessel as a direct order to stop.

As the shells used were nonexplosive, no damage was anticipated. One Sunday afternoon in 1942, however, a disastrous surprise was in store for the Narrows North battery. Point Atkinson had radioed the station that a fish-packer entering English Bay had refused to identify herself. An alarm sounded at Narrows North and the men rushed to their positions to fire the warning gun ahead of the vessel.

At the last minute the packer's captain stopped, but it was too late. The shell was deflected by a wave and canted off across the water, striking the hull of a newly launched freighter, the *Fort Rae*, just above the water-line amidships. The shell continued across the hold and hit the other side of the hull sideways, leaving a larger hole under the waterline. The freighter was out for speed trials, and it was not until after they were fin-ished that the ship's crew realized the hold was flooding. The *Fort Rae* was beached just east of the Lions Gate Bridge.

Late in 1944 the government decided to remove the guns and search-lights at Point Atkinson and reduce the crew sizes to 20 men to cover the other three forts, so that soldiers could be released for more active duties.

When Japan surrendered on August 14, 1945, Narrows North was immediately abandoned and the camp was eventually mostly demolished. Stanley Park guns were also removed and most of the huts razed. The officer's mess at Ferguson Point later became a tearoom.

In 1945 the government donated the Point Grey camp to UBC and the huts became additional lecture rooms and student accommodation, called Fort Camp. They were torn down in 1973–4 to clear a site for the Museum of Anthropology. Because coastal artillery was no longer considered a viable defensive force, the gun emplacements were also destroyed, although two of them and a powerhouse are still on the top of the point, and two searchlight towers and another powerhouse remain on the beach. These are commonly referred to by Vancouverites as "the gun towers." The No. 1 Gun pedestal on the university grounds has been preserved as a memorial to Vancouver's World War II defenders.[5]

The Royal Canadian Air Force was also involved in preparations for BC defence, but its mandate was the entire west coast. The Jericho Beach Air Station began recruiting men from around Vancouver. Lewis guns and bomb racks were fitted to its Vickers flying boats and a storage magazine for explosives was set up.

In 1938 Western Air Command was initiated, with headquarters at the Jericho Beach station. After war was declared the Western Air Command moved to Victoria, but activities at Jericho increased greatly and buildings were added. New planes arrived, and the older flying boats were used to train pilots before their assignments to units. This included bombing practice over the outer harbour, where the airmen dropped smoke bombs into the water, sometimes causing residents to think a small boat had exploded. Mechanics carried out major repairs and maintained all of the flying boats operating along the coast. In 1941 the base expanded when Vancouver city council permitted the Department of National Defence (DND) to take over more land at Jericho along with a parcel at Kitsilano Beach. The next year, because of the increase in personnel and activities, part of the Jericho Country Club land and an additional 56.6 hectares were added.

After the threat of Japanese invasion faded in 1943, the DND removed the coastal emergency status and made plans to disband nonpriority stations. With the end of the war military personnel were reduced, but the DND designated the Jericho and Kitsilano Beaches as permanent military bases in March 1947. The Jericho base became the BC area army head-quarters during the 1950s.

The Canadian government owned 62 hectares at Jericho Beach and 16 more hectares at Kitsilano, all prime waterfront land. Early in 1960 "the Battle of Jericho Beach" began with the City of Vancouver requesting the Canadian government to give up its claim to the property. Eventually, in June 1969, Ottawa signed over ownership of the land north of 4th Avenue—about 31 hectares—for $1, with the proviso that the city would develop it into a public park.

Through the next few years the station's buildings on that strip of land were demolished. The only sign that remains of the former waterfront base is the concrete apron that fronted Nos. 2, 3, 5 and 6 hangars, used today as a viewpoint for English Bay and the North Shore mountains.[6]

The Dominion government created the Royal Canadian Naval Volunteer Reserve (RCNVR) in 1923 in place of a complete naval service. The Vancouver Half-Company came into being later that year. It recruited and trained reservists at leased space in the Royal Vancouver Yacht Club buildings in Coal Harbour during the 1930s. The group used rooms allocated to the Vancouver Rowing Club.

After Canada declared war, the RCNVR undertook an ambitious recruiting and training program and added barracks to its Rowing Club headquarters. Before recruits were posted to naval duty, they received training in details of the naval service, seamanship training and drill. The instructors also trained volunteers from the Royal Vancouver Yacht Club in such skills as signalling and navigation. These members kept their yachts prepared to offer assistance if notified of a wartime emergency.

On November 1, 1941, the Vancouver Division of the RCNVR was commissioned as HMCS *Discovery*. As the number of recruits multiplied because of the war, the need for a larger headquarters building and barracks became essential. The ideal location was Deadman's Island in Coal Harbour, land that had been made part of Stanley Park's military reserve around 1860. The DND took possession of the island on July 24, 1942, and plans for the RCNVR buildings were laid out. The official opening of Deadman's Island as HMCS *Discovery* took place on October 21, 1944.[7]

The declaration of war in 1939 precipitated Canada into an emergency situation where naval expansion was essential, but British shipyards were no longer available to construct Canadian navy vessels. Government contracts for most of the minesweepers were signed with Burrard Dry Dock and North Van Ship Repairs Ltd. on Burrard Inlet's north shore. Passenger liners such as the *Empress of Canada* and the *Empress of Russia* were converted to troopships.

The greatest need, however, developed in 1940 when at one point more cargo ships were being sunk by the Germans than were being built. In April 1941 German U-boats sank 134 Allied and neutral ships, well beyond the number of those being constructed. British yards could not handle the demand for more ships to carry essential food and supplies, so Canadian shipyards were approached with orders for massive production of steel cargo ships.

Of the 78 vessels ordered by the British government, a contract for 38 went to Burrard Dry Dock, family-owned and the oldest company in the business on the West Coast, and 28 to North Van Ship Repairs. Expansion of their existing facilities was essential.

The *Fort St. James* is launched at Burrard Dry Dock in North Vancouver on October 15, 1941, under the wartime shipbuilding program. *NVMA 27-2395*

Burrard Dry Dock tripled the size of its North Vancouver yard at a cost of $3.5 million, then focussed on developing a piece of land owned by the Wallace family on the south shore at the foot of McLean Drive in Vancouver. Berths replaced a rocky beach and squatters' shacks. This yard, Burrard South, was able to handle the construction of four 10,160-tonne cargo ships simultaneously when it opened in September 1941. The company expanded Burrard South to Lapointe Pier in 1943, just east of the south yard, to renovate aircraft carriers.

North Van Ship Repairs was a smaller but very efficient yard west of Lonsdale Avenue, not far from Burrard Dry Dock, on the same site Lyall's Shipyard had occupied during World War I. By 1944 it had launched its 28 freighters.

West Coast Shipbuilders Ltd., set up east of the Cambie Street Bridge on False Creek, was formed by a group of BC businessmen to build steel cargo ships. It launched its first freighter in April 1942 and finished 56 more before the cargo ship program came to a close.

At the peak of the building boom reporters and newscasters referred to Burrard Inlet as the "Clydesdale of the Pacific." Not only was the number of ships noteworthy, but the workforce expanded at a phenomenal rate. At Burrard Dry Dock 14,000 employees, eight percent of them women, drew wages in 1944 from both yards combined. The three North Vancouver ferries in service, *No. 3*, *No. 4* and *No. 5*, were taxed well beyond their capabilities to carry the crowds to and from Vancouver, and an extra ferry was purchased from Washington state to help. In North Vancouver alone, several hundred homes were built to house workers and their families.

Along with the increased shipbuilding workforce, Vancouver's secondary industries grew. Plants developed for steel fabricating, marine boiler and auxiliary machinery construction, and for making masts, rudders, gun mountings, cargo winches, wire rope hawsers, bolts, rivets and propellers. Services also had to be supplied for the ships' crews—tables, chairs and kitchenware. Ship painting and house construction added to the incomes of thousands of workers who had suffered economically during the Great Depression.

In 1943, as the need for extra ships lessened, some contracts were cancelled and employee layoffs began, with cutbacks to five- rather than seven-day work weeks. The boom was coming to an end. Burrard Dry Dock's south yard launched its last ship in January 1946, and the yard

The victualling ship *Fort McDonell* and the Victory-type cargo ship *Bowness Park* under construction at Burrard Dry Dock on September 27, 1944. *NVMA 27-2310*

closed. West Coast Shipbuilders dismantled its equipment in 1947 and sold the land on False Creek to Arrow Transfer Company Ltd. North Van Ship Repairs remained in business until Burrard Dry Dock bought it out in May 1951 for $1.25 million. The new owners dismantled the berths and moved the machinery to their own yard.

Between the two world wars the British Columbia shipbuilding industry had built no ocean-going steel freighters or warships and employed only a few hundred men for repair work. Within two years the international emergency had propelled it into becoming one of the dominant West Coast industries, one that was a definite factor in the Allies' sea victory and contributed greatly to BC's economy and growth.[8]

False Creek

Economic growth during the war greatly benefitted the industries on False Creek; at least 27 of them became deeply involved in providing war supplies. The factories on Granville Island hummed with activity 24 hours a day, producing antitorpedo nets, minesweeping ropes and rigging ropes for merchant ships. Women worked in the factories, and Granville Island was declared essential to the war effort and closed to the public by 1942 to "guard island industries against saboteurs."[9] West Coast Shipbuilders at the east end of False Creek experienced a frenzied boom, building Victory-type ships for the war. All industry on the creek operated in a smoky, dirty atmosphere with a poor water system and constant fire danger.

The war also had the effect of sidetracking plans for improving what was called "a filthy ditch" and "a slop basin for the main harbour." Frederick J. Hume, running successfully for Vancouver mayor in December 1950, argued that False Creek should be filled in. He reasoned that this would reduce smoke over the city, provide more land for industry and parking and eliminate the need for costly bridges, although the Granville Street Bridge plans were already underway. In 1951 the 80 companies based on False Creek had an annual business volume of $90 mil-

West Coast Shipbuilders yard on the southeast shore of False Creek, during World War II. *CVA BO. P.167 N.219 #2*

lion, and they had invested more than $40 million in buildings and equipment. Thousands of barges, boats and log booms used the creek annually.

In 1949 the city engineering department had begun a study of the creek's potential. Hume continued to promote reclamation until the study was released in 1955. It said complete reclamation would be economically impractical: the new land would be worth only $10 million, half the cost of reclaiming it. Compensation to existing industries and the legal fees for eliminating the waterfront land rights would bring the total cost to about $50 million.

Plans for a complete reclamation were shelved, but a new False Creek Development Committee was formed in 1956 and studied other recommendations. Construction of a fisherman's wharf east of the Burrard Bridge began in 1957, taking over booming grounds from Rat Portage Lumber Mill, and the fill was used to reclaim land between Granville Island and the south shore, turning the island into a peninsula. In the meantime, plans for the creek's cleanup were discouraging businesses from upgrading. Many closed, while new industry was not interested in starting up at such a "bad address." Only three sawmills were still in operation by 1963.

Hundreds of squatters' shacks and floathomes had been the normal sight around the False Creek shore for many years. The area had been called Bennettville after R.B. Bennett, prime minister during the Depression. As part of the cleanup process, and after a typhoid scare and a horrible murder on the False Creek flats, the last of the waterfront residents was moved out in the late 1950s.

The next 20 years would see major changes in what had been the industrial centre of the city.[10]

Lighthouses

The secluded life of the Point Atkinson lightkeeper and his family came to a sudden end after the war began. The point became an important military site, upsetting the Dawes' quiet routines.

Daily, every two hours from sundown to sunrise, Ernie Dawe or his assistant climbed the three-storey tower at the lighthouse to hand-wind the system of weights that revolved the flashing light. Dawe had been lightkeeper since 1935, and even before his tenure a 500-candlepower oil lamp with a five-centimetre mantle, similar to those used in early homesteads, had generated the light. Giant prisms, like glass venetian blinds, encircled

Point Atkinson Lighthouse at the entrance to Burrard Inlet, circa 1940, showing the fog alarm building. The hexagonal light tower was built in 1912. *CVA OUT. P.420*

the lamp and increased the beam to 100,000 candlepower. During the day, Ernie had to enclose the tower's window with canvas curtains for protection from the sun's intense heat, magnified by the plate glass. One day his shirt caught fire while he was working in the tower's top room.

The Dawe family's life changed abruptly in October 1941 when the government installed a defence battery and military housing at Point Atkinson. Eighty soldiers occupied newly constructed barracks in the woods behind the lighthouse and practised their gunnery skills with the Mark 1, an eight-kilogram cannon that stood on a concrete base in front of the radio room. A powerful searchlight mounted on a concrete bunker was ready for night reconnaissance. Staffed observation posts and a radio communication system provided 24-hour-a-day surveillance.

If any ship entering the harbour failed to identify itself to the patrolling naval launches, one of the land-based cannons, called "examination guns," was to fire a shot across the bows and ultimately sink the offender if it failed to stop. Fortunately the facility never needed to defend the harbour, although a Japanese submarine allegedly shelled the Point Estevan Lighthouse on Vancouver Island in June 1942.

After the war the Dawes' life returned to its peaceful routine, with the benefit of the army-constructed road leading to the point. The barracks buildings, still maintained, are now used for children's camps and a nature house.[11]

Alfred Dickenson, the keeper at First Narrows light and fog station, was not well, and during 1937 had to take a holiday to recover from his nervous condition. A letter he sent to the Department of Transport in Victoria on February 16, 1942, gives insight into the cause of his problems:

> The rotten condition of bulk-head, and unfinished condition of part of West bulk heads, a disgrace to show visitors around, in fact dangerous, a terrible looking mess. Also the "Home Lighting Plant" it gets on my nerves for it sounds like a cement mixer...I used to take a pride in this station, in fact spent my own money on improvements, and was proud to show visitors around, but this sloppy repair work and being told "We are not going to spend any more money on this place." has changed my pride and pleasure to one of disgust. I would like a staunch 20 foot gas-boat, also a garden, these are my ambitions...

Although he and his wife wanted to leave the station, Dickenson cancelled several of his requests for transfers. At last, on February 23, 1946, the government informed him by letter:

> The remote control system of operating lightstation at First Narrows has now been completed and when final arrangements have been made to transfer the operation of the station to the Signal Tower on the [Lions Gate] bridge it is the intention of the Department to discontinue having a resident operator at the [lighthouse] site...

Dickenson set to work building crates for the move with driftwood he collected around the mouth of the Capilano River. He and his wife travelled by boat on June 15 to the light station and seven-room house at Sheringham Point on the southeast coast of Vancouver Island.[12]

Alexander McLeod took over the duties at Brockton Point station in 1936. On July 16, 1940, he was heading across the narrows in his dinghy to service the Calamity Point beacon when he fell overboard and drowned. His replacement, G.B. Kilgour, stayed until 1956, when he died.

Ships and Boats

The sandy tidal flats at Spanish Bank, named for the ships from Spain that anchored there in 1792, have long been an irresistible attraction for swimmers and children. Aiden Butterfield, a West Vancouver resident, remembers that when he was a boy in the late 1930s they were used for boats:

> Each spring, part of our Japanese Canadian fishing fleet would appear on the tidal flats at Spanish Banks. I would wake up one morning and there they would be, several hundred small trollers and seiners scattered all over the area. If the tide was in they would be riding at anchor, but if it was out they would be sitting on the sand, in various degrees of list, held up by odd pieces of lumber and driftwood.
>
> Natural curiosity carried me out to the flats, where I would walk among the boats and talk to the people. They showed me how their boats ran, from the one- or two-cylinder engines to the propellers, let me watch as they scraped the barnacles and seaweed off the bottoms, recaulked the seams, and repainted. I observed, fascinated, as they repaired their engines, with parts scattered all over the cabin floor, and the men all hunkered down in the bilge trying to get something in or out of a difficult place. Other repairs would also be made to decking, rigging and fishing gear.
>
> These were family-operated boats, and during the season the whole family would live on board in order to help with the work. The living quarters were all scrunched up in the foc'sle, under the deck at the bow, with the kitchen facilities in the wheelhouse, which is where just about everything else was kept too, except the fish! To this day I find it quite extraordinary how families of four, five and six people could live in such small, cramped quarters. After about a week most of the boats would be gone and within 10 days they were all gone.
>
> This annual event came to an end in 1941, probably with the bombing of Pearl Harbour and the internment of these warm, friendly, hard-working people in 1942.[13]

The government ordered 22,000 Japanese Canadians interned in the interior of BC and confiscated their fish boats, homes and property.

In 1946 the *Vancouver Sun* reported:

> Vancouver's sturdy, bright-red fireboat, the J.H. Carlisle gave land-based firemen a 6,500-gallon-a-minute assist Monday afternoon at the Joseph Chew Shingle Mill fire, 601 West Sixth. In command of Capt. Charles Ellinor, the floating pumping station was heading across False Creek from her Drake Street berth when the alarm was given. After a loaded lumber scow was towed away from the company dock, the J.H. Carlisle moved in close to shore, pouring water on the flames from No. 1 monitor.[14]

The 18.3-metre *Carlisle*—named after Vancouver's first fire chief, who had served for 42 years—had been launched on August 14, 1928, at Burrard Dry Dock in North Vancouver. Vancouver city council and the Board of Trade had been lobbying for a fireboat on Burrard Inlet for years but the False Creek business property owners mostly financed this first one, making annual contributions to a fireboat fund. The City of Vancouver paid for her operation and maintenance. The boat was mandated to provide fire-fighting services only in False Creek, where oil-soaked wooden buildings were an invitation for fire.

If anything, the new boat made the demands for the same service on the rest of Burrard Inlet even stronger. In 1931, in response to public pressure, the Harbour Commission had the old 28.7-metre steam whaler *Orion* converted into the fireboat *Pluvius* and berthed at the old Hastings Mill site.[15] Although far from modern, the *Pluvius* was successful in fighting several ship- and land-based fires before she was retired on February 28, 1937, and later sold for scrap. Two fire barges were temporarily in service from mid-1945 until March 1951.[16]

The following month, Vancouver's *Fireboat No. 2* tied up at her berth in Coal Harbour. The 26.5-metre-long hull was welded steel and the shallow two-metre draft was designed to allow coverage of a maximum harbour area. Five pumps could shoot out a minimum of 68,190 litres of water per minute.[17] She fought many blazes on the harbour successfully and was considered the most powerful fireboat in the world, but within very few years she developed excessive vibration, corrosion of the steel hull, a burned-out crankshaft and problems with four of the five engines.

Probably the most serious complaints were about situations involving fires on the North Shore or ships outside the inner harbour, which *No. 2*

CPR Pier D at the north end of Granville Street burns on July 27, 1938. It was destroyed and never reopened. On left are Piers B-C. *CVA CAN. P.187*

was not free to attend without a special resolution of city council. Fires were to be ignored unless they directly endangered Vancouver. Council again was under pressure, this time to construct another fireboat that would be responsible for the safety of shipping in or within reasonable sailing distance of Vancouver's harbour.

One of the few times the *J.H. Carlisle* fought a fire in the inner harbour was on March 6, 1945, the day Vancouver came close to having its own Halifax waterfront explosion. The *Green Hill Park*, a Victory-type ship built by Burrard Dry Dock, was tied up at Pier B at the north end of Burrard Street. Longshoremen were loading a variety of cargo such as lumber, newsprint, chemicals, distress signals, food and aircraft spare parts. At approximately 11:50 a.m. a fire broke out in number 3 hold. As the workers raced to get out, a tremendous explosion rocked the ship. Three more blasts followed.

Debris rained on buildings and streets. Pickles from the cargo fell like green hail. Hundreds of windows shattered in buildings from the waterfront to Georgia Street. The fire that erupted into an inferno on the ship threatened to spread to the docks. Ambulances raced to the disaster. Six longshoremen and two crew died, 19 men were injured and flying glass sliced into dozens of office workers.

Captain Cyril Andrews was in command of the Gulf of Georgia Towing Company tug *Cuprite*. He recalled:

> A scow was tied up beside the ship where the men had been loading lumber. I had just received instructions to turn the scow around when the first explosion blew me out of my wheelhouse. I was trying to pick up men from the water and the same thing happened twice more. I didn't know until a week later that I had a concussion. Men were climbing down ropes dangling from the ship's side, but were dropping like grapes from a vine at each explosion.[18]

Smoke and flames billow from the *Green Hill Park* after an explosion ripped through her on March 6, 1945, while she was tied to Pier B at the north end of Burrard Street. Tugs towed the flaming freighter into the outer harbour. *VMM*

George Grey brought up his tug, the *Sumas*, and towed the burning scow out into the harbour while another tug pulled the *Bownis Park* away from the dock and grave danger; it was tied up at the *Green Hill Park*'s stern. At the first indication of this disaster the *J.H. Carlisle* had been ordered from her berth in False Creek and was steaming through First Narrows, pumps primed and ready to begin pouring the first of nearly 41 million litres of water on the flames over three days and nights.

Frantic to move the burning ship away from the dock, towboat crews quickly attached lines and the tug *RFM* pulled her away from the pier with as much speed as she could muster. Captain Andrews on the *Cuprite* and another tug pushed against the hull to try to keep the blazing wreck on a straight course. He recalled: "I was only 15 feet away from the ship's side and didn't know whether she would explode at any minute." In spite of the danger to the Lions Gate Bridge, the tugs pulled the wildly swinging hulk into First Narrows, where she grounded once. The bridge controller was attempting to divert water traffic by shouting through his megaphone, but no one could hear him. Although the tugs succeeded in controlling the ship's passage through the narrows, she continued to swing out of control and beached on the shore near Siwash Rock.

With the flames extinguished and the fire-blackened and damaged ship cooled down, tugs towed her back to the harbour and tied her up at Ballantyne Pier. The insurance underwriters judged the vessel a total loss; it would have cost more to repair than she was worth.

The federal government held a hearing to investigate the disaster. Based on available evidence, the commission found that the explosion was caused by "improper stowage of combustible, dangerous and explosive material in No. 3 'tween decks and ignition thereof by a lighted match." Confirmed by a deathbed confession many years later, the commission's assumption was that some longshoremen had broached barrels of over-proof whiskey and had dropped a match while attempting to provide light in the area. Flares stowed on top of the barrels ignited.

The *Green Hill Park*'s life was prolonged when a Greek shipping com-pany bought the hulk and sent her to Burrard Dry Dock for repairs. She continued to work the seas into the 1960s.

The peace of the afternoon of May 2, 1959 was shattered by a boom that echoed between the shores on the outer harbour. The 134.3-metre Norwegian freighter MV *Ferngulf* was heading west out of the inlet when, just south of West Bay in West Vancouver, an explosion rocked the ship. A dark cloud of smoke erupted from the funnel and hung over the water. Fire had broken out in the engine room, killing two crew members and injuring several others. Despite the possibility that a fuel tank would explode, private boats congregated around the freighter to provide assistance. The ship's SOS was answered by navy vessels that lent a hand to fight the fire. The *Ferngulf* was later towed to Burrard Dry Dock in North Vancouver, where she was repaired and able to resume her sea duties.[19]

During the rescue, *Fireboat No. 2* was unable to leave its berth in the inner harbour because of standing regulations. Norway formally complained about the lack of assistance, adding fuel to the argument that fireboats should be available throughout the entire harbour.

The day was routine at the Ioco wharf. At 8:30 a.m. on June 15, 1953 the tanker *Argus*, part of the Union Steamship Company's fleet, was taking on 909,200 litres of high-octane gas and fuel oil. The flow stopped for a few minutes because of a breakdown in the pump room. The timing of that interval was miraculous. It saved the town of Port Moody and the entire eastern end of Burrard Inlet from being engulfed in a conflagration.

A few minutes after the pump had stopped, an explosion sent flames shooting through the engine room, injuring four of the crew. Their shipmates pulled them to safety. Chief Engineer Walter Haskett closed the hatches to seal off the gas and oil, and started up an emergency carbon dioxide system. At dockside Captain Bill Boyce made certain all of the crew were ashore and being cared for, then boarded the ship. In spite of flames blazing near him, he cast a line to the tug *Sea Chief* and steered the *Argus* while she was towed out into open water. With perfect timing, he then cut the tow rope and jumped onto the tug.

Police barricaded off two kilometres of the highway on the south shore and commuters watched as the floating bomb drifted with the tide. At 10:30 a.m. two more explosions rocked the vessel. The fire gradually burned itself out. The remains of the *Argus* were towed to a nearby tidal flat and grounded; the ship's glory days were over. Straits Towing later bought the hull and used it as a barge.[20]

Two years after opening its Ioco refinery, Imperial Oil was the first company to establish a floating fuel-service facility in Vancouver harbour. In 1917 its gasoline scow began to serve ships and boats with Premier motor gasoline at Coal Harbour. Home Oil was the next to provide a floating service, in 1934, and Shell Oil opened a float in 1935. Shell's was a 24-hour facility with restrooms, city water and telephones, and provided gasoline, diesel fuel and other petroleum products to watercraft and planes. Standard Oil later added its barge.

Home Oil opened an enlarged service station in 1947, with a capacity of 245,484 litres. The same year Shell installed a more modern facility with a capacity of 363,680 litres. In 1953 Imperial Oil raised and refitted one of its barges that had sunk after hitting the Second Narrows Bridge. The newly renovated Esso floating fueler replaced the old station and had a capacity of some 818,280 litres, with sleeping and eating facilities for the staff.

In August 1959 Texaco Oil Company added its $125,000 floating station on the water just east of the Nine O'Clock Gun. The green-and-white, 356-tonne, steel-welded barge announced its presence with a 17-metre-long sign and a circular six-metre Texaco star logo. The on-board tanks contained 468,238 litres of diesel, Skychief and Firechief fuels, outboard mix and stove oil.

Pennants and flags snapping in the breeze, white hull gleaming, the RCMP Arctic patrol ship *St. Roch* entered Burrard Inlet on October 12, 1954, at the end of her last voyage.

In 1940–42 she had become the first ship to traverse the Northwest Passage through the Canadian Arctic from west to east. She was also the first vessel to travel the passage in both directions, the first to do so in one season, and the first to circumnavigate North America (via the Panama Canal).

Because of the vessel's importance to Canadian maritime history, a Vancouver group had formed the St. Roch Preservation Society in 1954. One of its first successes was persuading Vancouver city council to purchase the ship for $5,000—the price of the fuel required for the *St. Roch* to sail from its moorage in Halifax to Vancouver.

While arrangements for a permanent moorage were being discussed, the 31.6-metre ship anchored in Coal Harbour for four years. Originally the plans called for berthing her beside the Stanley Park causeway, with a descriptive memorial. After the Native Sons of BC, Post 2, proposed construction of a maritime museum as Vancouver's commemoration of BC's centennial in 1958, the St. Roch Preservation Society prepared elaborate plans that featured the *St. Roch* as a centrepiece for the museum.

The RCMP boat *St. Roch* arrives in Burrard Inlet on October 12, 1954, completing her voyage from Halifax. *VMM HSUS-50-07*

On July 17, 1956, the city agreed that as its centennial project it would allocate $300,000 toward building a maritime museum that would house the *St. Roch*. Plans included enclosing the ship in a simulated Arctic environment, the "Arctic Circle," with an enclosed "Northwest Passage" connecting it to the museum. Because of expense, the artistic plans for the ship's protective covering were scrapped and the *St. Roch* sat out in the open air, beached at the foot of Cypress Street on a concrete dry dock. The Vancouver Maritime Museum itself officially opened on June 11, 1959, at Kitsilano Point.

The ravages of wind, rain and salt air gradually caused such deterioration in the ship that an A-frame roof was constructed over her in 1966. Visitors to the museum, rated one of BC's top 10, may climb aboard the *St. Roch*, go below to the cramped crew quarters, and try to envisage themselves trapped in Arctic ice for months at a time.[21]

The submersible *Ben Franklin* awaits cleanup in 2000 at its new home, the Vancouver Maritime Museum. The peaked roof shelters the *St. Roch. DA*

The war years dramatically increased the number of passengers using ferries across the inlet, and most of the new commuters were involved in the shipbuilding industry. Until 1931 the North Shore ferry fleet consisted of the *No. 1*, *No. 2* and *No. 3*. That year the *No. 4*, 39.6 metres long, was built by Boeing Aircraft of Canada Ltd. at its Coal Harbour yard. The *No. 4* carried a maximum 400 passengers and 26 cars. The *No. 1* and *No. 2* were taken out of service and sold.

Harvey Burt, a native of North Vancouver, crossed on the North Vancouver ferries countless times as a child and young man. He thoroughly enjoyed peeking down the hold into the engine room and standing on the deck with the wind blowing in his face. One not-so-pleasant memory stayed with him:

Both the men's and women's sides of the ferry were narrow, built where the hull overhung the water, with seats along both walls. There were urinals in the middle of the men's room, enclosed by walls. It was a particularly odious place. As you'd go in the door you'd get the stench of tobacco smoke, cigar and cigarette, urine, and whatever smell came from the spittoons. It was a terrible experience to go in. I would rather have stayed outside on the deck.

There was a small store in the men's section selling chocolate bars and cigarettes. A youth dressed in white would also go around selling candy, etc., from a tray hung by a strap around his neck.[22]

With the great increase in traffic because of the wartime workers, more ferries were necessary and the *No.* 5 was constructed at the North-West Coast Salvage and Contracting Company yard on False Creek in 1941, with a capacity of 600 passengers and 30 vehicles. She had two wheelhouses, one fore and one aft.

With the gradual decrease in ferry traffic after the war, the North Vancouver ferry service was discontinued in 1958. The following year Harry Almas, a Vancouver restaurant owner, purchased the *No.* 5 for $12,000 and renovated her as a floating restaurant, the Seven Seas. She was moored permanently at the foot of Lonsdale Avenue in North Vancouver, at the same location where she had picked up passengers for 17 years. Almas spent more than $100,000 on the boat before the restaurant opened in November 1959, including the cost of kitchen equipment and the laying of a 73-metre, 2,177-kilogram undersea power cable. The large red-and-blue neon sign on top of the boat announced "Seven Seas Seafoods" until January 12, 2001, when the historic restaurant closed its doors.

The summer season was underway on May 24, 1935, as flag-flying vessels filled with holidayers sailed out of the harbour, but all Union Steamship Company boats remained tied up at the Vancouver docks. The company's crews, members of the Seafarers Industrial Union, were on strike for improved working conditions, including the reduction of 12-hour shifts to nine hours.

Although this dispute was settled within a week, the crews again went on strike two weeks later, in support of striking Powell River longshoremen. The workers were out for six months with no strike pay or hope of finding other employment. The company was able to get a few boats out during this time with strikebreaker crews.

During the war several Union vessels had their hulls repainted camouflage grey. Armour was added to the bridges and they trailed antitorpedo devices, but none of the coastal vessels suffered enemy attack.

Union Steamship Company ships sit idle at the dock after the company's crews went on strike in 1935. *CVA WAT. P.83 N.78*

After the war the company purchased three Castle-class corvettes from the War Assets Corporation at a much lower cost than new boat construction. Union intended to use the upgraded vessels as white-painted luxury liners, but their design was not appropriate. They used too much gas, had only half the usual cargo space and were difficult to manoeuvre. They became known as "the white elephants," used only in summer months for tourists.

November 6, 1949 was a dark day in the company's history. The steamer *Chelohsin*, crowded with passengers, was heading through the outer harbour in the dark and a patchy fog. The vessel's radar had died a few hours before, but Captain Alfred Aspinall decided he would attempt the tricky passage through First Narrows anyway. He had passed through many times before.

With a resounding bump the boat hit rocks just off Siwash Rock, holing the hull. The crew and passengers abandoned ship but reached the

Stanley Park shore safely. Declared a total loss, the *Chelohsin* sat abandoned on the rocks and the company put her up for sale, believing her unsalvageable. However, an amateur salvager bought the vessel for $1,600, had her towed to the Evans, Coleman & Evans dock at Vancouver, then sold her for $25,000 to a scrap merchant from San Francisco.[23]

Throughout the 1950s the company's business and morale went downhill. When the Union vessel the *Catala* nosed into the Vancouver wharf in January 1959, it was the last time a ship carried passengers for the company. After 70 years of legendary service to the BC coast, providing a lifeline to isolated settlers, Union sold its fleet and floating equipment to the Northland Navigation Company on January 14.[24]

So sincere was the public's regard for Union's services that the passing of the company was viewed almost as a calamity. The familiar red-and-black funnels and the ships' distinctive whistles—a long, two shorts and a long—became only a memory.

English Bay

Aiden Butterfield's memories of the Japanese Canadian fishing boats at Spanish Bank included his enjoyment of a little park beside the beach:

> Blanca Street never did go all the way down to Marine Drive. It stops at the top of the bluff and forms a bit of turnaround and parking lot. From there, in the '30s and '40s a switchback trail led down to Marine Drive and the beach, and once you were there the old parks board bathhouse was just a few yards to the left. Beyond that and heading for UBC, Marine Drive rounds a corner, and there, directly to the left, lay a valley with a creek meandering through it. On both sides of the creek were lawns, weeping willows, little bridges, walking paths and picnic tables. On a hot summer day, this was truly an oasis of cool, quiet beauty. On the road at the entrance to this delightful little park was a typical small store-cum-restaurant where the young gathered to drink sodas, milkshakes, Coke or other beverages, where they could sit at small tables or booths and play the jukebox. The place was known as the Rob Roy.
>
> In the parking lot outside the store occasionally was to be found an old horse-drawn carriage, but without the shafts. It was big enough for a person to stand upright. It rested on large wood-

en-spoked carriage wheels and had a door at the end of the carriage where the drivers would have normally sat. From there a set of steps led down to the ground. It was brightly painted red and gold and had been converted into a popcorn stand. The owner of this little enterprise was an Englishman who consistently dressed in jodhpurs, riding boots and jacket, no matter what the weather.

The small, quiet park was in disrepair during the '30s and was gone, buildings and all, by the end of the '40s. Such a pity. But the area was inside the UBC Endowment Lands and I guess they just did not want it there any more. The last time I saw it, it was all overgrown, hiding the valley so that nobody would even know it was there.[25]

When the City of Vancouver constructed the Kitsilano Beach outdoor salt-water pool in 1931, it was the largest of its type in North America. Four years later the city built the Kitsilano Showboat stage adjacent to the pool. Plays and musicals enacted in the open air attracted hundreds of spectators. Sitting near the shore of English Bay, with the city lights reflecting in the water and the music echoing over the harbour, residents and tourists alike considered it a favourite evening entertainment. In 1954 the stage was rebuilt in the form of a Mississippi riverboat. The size of the audience grew to 100,000 people annually.

The beaches around English Bay were preserved and maintained for the enjoyment of the public, but a worrisome problem was always threatening: pollution from raw sewage entering the inlet had caused beach closures in 1911, and in the late 1940s the beaches and waters near the shore were again polluted. In 1956 the Greater Vancouver Sewerage and Drainage District was set up and it recommended the development of sewage treatment plants. New tunnels carried the sewage from Point Grey and Kerrisdale to new treatment plants at Iona Island on the Fraser River, and in West Vancouver near the First Narrows shoreline during the 1960s.

Indian Arm

Indian Arm had attracted recreational sailors for many years. Regattas had started at Woodlands in 1912 and since 1925 Deep Cove had hosted an annual regatta, with several thousand visitors watching and participating in sailboat and rowboat races, diving, swimming and canoe races and seashore tilting. Although the celebrations were cancelled during World War II, the Deep Cove Carnival and Regatta again attracted visitors and competitors in June 1947. By this time the Vancouver Power Boat Association was participating, holding its Gold Cup Speed Races there for several years.

During the 1950s, with improved transportation into the area Deep Cove became very popular as a residential and recreational district. Panorama Park on the shore enticed swimmers and picnickers with its bathhouse. The fine harbour became home to the Deep Cove Yacht Club.

Although not much more than a kilometre long, Bedwell Bay, a small cove on the arm's east shore, was selected by the War Assets Disposable Corporation as a storage area for hundreds of boats and ships—decommissioned destroyers and minesweepers, barges and small boats. The old dredge SS *Mastodon*, converted to an oil tanker in 1942, joined the moored fleet in 1946. A watchman daily inspected the vessels from his sad old fish boat. Gradually the vessels were sold at auction for a fraction of their original worth. At the end of the 1950s those that remained were taken to a scrapyard in Victoria.[26]

Burrard Inlet's harbour is ice-free year round, but Indian Arm has had its share of freeze-ups. For 10 days in January 1949 the upper reaches of the arm were made impassable by thick ice. To enable tugs and ferries to get through, a steel tug was sent in to break the buildup. One year later Deep Cove harbour was covered with ice for the first time in memory.

Over the years, the isolation of residents on Indian Arm has prompted unique services to provide necessities. Madge Winfield's nameless store boat was one of several. The *Weekend Magazine* in 1954 shared that craft's story:

> When housewives in communities along the fiord-like North Arm of Burrard Inlet...hear two loud blasts on an automobile horn they pick up their shopping bags and troop down to the wharf in time to meet the store edging in.
>
> The store is a converted, 28-foot gas boat, operated for the past six years by Madge Winfield, a former piano teacher from Griffin, Sask., who deserted the keys for the quays.
>
> The previous owner called this floating grocery store The Seabiscuit, which was apt enough, but now it is nameless for it is Madge who is the personality and not the boat. "Here comes

The 160-hp tug *Our Best* attempts to clear an ice jam with three boomsticks (logs strong enough to retain log booms) attached to its hull in an elongated V, after the inlet's surface froze at Port Moody in 1942. *Captain Cecil J. Rhodes photo*

Madge!" say her customers, and the way they say it is a measure of their regard for the cheerful quiet-spoken girl who has rarely failed to deliver supplies on promised days . . .

She likes to regard her customers as friends and neighbours, and the only complaint she has against any of them is that the occasional summer visitor will put paper money on her counter, forgetting that a playful breeze is waiting to whip it away.[27]

Madge visited 25 different wharves five days a week in summer and three in winter, delivering supplies to retired people, loggers, caretakers, powerhouse workers, campers and cottagers. When she took over as skipper she was totally inexperienced: she used to approach a wharf, then let the wind blow her in. Gaining confidence, she learned to handle strong blows and rough water and survived several near accidents. Her top-heavy boat carried groceries and vegetables. She would take special orders for meat, get cheques cashed, have prescriptions refilled, buy books and magazines and take films to be developed, all for no extra charge.

Harbour Navigation had continued its ferry and water-borne post office services since 1920. Captain Doug Stalker was still the postmaster, sorting the mail at the Gore Street dock in Vancouver, but it was Captain John "Paddy" Gilmore who mainly made the runs in the early 1950s, then Captain Andy Taylor on the three-days-a-week winter run and Stalker on the summer daily runs. In 1958 the *Scenic* was renovated with a new engine that managed 12 knots.

The company also maintained resort facilities at Wigwam Inn and recreational attractions at Belcarra Park. Its six excursion vessels were available for transport—the *Hollyburn, Harbour Princess, Lady Rose, Scenic*, the former cabin cruiser *Uchuck No. 1* and the *Thunderbird*. In September 1950 the Young estate in Madison, Wisconsin, offered Wigwam Inn for sale for $23,500, to include the 65 hectares on which the inn stands and 6.5 hectares bordering the Indian River. Harbour Navigation, which had leased the property since March 1935, purchased it on June 14, 1951, and set up Wigwam Inn Holdings Ltd.

The venture proved unprofitable. In March 1960 an American syndicate based in Salt Lake City made overtures to the failing Wigwam Inn Holdings Ltd. regarding purchase. The Americans had plans to convert Belcarra Park into a miniature Disneyland and Wigwam Inn into a mil-

MV *Scenic* arrives at Wigwam Inn on Indian Arm in 1956, delivering mail and passengers. *RC*

lionaires' yacht club. The sale fell through, fortunately for local residents but not so happily for Harbour Navigation. The holding company went into bankruptcy in 1963.

A further example of abandoned dreams on the inlet arose from a proposal made in 1954. Officials of West Vancouver, North Vancouver district and North Vancouver city approved in principle a plan to build a bridge across Indian Arm. An upper-level road from Taylor Way (named for Fred Taylor) in West Vancouver would cross North Vancouver, run to Cove Cliff between Dollarton and Deep Cove, cross on a new bridge to the east shore just south of Bedwell Bay, pass north of Ioco and continue to Port Coquitlam and what was then called the Pacific Highway. The provincial government disregarded the plan, but it wouldn't be the last creative attempt to solve the traffic problems of the North Shore.

Second Narrows Bridge

The story of crossings at Second Narrows involves one accident after another. The first bridge was variously referred to as "the Bridge of Sighs," "a target for tugboats" and "the most bunted bridge in the world." After the rebuilt span opened in 1934 the number of marine mishaps was reduced, but major crashes still occurred.

In July 1952, a barge loaded with heavy fuel oil turned over and sank in the strong tides, nearly taking her tug with her and landing on the bottom against one of the main piers. On June 15, 1954, the Norwegian freighter *Bonanza* was caught in a fierce riptide that hurled the 10,160-tonne vessel broadside against the bridge supports, moving the main reinforced concrete pile at the north end about 18 centimetres. The bridge was closed for nearly two weeks, adding 3,000 cars to the Lions Gate Bridge's daily rush-hour traffic and causing huge lineups for the North Vancouver ferries.

With the increase in population, the number of cars using the Second Narrows Bridge and the fear of further marine accidents, the government decided a replacement was necessary. The long-shelved plans for a dam and causeway across the narrows were reintroduced, but engineers advised that a new bridge would be much more economical.

A ceremonial concrete pouring for the new Second Narrows bridge was held on July 12, 1956. Construction went well—until 3:40 p.m. on June 17, 1958. The *Vancouver Sun* reported next day:

It couldn't happen. But it did. Three hundred and seventy-five feet [114.3 metres] of the new Second Narrows bridge anchor span thundered into Burrard Inlet Tuesday afternoon, tearing its concrete foundation as if it were cardboard and dropping a 282 foot [86-metre] deck truss span into the water behind it.

Workers had been finishing the anchor span and were nearly ready to start on the main 335-metre cantilevered arch. Of the 79 men working on the bridge, 18 fell to their deaths (including two engineers involved in the structural plans) and 20 were injured. A diver searching for bodies was drowned. Five more men subsequently died from injuries sustained in the accident.

Damage was estimated at $3.5 million and construction was delayed for eight months. An inquiry board later ruled that the temporary structure holding up the half-finished outside span was not strong enough to support the steel beams. On July 7, families watched from a wooden jetty as red roses, one for each of the men killed, were dropped into the water around the wreckage as a symbolic act of remembrance.

The new Second Narrows Bridge after it collapsed in 1958 while under construction. This view was taken facing south. *HF*

The steel contractors, Dominion Bridge Company, brought in a huge floating crane to clear the twisted wreckage. What remained of the heavily reinforced concrete-and-steel pier number 14 was blasted apart with 360 kilograms of Forcite, and construction eventually continued.

The new Second Narrows Bridge opened officially on August 25, 1960. At 948 metres long and 24.1 metres wide, it was the longest bridge in western Canada, and second in size in Canada only to Quebec City's cantilever bridge. The cantilevered main span provided a minimum ship-channel overhead clearance of 44 metres. The final cost was $23 million.[28] A bronze plaque on a 3.7-metre-high monument at the south end of the bridge was erected as a memorial to the men killed during construction.

The old bridge could not compete with the modern new span, even after reducing tolls in a mini price war. Closing to highway traffic in 1963, it continued to experience damage from ships and was finally replaced by a larger railway bridge with a vertical lift span in 1969.

On June 17, 1994, the Second Narrows Bridge was renamed the Ironworkers Memorial Second Narrows Crossing as a testimonial to the men who died in 1958.

People have wondered why disaster seemed to plague the site. One reporter came up with his own suggestion in the Vancouver *Province*, in an undated clipping:

> There was a tiny island where the crumpled leg of the New Second Narrows Bridge was built. (The islet was removed in 1923 to provide fill for Ballantyne Pier, building at that time.)
>
> Indians kept away from this islet and called it HWA-HWOI-HWOI, the sinister place. It had been haunted ever since a medicine man from a strange tribe was found lying on the island. The islet stretched up to about where the old Second Narrows Bridge is.

The Port

When the harbour was shrouded in fog, a loud but mysterious voice could be heard intermittently in the vicinity of the Lions Gate Bridge. An observation and signal station was perched on top of the span, like a small green cottage high above the traffic, with the goal of ensuring safety for the ever-increasing number of vessels using the port. Operated by the National Harbours Board, the station housed watchers 24 hours a day. Their duties were to keep a list of all ships entering and leaving the harbour, to signal the ships' captains and to keep a daily log of weather and any unusual event.

During the day ships would identify themselves by hoisting code flags as they approached the span. At night the bridge watchers would shine searchlights down onto the ships' names. When fog made the entrance dangerous, the captains could follow a voice-directional bearing, focusing on a powerful loudspeaker high above them from which the signalmen were calling.

Yardarms extending out from the station indicated the status of the channel—one black ball hanging from the south yardarm signified one or more ships entering the harbour; two black balls indicated vessels with tows; outgoing ships were indicated by red signals like inverted ice-cream cones, suspended from the opposite yardarm. Red lights for the cones and white ones for the balls were used at night, and if the channel was obstructed an emergency signal was used.[29]

After World War II the most important addition to the port was the construction of Centennial Pier, just west of Ballantyne Pier, where the old Hastings Mill had operated. Although the landfill had been started in 1930, the Depression and war interrupted construction of the wharf and work on it did not resume until 1956. When berths numbers 1 to 4 were completed in 1958, the name Centennial Pier commemorated BC's 100th anniversary. The facility had four portable cranes, outside storage of 23,255 square metres and shed storage of 18,580 square metres. Berth number 5 opened in December 1964 and number 6 on June 1, 1970. The total cost was $5 million.[30]

In its May 28, 1957, report the National Harbours Board, which had taken over from the Harbour Commission in March 1936, gave specific data about the port facilities. During 1956 more than 1,500 ocean-going commercial ships and more than 33,000 coastal passenger and commercial ships entered the harbour. More than 700,000 passengers landed and 26 deep-sea shipping companies had offices and acted as agents for eight lines of about 30 nations. Four yacht clubs were on the harbour, and the number of pleasure boats exceeded 10,000.

The board's 1958 report included even more details of how dramatically the port facilities had increased since the war:

> ... The entrance channel to the harbour, which is open the year round, has a minimum depth of 39 feet. The National Harbours

McKenzie Barge and Derrick Limited dredges First Narrows, circa 1950. The tug *Percy McKenzie* is on the left. *MBMW*

Board has piers, wharves and jetties with about 9500 linear feet of berthing, providing 17 deepsea berths and 3 berths for coastal shipping, also 6 transit sheds with an aggregate floor area of about 576,000 square feet. The Board's 4 grain elevators have a total storage capacity of 9,779,500 bushels, a combined loading capacity of about 200,000 bushels per hour and 1 and a half miles of conveyor galleries [altogether seven elevators on the inlet, with a total capacity of 20 million bushels]. Besides, there are storage tanks with a capacity of over 870,000 imperial gallons for the handling of fish and vegetable oils, open wharves, booming grounds and scow pools for the storage and shipment of timber. Three special wharves are also provided for the fishing industry, one being complete with a shed, a small ice plant and freezing equipment for processing fish. A 40-ton fixed derrick is installed on Lapointe Pier.[31]

CHAPTER 7

EXPANSION, RECLAMATION AND PROTECTION: 1960–2001

As home to the Port of Vancouver, Burrard Inlet is subjected to heavy industrial activity and consequent waste discharges... [D]espite large efforts towards control and treatment of such discharges, as well as those from stormwater outlets, municipal combined sewer overflows, industrial process effluents [and] urban runoff... contaminants exceed the Canadian Environmental Protection Act criteria for acceptable levels in sediments.

—Patrick McLaren, *Sediment Transport in Vancouver Harbour, 1994*

I n the early years, most of the shoreline around the harbour was composed of fairly shallow water drying to rocky mud flats at low tide. Over time, sections of the waterfront have been reclaimed for use as port terminals and recreational areas. Today gigantic ships can moor directly beside the loading docks at Ballantyne and Centennial Piers, Lynnterm and Neptune Terminals, grain elevators and many other industries. False Creek has been transformed into a community-based centre. The shorelines at West Vancouver and Port Moody are popular destinations. The face of the harbour has changed.

West Vancouver

West of the Capilano River, Ambleside Park in West Vancouver is a popular area for many thousands of visitors. Beaches, a waterfront sidewalk, lagoon, pitch and putt, playing fields and other attractions lure sport and nature lovers.

The land was not always so attractive. A long spit of gravel divided the Capilano River from the entrance to a large slough that snaked inland like a crooked finger and reached as far west as 14th Street. Boaters moored their vessels in the protected cove, and canoeists followed the narrow ribbon of water north past Marine Drive. The ferry *West Vancouver No. 5*, launched in 1915 and taken out of service the next year as a cost-saving measure, had been moved into the slough at high tide and abandoned there until she was needed again. West Vancouver's first municipal garbage dump, run by Peter Christy, was at the 13th Street end of the slough, the beginning of the addition of fill to the low land, which flooded at extremely high tides.

Ambleside, West Vancouver, in 1957. The original slough winds north to the present rail line. It was reduced to a lagoon in the 1960s and the rest of the slough was filled and converted to parkland, a par 3 golf course and playing fields, bordered by a seawall promenade. *WVMA 2270*

In 1943 the Department of National Defence built barracks just north of the present railway tracks at Ambleside for soldiers staffing the antiaircraft guns near the Capilano River. After the war, West Vancouver council purchased the huts from the War Assets Corporation and early in 1947 converted nine of them to provide 18 housing units for veterans and their families. The area was popularly called "the Army Huts," or "Diaper Lane"; West Vancouver parks superintendent John F. Wood, responsible for collecting rents there, was known as "the Mayor of Diaper Lane." Because these huts were built on low ground, the surrounding land was flooded several times a year and then food supplies had to be brought in by rowboat. By 1961 some huts had been destroyed and others moved and used for public works buildings.[1] One hut remains at Ambleside, used first as the Capilano Rod and Gun Club building, then as the Ambleside Youth Centre.

On June 1, 1961, Heinz Berger became assistant superintendent and municipal landscape architect for West Vancouver parks. He recalls that one of his major projects was the land reclamation at Ambleside. Working with a very small budget, he used ingenious cost-saving measures. The present sports fields and the pitch and putt fairways are built on wood waste—sawdust, bark and end cuts—from L and K Lumber, a North Vancouver sawmill. East of the golf course, as far as the Capilano River, the

Army huts at Ambleside, circa 1943. After an antiaircraft base was established at Narrows North, the huts were built to house the soldiers. Water from the original slough came close to the homes' foundations. *WVMA 2200*

low areas were filled with soil and concrete removed from West Vancouver construction sites. Miller's Cannery, located in the municipality, provided the roadbed on top of the materials—a one-metre-deep layer of oyster shells, a malodorous deposit that sweetened after a few weeks.

The present lagoon was formed by dredging the south portion of the slough, which had become a "stinking mess" from septic tanks on Sentinel Hill overflowing into it. The resulting muck was piled up for use on the future pitch and putt. As it was very salty, sprinklers sprayed fresh water over the soil day and night before it was ready to be mixed with sand and spread for a grass base. Old railway ties lined the lagoon's banks. The West Vancouver Garden Club donated funds to build an island in the lagoon to encourage safe waterfowl nesting and to establish a feeding house.

To keep salt water from entering the lagoon uncontrolled, a special gate was designed by Swann Wooster Engineering that allowed water in or out depending on the level of the pond. A pipe runs under the seawalk just south and east of the lagoon. Within two years fish were making their home there. Today, swans and seabirds of many species flock to the sanctuary.

In 1968 the municipality started construction of the seawalk. Today the walk runs from the pier at Dundarave east to John Lawson Park, takes a short diversion away from the water, then rejoins the seawalk at Ambleside. The entire route is a tribute to Heinz Berger and the forward-looking council of the day.

Stanley Park Seawall

A short distance across the entrance to the inner harbour from Ambleside, the seawall at Stanley Park is a popular 8.9-kilometre recreational walkway that has been reclaimed and chipped out from the waterfront.

The first plans for a seawall and pathway were not grandiose. The initial stretch in 1917 was only 125 metres long and was reinforced with granite blocks to prevent wave erosion. When park superintendent W.S. Rawlings realized the path's potential, he recommended the same year a marine walk that would encircle the park in a unique combination of parkland and seawall. As federal funding became available the walk was built slowly, in sections. More than 2,300 men cleared and filled in 1920, mostly during the winter months, a peak construction period. During the Great Depression gangs of workers on relief chiselled, drilled and set in place

The Clachan restaurant at Dundarave in 1913. Run for decades by the Clachan sisters, the West Vancouver restaurant has had several owners over the years and a second storey has been added. In 2001 it was still in business, under a different name, at the Dundarave pier. *WVMA 1104 WV RAH*

Stanley Park seawall, 2001. The last section of the wall was completed in 1974, in the vicinity of Siwash Rock. *DA*

45.5-kilogram granite blocks. Work often took place at night as the men had to work around tide levels.

From 1931 to 1963, master stonemason James Cunningham supervised the construction and became a local legend. After retirement, even when he was in poor health, he would make his way to the seawall work area in topcoat and pyjamas and direct the job. He died in 1963 and the city erected a plaque in his memory at Siwash Rock,[2] where the last 2.4 kilometres were completed in 1980. His ashes lie in an undisclosed location somewhere on the seawall.

Alternative Lifestyles

Since the late 1800s, squatters had lived below the high-tide line in many locations around the inlet. False Creek attracted many during the 1930s, and the Kitsilano foreshore was home to several during the 1920s and 1930s. Until 1941, at the foot of Vancouver's Renfrew Street near Brighton Beach nearly two dozen families lived in 20 cabins on the foreshore, their tax- and rent-free existence allowing them to stay off relief and live in the fresh air, rather than in a squalid room in a tenement or rooming house. About 130 squatters were crowded along the Burnaby shore between the railway line and the inlet, from Second Narrows Bridge to Willingdon Avenue, and more were interspersed as far as Port Moody.

These were mostly single men, mainly pensioners and welfare recipients, saving money on rent and taxes, but there were also some families. The dwellings were as varied as their owners' imaginations (and incomes)—log cabins, shingled siding, driftwood, even cardboard boxes. Many had small porches, were brightly painted and had flowerpots in the windows. The adventurous residents enjoyed "living on the beach."[3]

Trudi Tuomi was eight years old in 1936 when her parents, Gus and Aune Rintanen, brought their family to Vancouver from the Prairies as they looked for work. The following year the Finnish family were delighted to find a home they could and did buy for $50. It was a two-room squatter's cabin at the Burnaby shoreline east of Second Narrows, on pilings below the high-tide line, with a deck, shed, wharf and a leaky rowboat. Their toilet was flushed by the tides, their fridge a crock sunk into the bank behind their house, and a wood stove provided ample heat. Burrard Inlet was their front yard and the CPR tracks closely bordered their steep backyard.

Squatters' shacks at 'Crabtown' in Burnaby, circa 1935. *BHS 204-441*

They had a constant supply of fresh water from an overflow pipe drain-ing the waterline that crossed the inlet from the Seymour watershed to Vancouver. Trudi and her sister Aili would row for almost a kilometre to the west to fill four buckets at the pipe. Trudi remembers that during World War II a guard was stationed at the pipes above the tracks to pre-vent enemy sabotage of Vancouver's water supply.

The Rintanens lived there for several years after Gus found a job. He built a sauna; they grew vegetables on the bank behind their house and kept chickens. Aune kept the tiny house spotless and put up frilly white curtains at the windows. A dog, cat and pet seagull joined the family. Their immediate neighbours were bachelors—Polish Joe, who kept pigeons and sold them to a Chinese market, and old Captain George, who walked with a seaman's rolling gait.

Trudi remembers the pleasures of watching the passing ferries—the *Hollyburn*, the *Harbour Princess*, the *Scenic* "with the fringe on top"—and listening to the passengers' singing carry over the water; the constant supply of free crabs and clams; rowing to picnics at the Seymour River or to Port Moody just for fun; the water always being available for swimming; visits to a nearby Finnish community where they learned old ethnic dances. To the girls life was good, though they had to walk nearly five kilo-metres to school and do their homework by the light of a coal-oil lantern.

Finally moving in 1947, the family sold the house for $200 and left their "magic years" behind them.[4]

In 1959 the National Harbours Board evicted the squatters and burned down all the shacks. At the same time squatters were removed from Lynn Creek Flats on the North Shore.

Harvey Burt and his wife owned one of the shacks northeast of Roche Point in North Vancouver. He remembers:

In 1951 my wife and I were looking for a spot to have a summer-escape place. I had heard about the shacks on Indian Arm, so we thought we would go down and see if there was an empty one there. We walked along a trail through cathedral groves of salmonberry bushes and came to some houses. We talked to people who had a place there and they turned out to be Margerie and Malcolm Lowry, the well-known writers. We told them we were looking for a place. Margerie said, "I think there's an empty house along there." We saw a sign with a telephone number, on a house the second north of the Lowry's. We were able to buy it for $100. There was no right of ownership, of course, it being a squatter's shack.

It was small, about the size of a small garage, and had space for a stove, table and a set of drawers, one of which contained a nest of mice. We also had an outhouse. A squatter's shack legally couldn't touch the land and was built between the low- and high-tide lines on stilts higher than the high-water level. Our house was built away from the land, but it had a porch connected by a plank to the shore.

There were about 20 shacks at that time, all east and north of Roche Point, and about four just west of the point. They were all burned down in 1958 by North Vancouver District.

Farther west were great mud flats. Some squatters had lived for years out on the flats because the water, even 100 metres out, was only about one metre deep. It was quite difficult getting to them, as you had to walk along planks nailed to logs—2 x 10s or 2 x 8s—and they'd sag. I visited there in the 1970s. There were some very interesting people down there. One was Dr. Paul Spong, who later worked in the orca whale field. The real characters were old guys, one called John Petrush, and another called Mike Bozzer.

Waterfront shacks between Second Narrows and Cates Park in North Vancouver, circa 1936. The one on the right was owned by the Chat family from Burnaby, who spent summers there. *Dawn L'Hirondelle Collection*

One of the last squatters' shacks on Burrard Inlet, 2000. The high tide reaches under the foundations. *DA*

Squatters' shacks between Dollarton Highway and Burrard Inlet, west of Burrard Reserve, circa 1958. *NVMA 10513*

Mike was deaf and had a speech impediment and when I met him he was quite old. I met Petrush only once or twice. He was a remarkable man, apparently. He made violins, and some of them were played by the Vancouver Symphony Orchestra. He lived next door to Mike Bozzer, and those two shacks were close to shore. Mike's was made of lumber he had found on the beach and had a lot of windows on the south side.

He and John Petrush had had a fight. He thought John had stolen one of his windows. They never spoke to each other after that, for years. John built a boat there and took it around to Marpole and later died aboard it. When old Mike heard about his death, he said, "Did he ever say he was sorry for stealin' that window?"

I used to take my dog down to the flats and I'd see Mike wading through the seagrass, his white hair ruffling in the breeze, collecting lumber from the beach. He had a peculiar walk, swung his legs to the side. On December 23, 1971, district crews had destroyed some of the shacks. In 1973, under pressure, the rest of the squatters gradually moved out and the North Vancouver District council had all of the buildings destroyed.

All except Mike's. It was at 2793 Dollarton Highway where the Crab Shack used to be. They left his place because he was an old man.[5]

In February 1973 Lyttle Brothers Ltd., which owned the property, arranged a court settlement with the squatters under which they would receive $500 if they left by March 28 and removed their shacks or made them unlivable, and cleared the area of garbage. Mike Bozzer later moved to a Vancouver retirement home at age 84. His two-storey clapboard home, with an enclosed courtyard and three sheds, was demolished at 7:00 a.m. on Friday, September 19, 1986, despite appeals that it should be saved for its value as an example of a forgotten lifestyle.

Malcolm Lowry squatted on Indian Arm near Roche Point from 1939 to 1954 and there wrote his renowned novel *Under the Volcano*, published in 1947. He was a reclusive alcoholic viewed by many people in the Dollarton area as eccentric, but he and Margerie enjoyed the companionship of close friends, several of whom were also writers, often drinking, laughing and discussing their work. Those days had a great influence on Lowry's writing, but in 1954 the couple were forced to move with the other squatters and went to England, where he died in 1957.[6]

Industry

Just to the west of the Ioco storage facility at Port Moody, on the north shore of Burrard Inlet, tall chimneys and plumes of steam mark the Burrard Generating Station. Not as well known or as long established as its close neighbour, Ioco, the plant was built in several stages from the end of the 1950s to the middle of the 1970s. It generates electricity through the use of natural gas, which is burned to produce high-pressure steam that passes through turbines that drive a generator. The station could supply 700,000 homes with power, but is used to back up BC Hydro's other

Burrard Generating Station, 1999. It was built on the North Shore at Port Moody in the 1950s to produce electricity. *JH*

resources. Usually it's in service from late spring into early autumn, allowing hydroelectric plants' reservoirs to refill with water from spring runoff, but it can run at any time.

Over the years the plant has had some negative impact on the environment—air emissions of nitrogen oxides that affect air quality, carbon dioxide that contributes to global warming, chlorine in water effluent discharged into Burrard Inlet and plant noise. Hydro initiated a $200-million Burrard Upgrade Project in 1993 and addressed most of these concerns, working closely with public representatives including a Burrard Community Liaison Committee that was reorganized in 1997 with a local group, Residents for a Better Port Moody. As of 2001 BC Hydro had submitted to the Greater Vancouver Regional District a draft plan for dealing with the carbon dioxide emissions.[7]

During the 1960s the Burrard Dry Dock shipbuilding and repair facilities continued to dominate the North Vancouver shore east of Lonsdale Avenue. Yard modernization in the 1950s and early 1960s had cost about

$3 million and greatly improved steel ship construction practices. After its shipbuilding operations lost $42,000 in 1971, and because of the uncertainty of winning new contracts and other matters, the Wallace family decided to sell the company after nearly 80 years in business. In 1972 Cornat Industries purchased the company for $10 million and all Wallace family members gave up their positions. In 1978 the Vancouver and Victoria Burrard Dry Dock divisions amalgamated under a new name, Burrard Yarrows Corporation. In 1985 the name Burrard Dry Dock was dropped, replaced by Versatile Pacific Shipyards Incorporated.

The yards were busy during the 1980s with new ship construction, conversions of two ferries for BC Ferry Corporation, the *Queen of Saanich* and the *Queen of Esquimalt*, and an extension of the ferry *Queen of Alberni*. The ferries *Queen of Vancouver* and *Queen of Victoria* each had a deck added in 1981. P&O Cruises of Southampton commissioned the company to upgrade its cruise ships the *Island Princess* and the *Pacific Princess*.

In the early 1990s, business slowed. Despite the company's attempts to secure contracts and expand beyond shipbuilding, in December 1992 its last North Vancouver employees were let go and in 1994 the Victoria Division closed.[8]

The company's old North Vancouver construction buildings lay idle after 1991, gradually weathering away. In 1990 the City of North Vancouver considered the possibility of a change in the use of the site while maintaining its historical flavour; a heritage inventory was conducted in 1991. Subsequently the city initiated a land use study with the owners, completed in 1997. The resulting proposal reflected the location's history and included commercial, residential and cultural buildings on the approximately five-hectare site.

Plans in 2001 included development over the next 10 years of more than 92,900 square metres of floor space for a hotel, apartments, cafes, retail space and offices. Eight former shipyard buildings were to be used in the heritage precinct; the old 3,530-square-metre machine shop was to house a public facility, possibly a museum. Waterfront walkways, open plazas and access to two heritage piers were planned to maintain the industrial quality of the buildings and their environment, similar in character to Granville Island.[9]

Although the Wallace family owned the largest North Shore shipbuilding company, smaller family firms also were successful. In 1948 Allied Builders opened on False Creek under the ownership of Arthur McLaren.

The Seven Seas floating restaurant in 2000. Formerly the *North Vancouver Ferry No. 5*, the restaurant opened in 1959 at the foot of Lonsdale in North Vancouver; it closed in January 2001. In the background is the *Cape Breton*, a former Victory ship whose stern and engine have been removed for historical display at the new North Vancouver Museum facility. *MP*

He had been general manager of West Coast Shipbuilders Ltd. since 1946, following "W.D.," his father, in that position. Arthur had inherited a love of ships and shipbuilding and his dream was to make "really good ships." In 1967 McLaren moved the business to Harbour Road in North Vancouver, just east of the Second Narrows Bridge. As Allied Shipbuilders Ltd. the company has built tugs, barges and coastal commercial vessels. Arthur, later joined by his sons Malcolm, James and Douglas, also designed and built ferries, freighters, fish boats, tugs and barges. By 2001 the company had constructed 258 vessels of up to 10,000 deadweight tonnes, including seven BC ferries.[10]

Farther east, along Dollarton Highway in North Vancouver, a faded sign with the name "Matsumoto" on a large, obviously old wooden building sat until at least 1988 between the road and the shore. Behind that name was a family story of courage, resolve and success.

Allied Shipbuilders yard in North Vancouver, 1969. The ferries *Tachek* and *Quadra Queen* are on the ways, with the Second Narrows Bridge in the background.

Ichijuro "Phillip" Matsumoto had left Nagasaki, Japan, in 1920 and settled in Prince Rupert, where he built wooden fishing boats. During World War II he and his family were interned in the Kootenay district and his shop and machinery were confiscated. After the war he and his son Isamu ("Sam") started a small-boat business in Nelson, then moved to North Vancouver and founded Matsumoto Shipyards Ltd. in 1950. The business was very successful, building with wood and steel and pioneering the construction of aluminum vessels. Their contracts ranged from luxury wooden cruisers to Coast Guard patrol boats and fireboats for Mexico. Ichijuro died in 1978 and Sam continued to run the company with his son, Ken. They were proud of their family tradition of designing and building boats to meet individual needs.[11]

The business closed in 1988 and was purchased by Noble Towing, which built steel tugs and carried out repairs. In about 1995 Allied

Matsumoto Shipyards, circa 1955. The company opened on the North Shore in 1950 and was very successful in constructing wooden, steel and later aluminum vessels.

Shipbuilders rented the facility, now Dollarton Ship Yards, and today build and repair ships there, as well as at its yard farther west.

McKenzie Barge and Marine Ways Limited, on Dollarton Highway east of the former Matsumoto yard, has operated as a family business for 78 years. In 1922 John Kenneth "J.K." McKenzie opened McKenzie Barge and Derrick Limited on the waterfront at the foot of Victoria Drive in Vancouver and ran it with the assistance of his daughter Margaret and sons Ken, Ralph and Ross.

Margaret worked in the office from day one and continued to be involved until 1998. At age 92 she recalled the first of those offices as being a tiny hole in the wall, always too hot or icy cold, with room for only a desk and a small pot-bellied stove, no bathroom. When customers arrived to talk business, they had to sit outside on a stack of lumber. At that time the company had one barge with derrick, the *Number One*; the barge was rented out and the derrick was mainly used for lifting loads.

In 1928 the company built and launched its first tug, the *J.K. McKenzie*, which worked the BC coast for years. Margaret fondly remembered her as "a saucy little tug." When she sank near Powell River, the family's efforts to salvage her were unsuccessful.

The company also built and sold wooden scows, 10.36 by 27.4 metres, small by today's standard 70 metres. Yearly maintenance of the barges included copper painting on the outside below the water line to prevent teredo worm infestation, and pumping concentrated salt brine into the hull to control dry rot. The family bought two used dredges, then built their own, the *McKenzie*, their pride and joy. It performed well and still operates. The company's fleet was painted a distinctive barn red.

In the early 1930s the McKenzies opened a second yard at 3919 Dollarton Highway. The land was covered with apple trees and the family called its holding "The Ranch," even growing potatoes there in the rich soil. Dollarton Highway had only recently been constructed in North Vancouver and was a bumpy lane. Telephone service was undependable. The family built small tugs and wooden barges there for their own dredging operations and a cookhouse supplied lunch to their employees.

During World War II the company constructed wooden Glen-class tugs for the Department of National Defence, and after the war barges for Vancouver Tug, Gulf of Georgia Towing and other companies, but its main business continued to be dredging. "You name it, on Burrard Inlet we dredged it," said Bob McKenzie, grandson of the founder.

In the late 1950s McKenzie started steel construction, mostly barges in the new company colours of orange and grey. In 1971 it closed its Vancouver yard and sold the dredging equipment to Fraser River Pile and Dredging.

The family company's name changed to McKenzie Barge and Marine Ways Limited and during the 1970s concentrated on new construction and repair of coastal vessels. Bob McKenzie took over from his father Ralph as president in 1976 and he and his brother Brian, yard manager, still operated the business with their sons in 2001, focussed on maintenance and repair and renting out a small fleet of charter barges.

Wooden barges needed annual maintenance and McKenzie handled 200 a year; today's steel barges require work only once every two to four years. "There will always be a future for shipbuilding and repairs on the BC coast, but it has cut down from where it used to be," said Bob.[12]

False Creek

During the 1960s and 1970s, political decisions and forward-looking planners transformed the False Creek industrial eyesore into an attractive community-based centre. In 1967 the BC government exchanged a 4.85-hectare parcel of land it owned on the creek's north shore for an equal-sized parcel owned by the CPR on the south shore, leaving the province with a long, narrow strip of land along the south shoreline. The following year the government gave all its holdings on the south shore (34.6 hectares) to the City of Vancouver in exchange for $400,000 and some land in Burnaby that the province needed to expand Simon Fraser University. The city now owned nearly all of the south and east shorelines of False Creek and was keen to develop the land.

City council was split on whether to develop an industrial area or a landscaped parkland. Public opinion was strongly in favour of the greenbelt, and when the Roberts Bank port facility south of the city was announced council members recognized that False Creek would not be used in future as an extension of Burrard Inlet harbour. They also recognized that improved landscaping would encourage high-density housing on Fairview Slopes in Vancouver, increasing tax revenue. Tourism would add to the economy.

In 1968, city council voted to remove False Creek's industrial designation, significantly affecting its future. Within the next 15 years the CPR removed its yards from the north shore of False Creek and tore down its Kitsilano trestle over the creek. Almost all industry was removed from the shore west of the Cambie Street Bridge and leases were running out. The air and water gradually cleared of pollution, and fish and waterfowl returned.[13]

Near the mouth of False Creek, Granville Island was still occupied by industry. The National Harbours Board controlled the site and Ottawa realized, in the early 1970s, that the island would have to change to reflect the False Creek renovations. In 1973 Vancouver MP Ron Basford was made minister responsible for Canada Mortgage and Housing Corporation. As Granville Island was part of his own riding, he took a keen interest in having it controlled by CMHC and went ahead with plans to make it a "public place." The federal government provided $25 million for the upgrade and Basford set up the Granville Island Trust, composed of local residents, to monitor the project.

Houseboats on the southeast shore of False Creek, 2000. *DA*

A seawall was built and business leases were bought out. Long-established industries left—Allied Engineering, Arrow Transfer, National Machinery and finally BC Equipment, which had operated there for 60 years. Development proposals were called for and unique plans made for an urban park that would incorporate the old commercial buildings as a reminder of False Creek's industrial past.

In 1978 Vancouver city council approved the plans and the rejuvenated Granville Island was born. Wherever possible, new construction followed original building designs: walls look like the old corrugated tin siding, the over-sized industrial doors and huge wooden posts remain, as do the railway line, bollards, steel pipes, docks and building hardware. Cars follow the old roadway and pedestrians have to keep to the sides—sidewalks were not part of the old Granville Island and are not part of it today.

The old Arrow Transfer building became Bridges seafood restaurant, and the British Ropes and Westex factories became the Emily Carr College of Art. Micon Products, producing drill bits for mining, and Ocean Cement remained and continue to operate. The food market, children's stores, restaurants, art studios, boat works, live-aboards, theatres, a water park and dozens of shops form a lively melange that attracts an estimated eight million visitors a year. The island's development inspired Lonsdale Quay and Waterfront Park to the west of it on the North Shore, which opened for Expo 86, and waterfront markets at New Westminster Quay and Bridgepoint in Richmond.

In 1986 Vancouver proudly invited the world to False Creek. Expo 86, celebrating the city's centennial, was held on the creek's north shore on the former CPR land.[14] After the Expo buildings were cleared from the land, controversy arose when Premier William Vander Zalm offered to sell the 84-hectare site to entrepreneurs, instead of having it developed by a Crown corporation. Li Ka-shing, a Hong Kong billionaire, made the highest offer, $320 million to be paid over 15 years.

For more than a year Vancouverites voiced strong complaints against the deal, alleging that it had been made under a cloak of secrecy, in a suspiciously short space of time and for too low a price. When Li's company, Concord Pacific, released plans for the site it revealed a design for the largest development scheme in North America, a $3-billion project. It included high-rise towers, parks, marinas, a residential neighbourhood and a seawall bordering False Creek.[15] The original CPR roundhouse was redesigned as a community centre. By 2010 the population on this spectacular site is expected to reach 15,000.

The 35-hectare site at Kitsilano Point, from Burrard Bridge west to Jericho, now includes Vanier Park, the Vancouver Museum, the H.R. MacMillan Space Centre, the Vancouver Maritime Museum, Seaforth Armories, Molson's Brewery and other buildings. The tangled history of the original aboriginal Reserve No. 6 land there, the village of Snauq, and payments to the Squamish by provincial and federal governments over a period of nearly 90 years has led to what had once been dubbed "the Infamous Kitsilano Affair."[16]

Although a traditional village, Snauq was home to only 17 Squamish families by 1913. BC Premier W.J. Bowser, influenced by a real estate boom and a grandiose scheme for new harbour facilities at the point, offered the families a cash payment of $11,500 per person if they would pack up and leave. He did not inform the federal government of his actions.

In April 1913 the families were removed by barge with their belongings, including the bones of their ancestors. The last person to leave was

"Old Man Jim," one of the oldest members of the band, who went to live on Indian Arm. Others set up new homes at reserves on the North Shore and Squamish. When the federal Indian Affairs Department heard about the "bribe," the government labelled it an "illegal inducement" and refused to deliver title for the land to the provincial government, or to allow industrial development there.

The land lay idle for many years, although small sections were alienated for the Burrard Bridge and CPR right-of-way, with payment for these going to the Squamish band. In 1947 the federal government, to clear its books of the original "inducement" records, offered a large payment to the BC government. From then until 2000, discussions, arguments, claims and counterclaims involved both levels of government and the Squamish Nation.[17]

Finally, in 2000, the federal government offered the Squamish people a formal monetary settlement for their Kitsilano reserve land, plus former reserve land in Squamish and on the North Shore, for a total value of $92.5 million. Squamish Chief Gibby Jacob commented: "It's an awesome day. The sun is just beginning to peek from the clouds...our ancestors are smiling down on us."[18]

Coal Harbour

The face of Coal Harbour has changed since the removal in the 1960s and 1970s of the bustling industries, fire-trap buildings and old narrow wooden piers. The Bayshore Inn, built for $6 million, opened on March 27, 1961. Now the Westin Bayshore, it has more than 500 rooms and glorious views of the inlet and mountains. A large apartment tower development with gardens and waterfront walks is adjacent to the hotel. On the water, nearly 1,000 pleasure boats tie up at the grid of docks that mostly are home to the Royal Vancouver Yacht Club (RVYC).

In the remaining open water, commuter float planes land regularly—but not always safely. An AirWest plane flew low over Stanley Park at 5:45 p.m. on Saturday, September 2, 1978, heading for Coal Harbour. Its engine sputtering, it cleared the RVYC boat sheds, then made a sharp left bank, nosed into a small area of open water and flipped over. Both crew members and nine of the 11 passengers died.

Dennis Lee, a security guard at the RVYC, was one of the first on the scene. He told a *Province* reporter:

I was on the float (the yacht club walkway) and I got over to the plane as soon as I could. There was a little hole in the underside of the plane. I looked down, I heard a voice and saw a hand. I yelled for him to hold on. He got out. He was a real fighter.[19]

The plane was a regularly scheduled commuter flight from Victoria, delivering Japanese tourists to the Coal Harbour landing area.

Off the shore of Stanley Park, two remaining marine service stations—Chevron and Esso—dispense fuel to local boaters. They are now safe from projectiles shot out of the Nine O'Clock Gun.

On Sunday, May 12, 1974, the Texaco barge was peppered with a hail of rocks after the gun fired. A favourite pastime for some young people, evidently, was to throw rocks from the shore at low tide into the cannon's mouth. The Nine O'Clock discharge this time shot the rocks 275 metres to the barge, hitting a passing Coast Guard cutter and a police boat. Renovations to the gun solved that problem; the "boom" is triggered electronically and fires nothing.[20]

Indian Arm

For the last time, on October 31, 1970 the Burrard Inlet Travelling Post Office delivered mail to Indian Arm communities. Skipper Joe Blackmun paid farewell visits along the shore, guiding the 7.9-metre *Wee Willie* into the small docks. The Canadian post office had decided to cancel the service because the number of deliveries had dropped significantly. Some places, such as Woodlands and Belcarra, now had mail delivered to boxes nearby and many of the isolated spots were occupied only in summer. After years of memorable mail delivery, the end of the service took with it many memories. Harbour Navigation Company Ltd. continued to provide ferry service.

The peaceful and secluded cove at the head of Indian Arm had been the destination of many of the ships and boats carrying visitors over the years. Just after midnight on July 29, 1962, it was the site of a Royal Canadian Mounted Police raid. Two boatloads of officers descended on the Wigwam Inn and its outlying houses and offices. An undercover officer had been investigating for five months and had received bribes to provide "police protection" for illegal casino operations designed to attract millionaires to the hotel. The officers seized a large quantity of gambling

257

equipment and 300 cases of beer. A court later sentenced two of the Wigwam Inn promoters to six years in jail for bribery.[21]

The property was placed in receivership in 1963, and that year saw the worst devastation in the inn's long history. Vandals stripped the building of furniture, rugs, bar stools, bedding and dishes. They smashed the piano, shredded the wallpaper, ripped the green felt on the pool table and generally destroyed the building's interior. A watchman was put on guard and hopes rose for the hotel's future when a Fraser Valley farmer, Karl Zielke, bought and reopened it on a trial basis in the summer of 1964. However, the property again returned to the hands of a receiver.

In 1972 a North Vancouver contractor, Tony Casano, bought the crumbling wreck and its 62.7 hectares for what was believed to be $150,000. He hired a caretaker, Harley Beamish, who took up residence with his dog in one of the inn's ruined rooms with a small wood stove, a bed, and the walls encased in plastic sheets to keep out bad weather. Renovations began.

Parts of walls and floorboards had been torn up for firewood. The roof was leaking. Rotten wood and windows had to be replaced. Casano set up a sawmill at the rear, piped in water from an adjacent creek, set up a radio

When Tony Casano bought the Wigwam Inn and its land in 1972 the building was a wreck, with windows missing, the roof leaking and inside walls and floorboards torn out. *RC*

telephone and hired workers to assist. Rose Casano, Tony's wife, remembers that when they first visited the inn in 1972 the grand piano was visible underwater at the shoreline. As work progressed the couple allowed visitors to moor their boats, for a charge, rented out five canoes and made the shoreline available for picnics in summer. Casano eventually built two gazebos, one with a barbecue spit big enough to hold a whole pig.[22]

In 1980 Casano sold the property for $500,000 to five local businessmen. They renovated the inn to their specifications, adding a bathroom to every guest room, and opened it as a modern hotel with furnishings from the early 1900s. Room rates were $55 a night.[23] The business again was not successful and in 1986 the Royal Vancouver Yacht Club purchased the site as an outstation for its members.

Opposite the inn, on the eastern shore, another resort was popular with nature lovers. From the mid-1960s Harbour Navigation had operated the Granite Falls Holiday Resort. Visitors could dine and dance in a beautiful natural setting near the 40-metre waterfall where once men had quarried granite for the new city of Vancouver. From 1983 the resort operated under new ownership, and it was sold in 1993 to the provincial government for use as parkland.

The small community of Belcarra, nestled farther south on the eastern shore, officially became a village on August 22, 1979.[24] By then it was serviced by electricity and roads and most residents lived there permanently. It has retained its aura of privacy and isolation, a public telephone its only concession to anything approximating a commercial location.

Woodlands remains a small community north of Deep Cove, across the water from Belcarra and accessible by a steep, winding, paved road. Zellah and Jack Leyland moved there permanently in 1973, but Zellah had spent every summer of her life at the family camp. Her father and mother, Percy and Zellah "Teanie" Ward, bought the waterfront in 1909 from Hugh Myddleton Wood when they moved to BC after the Boer War.

Zellah recalled:

Before the road was built, my father used to come by water. The road's been there in some form, I think, since shortly after the First World War. The original one was very primitive, with bridges crossing numerous small creeks. Logs were laid across the road in the swampy spots so the cars wouldn't get stuck in the mud. It was called a "corduroy road." The paved one was put in only a few years ago.

The water was piped into our house from Ward Creek. Daddy erected a 1,000-gallon [4,546-litre] wood-stave tank to reserve the water, but we had to be careful to use as little as possible. About 1960 we switched to Ostler Creek, which never ran dry.

We used to take our garbage out [into the inlet] and sink it. We had to row out until we could see the Buntzen Power House, then drop our trash overboard. It was an unwritten rule to sink it. We filled cans and bottles with water until they sank.

We had a cooler on the back porch with a breeze from the water going through it. As a matter of fact, when our present house was remodelled from a cottage to a permanent home I insisted on having an old-fashioned cooler installed on the shady side of the house.

We used to get milk from the ferry boat that came every day from Vancouver. My mother made her own bread on a wood stove. If our milk went sour she'd make cream cheese with it. The milk kept fresh longer if it was brought to a boil. My sisters and I used to fight over the resulting scum on top—it was cream, beautiful.

The Ward family's summer home at South Woodlands on Indian Arm, circa 1950. Percy Ward purchased the land in 1910. *ZL*

My mother and my sister Lily sometimes picked salal berries at Wigwam Inn and made salal and apple jelly to put on bread or toast. Often my mother would ask me to row over to Racoon Island to pick her some salal berries.

I think I spent most of my time in a rowboat. I loved to row. Jimmy Underhill and I would have races. We'd bring the boat in as fast as we could to the dock as though we were going to crash. Then all of a sudden we'd dig the oar in so the boat would turn.

During the late 1950s my father divided the land equally between his four daughters. Jack and I built our own camp and used it every summer. It had a tiny living room and kitchen, a back shed and veranda. We brought the building material in by water. I remember that the bricks came down the hill on a chute and landed undamaged on an old kapok mattress. In 1973 we converted the camp into this house, and a permanent reservoir was installed with a pump and underground waterlines to serve the four homes on "Fire Lane number 2." We now have water piped in from North Vancouver, but we still pack our garbage out of here by car to dumpsters set aside for the local residents. We've lived here ever since.[25]

Boulder Island, just inside the mouth of the arm, was named for a large rock that used to sit on its west shore. Harvey Burt, a long-time resident of Indian Arm, recalls:

When I first knew the island, in 1937, I came up past here in a boat. When we passed Boulder Island the boulder was sitting on a flat shelf on the shore about 10 feet above water level with a steep drop below it. The rock itself was about six and a half to seven feet high, and about five feet wide. It was squarish, with a sloping top. It was a real landmark, one of the old glacial erratics you find sparsely scattered on the North Shore.

When we moved here in 1959 we had a view directly across to the island. In the early '70s, a shake mill called Viking was established on the Burrard Native band's waterfront. Workers from the mill decided to remove the boulder and use it as an anchor for their log booms. Some men came up here in a boat, pulling a scow, and they went to Boulder Island, drilled a hole in the rock with a compressor, then came back the next day and drove an iron peg into the hole. They snugged the scow up against the cliff, the tugboat put its line around the peg, and they heaved and heaved. Finally the boulder moved. It fell, breaking the line, smashed into the scow, damaging the bow, then rolled down into the water, way down. It didn't even leave a mark on the face of the cliff. The crew then started to try and pick up a rock on the southwestern corner of the island. It's still there with their iron rod in it.[26]

Concerned with the strong tidal currents through Burrard Inlet and their effect on ships berthing at harbour terminals, the National Harbours Board commissioned studies to consider the most effective means of reducing the strength of the flow. Dredging of First and Second Narrows was considered, but so was a dam and causeway across Indian Arm. In 1967 the Foundation of Canada Engineering Corporation drew up plans for a dam and causeway that would reduce tidal currents at Second Narrows from six to two knots, and at First Narrows from six to three knots.[27] The dam would turn Indian Arm into a fresh-water lake.

A dam had first been proposed before World War I as part of a rail line to be known as the "Port Moody-Indian Arm-and Northern" rail line and a charter had been granted, which the CPR had subsequently purchased. The 1967 proposal included a double-track railway from the CPR terminus at Port Moody and a four-lane highway from North Vancouver to Port Moody. Total cost: $29 million. The dam would stretch across Indian Arm from just north of Admiralty Point on the east to the northern limits of Roche Point, south of Deep Cove. This proposal was never carried out, to the relief of most Indian Arm residents.

The arm is still a favourite retreat for water lovers. At the northern end, Croker Island—the largest island in Burrard Inlet—attracts scuba divers to its southern wall with underwater visibility of up to 30.5 metres and a broad selection of marine life. Divers call the area "Paradise." Seycove Marina and the Deep Cove Yacht Club are popular havens for boaters.

The BC government created Indian Arm Park in 1995. As the area traditionally belonged to the aboriginal people, on January 16, 1998, after lengthy discussions the government and the Tsleil-Waututh Nation signed a co-operative management agreement for Indian Arm/Say-Nuth-Khaw-Yum Heritage Park. It parallels both sides of the shore from approximately North Woodlands and the village of Anmore north to the Indian River, encompassing 9,300 hectares. A wilderness area, it protects the old-growth forest, alpine lakes and the Indian River estuary and offers excellent wilderness hiking and camping opportunities.

Port Moody

The large bay that comprises the head of Burrard Inlet forms the centre of the City of Port Moody. City council has made a commitment to retain the three kilometres of the eastern shoreline and foreshore as the city's primary public open space. The Shoreline Park System reaches from Rocky Point Park on the south shore around the bay to Old Orchard Park on the north side. In 1978 and 1980 residents approved referenda dedicating that area as a public park, and by 1996 the city had acquired the necessary waterfront lands.

Besides the 50 hectares of waterfrontage, the intertidal area forms 40 hectares of environmentally sensitive space. A series of small parks had dotted the shoreline, and when the Head of the Inlet Park Development Committee was formed in 1985 its objectives included future plans for unifying and connecting the designated foreshore with a system of trails that

The northeast side of Shoreline Park in Port Moody in 2000, showing the remains of the Robert McNair Shingle Mill that operated from 1908 to the 1950s at the eastern end of Burrard Inlet. *JH*

would also provide access at several points. Natural features would be protected and enhanced.

From Rocky Point Park, east and north a series of natural areas were joined by trails and bridges. Pigeon Cove, an intertidal area, is an important roosting and feeding area for large flocks of band-tailed pigeons, with a swamp maintained in its natural state and crossed by a boardwalk. The Old Mill site on three hectares at the northeast corner was the location of the Robert McNair Shingle Company mill from 1908 until it burned down in the 1950s. Remnants remained in the form of cement pads, bricks, broken pilings, dikes, rotting sawdust and waste wood. The residue caused a strong sulphur smell, and the silty sediments in the intertidal area discouraged marine life.

Trails were cleared, the natural landscape maintained and a freshwater pond and meadow developed to attract nesting birds. Old Orchard Park on the north shore has been a one-hectare picnic site for many years, with a playground and beach, and is now the western terminus of the park system. Trails join the Town Centre Area, inland on the east, to the shoreline. This area provides a base for recreational activities and includes the city hall, library and community theatre. A fish hatchery has operated there since 1992.

Plans have been discussed for the intertidal area, which is highly important for the proliferation of sea and bird life. A number of log-booming leases are still viable there for the use of the Mill and Timber Company sawmill just west of Rocky Point Park. While the intrusion of human effluent into the inlet has been reduced for the better, the bottom debris deposited from log booms is still a problem. Studies have analyzed the physical composition of the inlet's bottom, water movements, and existing plant and marine life. The next major work planned for this park system is the redevelopment of Rocky Point Park.[28]

The Bridges

Another chapter in the history of Second Narrows bridges came to an end on May 6, 1969, when the Canadian National Railway officially opened its new 662.6-metre span. At a total cost of $32 million, the project included a 3,424.4-metre tunnel passing under Vancouver Heights in Burnaby, reducing south shore rail congestion by 30 percent and saving up to 10 hours on delivery of a boxcar from Port Mann on the Fraser River to North

For 10 years, three bridges spanned Second Narrows. Looking south toward Vancouver in 1969, the new Second Narrows Bridge is on the right, the old rail and car bridge is in the middle, and the new CNR rail bridge and a powerline tower are on the left. *NVMA 10006*

Shore industries. The new bridge had a lift span of 153 metres, the longest in Canada, and could be raised in two minutes.

CNR had purchased the first rail bridge for $1 in 1964; it had become obsolete after the Second Narrows highway bridge opened in 1960. In July 1970 the old bridge, which had been plagued by accidents, was dismantled. Its metal was sold for scrap and the concrete footings were blasted out of the water.

Lions Gate Bridge, the grand old lady of Burrard Inlet landmarks, had been feeling her age. Sixty or so years isn't terribly old, but her decks, planned for a 50-year lifespan, were worn out by the 60,000

The new CNR bridge at Second Narrows, 1969. At left is the original railway and car bridge, which was dismantled in 1970. HF

vehicles passing over them each day. Even her sparkling necklaces of 192 mercury vapour lamps, added in 1986 as a Vancouver centennial memento by the Guinness family, did nothing to improve her safety. Several proposals were studied, including a third crossing of the inlet and a widening of the bridge to include more traffic lanes.

In 1999 the BC government announced its plans to extend the bridge's life by replacing the deck and upgrading the Stanley Park causeway, at a cost of $100 million. Sidewalks were added on the outside of the bridge towers to widen the road width. Seismic upgrading was done in the spring and summer of 2000 and a new roadbed was being installed into 2001. The decision to renovate was received with mixed emotions, especially by North Shore residents who were not convinced that the project would end or reduce traffic lineups.

A cartoon by Len Norris, popular editorial cartoonist for the *Vancouver Sun* who illustrated amusing vignettes of life in West Vancouver. The caption reads: "On the other hand, if they are not going to use the place, we could fill it in and solve the crossing problem once and for all." *WVMA 286a*

The Environment

The profile of Burrard Inlet's inner harbour has changed dramatically over the last century and not only because of the growth in industrial sites. Intertidal mud flats had stretched far out from the shores at low tide, a great attraction for wildlife. From the time in the late 1800s and early 1900s that the foreshore on the south side was filled for CPR tracks, storage and docks, the Port of Vancouver's practice of reclaiming waterfront land for industry almost completely eliminated these salt-water mud flats. Only one small section, known as Maplewood, remained on the North Shore east of the Second Narrows Bridge in the 1960s.

Above the high-tide line on the north side of Dollarton Highway a sand and gravel company, Deeks-McBride Limited, operated a quarry from the 1920s to the early 1960s. The tidal flats at that time reached up to the road. Deeks had dredged a unique 48-metre-wide canal through the flats and out to deep water to enable its barges to carry sand and gravel from the site to the harbour. Shortly after the business closed, the National Harbours Board purchased the land from North Vancouver district, planning to fill in the mud flats and construct a deep-sea terminal—as it did in the 1970s at the Lynnterm site farther west.

The marshland and intertidal flats then became a controlled dump site for construction debris, most taken from Vancouver's West End when houses were demolished to make space for high-rise apartments. Accumulations of logs, lumber, tires, oil and garbage floating around the harbour had caused problems to navigation for years, since the number of sawmills had increased around the shores. During the 1960s a harbour tug towed a scow around the port and up Indian Arm, collecting the rafts of wood and junk and dumping them at the Maplewood site. As fill gradually covered the mud flats, the North Vancouver district council in 1967 made plans for a marina and townsite on the land. This announcement precipitated an unexpected, concerted public drive toward conserving the site for wildlife. North Vancouver district shelved its plans.

The natural resilience of the soil allowed plants and trees to sprout from the debris over the next few years, and this last five percent of estuarine wetland on the North Shore began to attract a wide diversity of wildlife to its pond and marsh. In 1987 a community organization, the Maplewood Committee, was formed and, with the support of the Western Canada Wilderness Committee, Vancouver Natural History Society and many other environmentally aware groups, launched a long and difficult campaign to make Maplewood a wildlife sanctuary. Because the Vancouver Port Authority (then the Vancouver Port Corporation) and North Vancouver district each owned parts of the land, approvals from both were necessary.

As a result of continuing public pressure, in 1989 North Vancouver district council designated Maplewood Flats a conservation area in its official community plan. The Vancouver Port Corporation seemed immovable in its refusal to make a similar concession. Finally, in 1991, the corporation agreed to lease its part of the property to Environment Canada for 49 years. In 1993 WBT Wild Bird Trust of British Columbia was incorporated to establish a wildlife sanctuary on the site. The Maplewood Committee became part of this new society.[29]

The 32-hectare conservation area at Maplewood Flats is a tribute to the group of citizens committed to preserving their natural heritage.

Ospreys return to their nest atop pilings in the salt marsh at Maplewood Flats wildlife sanctuary, April 2001. *John Lowman photo*

Thousands of volunteer hours have been invested in activities such as building, planting and clearing. The future may bring development of a nature house to complement Maplewood's "living classroom." The filled marsh, meadow, woodland and intertidal flats attract more than 214 species of birds and about 13 native mammals. For the first time in memory, a pair of osprey built a nest in 1991 on one of the pilings in front of the flats and reared two young. They have returned every year since, and every second year the Return of the Osprey Festival is held to celebrate not only their reappearance but also the achievement that made it possible: the first wildlife sanctuary on the North Shore of Burrard Inlet.

Formal efforts have been made to protect the inlet's marine, air and land environments. The Burrard Inlet Environmental Action Program (BIEAP), established in 1991, co-ordinates planning and decision making related to the improvement and protection of Burrard Inlet's environmental quality. Heavy industrial activity causes concerns regarding waste discharges, storm-water outlets, municipal combined sewer overflows and industrial-process effluents. Over the years contaminants such as cadmium, mercury, lead, zinc, copper and polynuclear aromatic hydrocarbons have exceeded the Canadian Environmental Protection Act criteria for acceptable ocean disposition levels.

BIEAP is supported by five funding partners—the federal Department of the Environment and Department of Fisheries and Oceans, Greater Vancouver Regional District, the BC Ministry of Environment, Lands and Parks and the Vancouver Port Authority. Its boundaries encompass 190 kilometres of marine foreshore and all inlet tidal waters. The Burrard Environmental Review Committee is made up of one representative of each partner and co-ordinates the environmental review of development projects proposed for Burrard Inlet.

Several ongoing research studies and projects have been carried out by BIEAP's supporting groups:

The Vancouver Natural History Society leads a volunteer birder program designed by the Canadian Wildlife Service to monitor bird populations on the inlet. Another volunteer group monitors intertidal ecosystems on the surface of, and underneath, rocks at eight sites.

The government of Canada, through the Department of Fisheries and Oceans, monitors fish habitat in intertidal marsh and riparian vegetation at 16 sites. It has sampled water to study chlorine-produced oxidant levels and toxicity in Burrard Inlet, and the effects of water chemistry on chum salmon off the Burrard Generating Station near Port Moody.

The government of British Columbia enforces waste-water discharge permits for all industries discharging effluents, carries out fecal coliform counts at all North Shore bathing beaches, and during 1997 monitored the impact from chlorinated discharges and assessed copper, lead and zinc levels in plankton.

Greater Vancouver Regional District studies have included the environmental impact in Burrard Inlet of combined sewer overflow from Clark Drive, Angus Drive and English Bay in Vancouver, the monitoring of three storm-water catchments for water quality and suspended sediment, and the collecting and analyzing of effluent samples from the Lions Gate waste-water treatment plant near the east bank of the Capilano River for organic contaminants and metals.

Municipal governments have also been involved in environmental issues related to the inlet. The City of North Vancouver sponsored a study in 1997 to record fish presence, species type, erosion, channel structure and so on, primarily in Mackay, Mosquito, Mission and Wagg Creeks. Port

Moody sponsored a feasibility study for protecting and preserving two wetlands on its north shore.

The University of BC and the Vancouver Port Authority have been conducting habitat studies. In October 1995, BIEAP-supported groups sampled sediment at 15 sites in the inlet for chemical and biological information.

For dry bulk terminals, such as those shipping grain or coal, the control of dust from material spillage is important; dust may be transformed from an air pollutant into water pollution, through waste water and contaminated storm water. BIEAP provides a "Best Management Practice Guide" for British Columbia Dry Bulk Terminals.[30]

With 29 ship-loading terminals on the inlet, contaminated ballast water from vessels could have a serious effect by adding pollutants to harbour water, as well as foreign aquatic species that could disrupt the natural food chain. Vancouver was the first port in Canada, and possibly North America, to make midocean ballast dumping compulsory. The Port of Vancouver Harbour Master's Office staff boards all deep-sea vessels entering the harbour to verify that bilge valves are sealed, and to inspect ballast water for pollutants. Treatment barges are available to retrieve contaminated or oily ballast. The Harbour Master's Office boat crews also monitor the water for signs of oil spills and/or pollution.[31]

The Port

Hundreds of hectares of what comprises the busy Port of Vancouver waterfront were made, not born. The early National Harbours Board instituted a program that has continued almost to the present day of dredging the tidal flats along the shore, then filling them for use as terminal facilities. The land gained helps to meet the needs of the increasing port traffic. Many docks and terminals are built on reclaimed land: in Vancouver, Centerm at Centennial and Ballantyne Piers, and Vanterm Terminal; in North Vancouver the 44.9-hectare Vancouver Wharves, Lynnterm, Seaboard Shipping and Neptune Terminals, and the businesses on reclaimed land at the foot of Fell Avenue, an area known as "Fell Fill."

The story of the development of waterfront land for Neptune Bulk Terminals (Canada) Ltd., west of Lynn Creek, illustrates the work involved in the reclamation process. In August 1966 the hydraulic suction dredge

Burrard Cleaner No. 2, a 15-metre-long skimming vessel, is towed stern-first in February 2000 by two fish boats with specially trained crews. Guide booms contain a Neptune Terminals canola oil spill that will be recovered by the skimmer. *Courtesy Burrard Clean Operations*

Neptune Terminals in North Vancouver, circa 1968, built on filled tidal flats in 1966–7. *Neptune Bulk Terminals (Canada) Ltd. Collection*

A 1946 aerial photo of the North Vancouver shoreline mud flats, with the Capilano River at left. Most of the inlet's mud flats have been reclaimed for commercial use. *Courtesy National Air Photo Library, with permission of Natural Resources Canada*

Sceptre Fraser, 49 metres long, began dredging material from the floor of Burrard Inlet and used it to extend the existing shoreline. This created 54 hectares of new waterfront land and deepened the moorage site to 15.2 metres at low water, a space that would hold six deep-sea ships. For 1,646 metres across the water side of the fill, more than 5,000 interlocking piles—each 16.5 metres long and weighing almost a tonne—were driven into the inlet's bottom, then joined to a concrete wall. The dredge suctioned up to 15,292 cubic metres of sand and gravel per day, an estimated

2.37 million cubic metres in total, and operated 24 hours a day, seven days a week, for about six months. The work was completed in 1967 at an approximate cost of $3.5 million. Neptune leased 28.3 hectares for loading and storage facilities for dry bulk cargo.[32]

The terminal is now the biggest multiproduct bulk terminal in North America and handles coal, potash, specialty grains, chemical fertilizers, canola oil and phosphate rock. It can store 600,000 tonnes of coal, 210,000 tonnes of dry bulk, 19,000 tonnes of canola oil and 25,000 tonnes of phosphate in each of two silos. Berth number 1, the coal dock, handles ships of up to 180,000 deadweight tonnes, and continuous-loop rail tracks permit railway cars to dump on-site. In 2000 the company had 250 full-time-equivalent employees.

CHAPTER 8

THE PORT OF VANCOUVER

Total tonnage through Port Vancouver hit its highest level ever in 2000. It was a record-setting year for the Port with 76.5 million tonnes handled, representing a seven per cent increase over 1999.

—Vancouver Port Authority, *Your Port & You*, Spring 2001

The driving force behind early European exploration of the BC coast was the search for a passage between the Atlantic and Pacific Oceans, a passage that would speed the transportation of trade goods to the Pacific countries from Europe and vice versa. Even though a passage through the northern Arctic waters was located eventually, the dream of such a route expediting commerce did not come to pass. The Port of Vancouver may now reasonably be considered the terminus of the Northwest Passage across Canada, accessed by land rather than by water, opening up trade with the Pacific Rim countries and their markets.

The Port

The Port of Vancouver is the largest and most diversified in Canada and trades more than $30 billion in goods with more than 90 nations. In 1998 the port's bulk exports, mainly coal and grain, encompassed 84 percent of all tonnage, at 60.6 million tonnes.

The major grain terminals—Cascadia (formerly Alberta Wheat Pool), JRI-James Richardson International (formerly Pioneer and Burrard), Pacific Elevators, Saskatchewan Wheat Pool and United Grain—ship the port's second-largest bulk commodity, after coal.

View of Vancouver from near Third Street in North Vancouver in 2000, looking across the Mission Reserve and the Mosquito Creek Marina, which is the second largest in BC and is operated by the Squamish Indian Band. St. Paul's two-spired church in left foreground. *MP*

A familiar sight on the harbour is the piles of yellow sulphur pellets at Vancouver Wharves on the North Shore and at Pacific Coast Terminals Company Limited in Port Moody. Sulphur is extracted from natural gas processing plants and exported around the world for use in agricultural fertilizers. Vancouver Wharves stores about 165,000 tonnes and Pacific Coast up to 220,000 tonnes. Both terminals also ship and receive other commodities.

In 1970 the first regularly scheduled container service into the port began with the entry of the *Golden Arrow* at Vanterm, a 30.7-hectare Vancouver container terminal. Now two berths, each 286 metres long with five cranes to handle containers, and others that are shorter, load and unload general cargo, forest and other products. Centerm at Centennial and Ballantyne Piers has six berths with five ship-to-shore gantries in all for lifting containers. The terminal also deals with forest products and general cargo.

The trend toward container transport has become so popular that the port handled more than 1.1 million foreign containers during 2000. Deltaport, 32 kilometres south of Vancouver's inner harbour and near the

Sulphur awaits shipment from Vancouver Wharves in North Vancouver, 2001.
Courtesy BCR Marine/Vancouver Wharves

Fraser River, is part of the Port of Vancouver and shipments to and from there are counted in the overall estimate.

Two chemical companies are located on the North Shore. CXY Chemicals imports bulk sea salt and exports caustic soda and sodium chlorate; Dow Chemical's terminal at Lynnterm deals in caustic soda solution, ethylene dichloride and ethelyne glycol.

Petro-Canada, Shellburn (Shell Canada), Stanovan (Chevron) and Trans Mountain-Westridge Terminals are on the Burnaby shoreline. The Imperial Oil storage facility, Ioco, is at Port Moody. All are sources for petroleum products, but with completion of the Trans Mountain pipeline the plants changed from refineries to marine, rail and truck terminals.

A tugboat with Tiger Tugz, a division of Straits Towing, tends a bulk carrier at the Cascadia grain terminal dock in 2000, with the Second Narrows Bridge in background. *MP*

Vanterm, the largest multipurpose terminal in the Port of Vancouver in 2000. On the left is a rubber-tired gantry used for moving heavy containers that are shipped around the world. *MP*

The southeast corner of Cates Park in North Vancouver in 2000, looking across Burrard Inlet to Trans Mountain–Westridge Marine Terminal. Note historic light beacon at shoreline. *DA*

Saskatchewan Wheat Pool elevators, 2000. On the North Vancouver shore near Second Narrows, they store a total 240,000 tonnes of grain. *DA*

Fibreco, 2000. The company receives and ships wood chips in bulk on the North Vancouver shore at First Narrows. *DA*

Aerial view in 1997 of Washington Marine Group companies Seaspan International Ltd. (left) and Vancouver Shipyards Co. Ltd. (right) on the North Vancouver shore. *Courtesy Washington Marine Group*

Ioco, 1999. The Imperial Oil distribution terminal on the north shore of Port Moody started business on the inlet in 1909 and operated as a refinery until 1995. *JH*

Alaska cruises are among the most popular tourism options in the world. Between May and September every year, for 17 years, Canada Place and Ballantyne Pier have accommodated some of the largest ships on the sea today, representing 12 cruise lines. In 2000 more than 1,050,000 passengers enjoyed over 333 sailings from home port in Vancouver. On average, every cruise ship that berths at the port injects $1.5 million into the BC economy.

Other enterprises vital to the port's operation include Vancouver Shipyards Company Limited and Vancouver Drydock Company Limited in North Vancouver; Seaspan International Limited and its Cates Tugs division and other towing companies without whose services the harbour would be crippled; ancillary industries that support port activities such as the Canadian Coast Guard, Canada Customs, dredgers, longshoremen, marine agents and surveyors, maritime lawyers, naval architects, oil spill experts, pilots, port wardens, railways, repair yards, ship brokers and chandlers, traffic control, truckers and water taxis.[1] All of these services, and more, make up a successful international port that is still growing.

Ships and Boats

Harbour safety is a paramount consideration for the Vancouver Port Authority and involves several groups of committed protection agents.

One of those, the firefighters, used the old *J.H. Carlisle* fireboat on False Creek until 1971, when she was finally retired and not replaced because land-based truck pumpers could provide even more water than the *Carlisle*. Vancouver *Fireboat No. 2* was left to protect industries and ships along the Vancouver shoreline, but the long-standing controversy over whether she should respond to fires in other municipalities continued to simmer.

Vancouver paid for extensive renovations to *Number 2* in 1972, including five new GM Detroit Diesel engines. It was by this time the only fireboat on the entire inlet. Despite threats by council in 1977 and 1978 to retire the boat unless the other municipalities contributed to its cost, Vancouver continued to pay until 1987, when *Fireboat Number 2* was finally retired. This drove the municipalities and the Port of Vancouver to agree to contribute to construction of five new fireboats. The port paid half of the $3.2-million cost and the rest was shared by Vancouver, Burnaby, North Vancouver city and district and Port Moody.

Celtic Shipyards, in south Vancouver on the North Arm of the Fraser River, constructed all five vessels. It launched the first white-hulled fast-response boat at the end of 1992, named *Fireboat 1*; similarly named, the other four took to the water during 1993. Each is 12.2 metres long, displacing 13.7 tonnes; two diesel 6/71 turbocharged 450 BHP engines drive Hamilton water jets and each craft can reach a speed of 30 knots. Water pumps provide 11,366.5 litres per minute.

Two of the boats are staffed by Vancouver firefighters and moor at Burrard Civic Marina in False Creek and a wharf near the foot of Main Street. City of North Vancouver firefighters operate a boat moored near Lonsdale Quay, and District of North Vancouver firefighters staff another at Lynnwood Marina on the North Shore. Burnaby and Port Moody together staff the fifth boat, based at Reid Point Marina.

This efficient harbour fire protection force came into effect 71 years after the first fireboat was launched.[2]

Some harbour services are focussed on enforcing and maintaining safety. People may not often notice the royal blue-and-white Harbour Patrol vessels on the inlet. They do their job without fanfare, providing services quite distinct from the Vancouver police boats. The Harbour Master's Office of the Vancouver Port Authority has operated them since 1997, when it took over responsibility from Ports Canada Police. The new service expanded to 24-hour coverage and operates with three boats, the *Brockton*, the *Kla-Wichen* and the *Takaya*.

The *Kla-Wichen*, a Vancouver Port Authority Harbour Patrol boat, in service on English Bay in 1995. This boat is responsible for pollution control related to ships entering the harbour. *D.A. Drew photo*

Each vessel has specific duties. The *Kla-Wichen* carries out general patrol and deep-sea boardings: the crew boards docked or anchored ocean-going vessels, acquaints the master or first officer with harbour rules and regulations, monitors ballast water disposal, and puts tamper-evidence seals on bilge systems to prevent dumping while in the harbour. Its crew also helps to co-ordinate safety at large marine events like regattas. The *Brockton*, a smaller, slower, more powerful boat, deals mostly with maintenance of docks and other facilities and removal of wood debris from the harbour. The *Nahnitch* was used for tours, patrol work and security at special events. Constructed of fibreglass, her hull was not strong enough to prevent damage if tied up to large freighters; the craft was replaced by a new aluminum boat, the *Takaya*, built in 2000 by Allied Shipbuilders.[3]

SS *Universe Explorer*, moored at Canada Place dock in 2000. She and other even larger ships must have a pilot aboard when entering or leaving Burrard Inlet. MP

Another safety oriented service focusses on the large ships in the harbour, some weighing as much as 60,000 tonnes, two city blocks long and as high as a six-storey building. The B.C. Coast Pilots Ltd., a partnership of BC pilots, supplies 106 marine pilots to help protect ships on the rugged BC coast, not including those for the Fraser River. The Pacific Pilotage Authority, operated by the federal government, assigns the pilots for specific duties. Ships planning to enter Burrard Inlet must have a pilot on board. (A "ship," as distinct from a "boat," is defined as a vessel of considerable size able to go on any ocean.)

The pilots board from a small pilot boat, five kilometres south of Victoria, then take over navigational duties from the ship's officers and direct the captain until the ship docks safely. The pilot's presence on board is indicated by a rectangular flag, vertically halved, half red, half white (the international letter "H" signal flag), flying from the highest point on the ship. When the vessel is ready to leave the inlet, the pilot boards from the dock or is delivered by water taxi to the anchorage.

The pilots are master mariners with a minimum of eight years' sea experience as licensed captains. They must write stringent examinations and serve an apprenticeship of at least 6.5 months, making approximately 105 trips before their acceptance as registered pilots. Their knowledge of the coast waterways goes well beyond charts. They must be able to navigate even if all of a ship's electronics are lost, and interpret the effects of wind and tides on the currents. The pilots communicate with the accompanying tugs and direct them as required when transiting narrow channels, or when the vessel requires docking assistance. With 13,000 assignments a year on the entire coast, the pilots' safety record is enviable—99.9 percent for all movements.[4]

The Canadian Coast Guard also plays an important role in enhancing safety on the waters of Burrard Inlet. The Vancouver Harbour Marine Communications and Traffic Services Centre (MCTS), located high in Vancouver Harbour Centre, provides a marine radio safety service (Vancouver Coast Guard Radio) to the boating community and industry, and vessel traffic service (Vancouver Traffic, or VTS) to large foreign-going ships, coastal commercial shipping and the towing industry. The Vancouver MCTS is a 24-hour operation that during a marine emergency also directs communications with the Rescue Co-ordination Centre in Victoria. Coast Guard Radio, formerly located at Vancouver Airport, and the VTS, formerly in the Kapilano 100 building in West Vancouver, combined into one operational unit in 1994 and moved to Harbour Centre.

Radio services such as a VHF channel 16 Distress and Communications Guard, marine weather information and notices-to-shipping broadcasts, and a pollution-reporting service are provided. Constant radar surveillance of vessel movements within the inlet and port approaches are microwaved back to the MCTS centre from locations on Bowen Island, the Kapilano 100 building in West Vancouver, and at Berry Point in Burnaby east of Second Narrows. MCTS also monitors via video camera on top of the Lions Gate Bridge and from the MCTS office itself. All commercial vessels of 20 metres or more in length are required by law to actively participate with VTS.

An additional MCTS service is operation of the Regional Marine Information Centre, which screens all vessels approaching Canadian and Puget Sound waters for defects and deficiencies, and provides clearances to enter our common waters.[5]

Ferries have been part of the inlet since the 1860s, but even before the new Second Narrows Bridge was completed in 1960 ferry service was eliminated, except for the service to Indian Arm. In September 1968 Harbour Ferries Limited instituted a new ferry service between Vancouver and North Vancouver. Initially MV *Hollyburn* and the *Harbour Princess*, painted blue and white to emulate the BC Ferry Corporation fleet, carried passengers for 50 cents one way. Later the 65-year-old MV *Scenic*, a former Indian Arm favourite, took over the service.

The ferries docked on a south shore floating pier at the foot of Burrard Street, surrounded on two sides by water or freighters and on the third by freight cars. Although the *Scenic*'s service was reliable it was slow, and the situation for passengers at the dock was less than ideal, especially when they were travelling in the dark. Access to the pier was a narrow stairway illuminated by a single oil lamp. At Bewicke Avenue in North Vancouver the landing facilities were even worse.

After three years, during which the *Scenic* carried up to 350 passengers a day and the company lost $60,000, Harbour Ferries closed the ser-

The former ferry *Hollyburn* in 2000 at its permanent berth in Coal Harbour, where it is used as an office by Coast Ferries/Harbour Tours. The Vancouver Rowing Club is visible at left rear. *DA*

SS *North Vancouver Ferry No. 1* in 2000. Launched in 1900 and retired in 1931, she has been used for many years as a home for the Palm family at Strawberry Island near Tofino, Vancouver Island. *DA*

vice on November 5, 1971.[6] The *Scenic* went on to ferry passengers between Nanaimo and Protection Island, then was laid up for several years. It was renovated for use as a ferry for Expo 86, with a 260-horsepower Nissan diesel engine and rated for 120 passengers. After the fair it sat idle until 1990, when it became the Fraser River Scenic River Tours vessel. The craft came to its final rest in February 1994, on the beach at Ladysmith.

Over the years other proposals for ferry service have surfaced. In January 1969 Harbour Ferries and Fleet Ferry Transit Limited proposed to initiate a three-ferry cable service on the inlet. One ferry would operate from Vancouver to North Vancouver, a second would cross Indian Arm from south of Deep Cove to Belcarra, and a third would travel from Indian River Drive in North Vancouver to a dock in Burnaby. They would operate by means of submerged cables. Touted as the answer to the inlet's transit problem, the plans never left the drawing boards.

On June 17, 1977, SeaBus initiated the first ferry service of its kind in the world when the orange ferries *Burrard Beaver* and *Burrard Otter* made their first crossings for BC Hydro (later they were operated by the Greater Vancouver Transportation Authority, now TransLink) between Vancouver and North Vancouver. Designed and built in Victoria, the ves-

A small False Creek ferry heads for Granville Island. AquaBus and False Creek Ferries both run commuters, shoppers and tourists across the creek.

sels are 34.13 metres long, with four diesel engines and a maximum speed of 13.5 knots. Together they can carry 3,200 passengers an hour, with a dock turnaround time of only three minutes. More than 11,000 riders a day make the trip in winter, and in excess of 19,000 daily in summer. During their years of service, neither SeaBus has been involved in a serious accident.

During 1986 seven temporary ferries emerged to transport Expo 86 visitors from Harbour Place in Vancouver to the Dream Ship central landing on False Creek. Among them were the former West Vancouver ferry *Hollyburn* and the old *Scenic*. Both had provided service on Indian Arm for Harbour Navigation. In 2001 the *Hollyburn* rested quietly on her laurels, tied up at the dock near the north end of Denman Street on Coal Harbour. Rebuilt for Expo 86, she houses the reservation and tour offices for Coast Ferries/Harbour Tours.

Tied up close by, the paddlewheeler *Constitution* and the *Harbour Princess* continue to provide harbour and Indian Arm cruises. The original wooden *Harbour Princess*, built in 1924 for Harbour Navigation, sank at its berth in North Vancouver in 1987. She was raised and sold to the operator of the Northern Lights Fishing Lodge for use as a barge for building materials.[7]

Deep within Burrard Inlet's waters lies a hidden history of ships and boats. Reports of more than 100 sinkings around Vancouver have been made over the years, a legacy of the thousands of ships moving in and out of the harbour. Most wrecks were caused by accidents due to human error, scuttling, or mere neglect. Many were tugboats or barges, while a number had been some type of warship.

One of the two SeaBus ferries, circa 1990. They have been carrying passengers between Vancouver and North Vancouver since 1977. *SeaBus Collection*

The Underwater Archaeological Society of British Columbia (UASBC) was founded in 1975 as a nonprofit volunteer organization to promote the science of underwater archaeology and to conserve, preserve and protect the maritime heritage lying beneath BC's coastal and inland waters. One of the society's most important tasks is to make inventories of shipwrecks and other submerged cultural sites, leading to their conservation and management, and assessment of their potential for educational or recreational use. The sites so far investigated throughout Burrard Inlet were selected for their historical significance, industrial or recreational impacts and accessibility.

Typically dives are conducted year round, with seven participants involved in each one—divers, some of whom are photographers, and people crewing the boats on the surface and/or recording artifacts. Ship remains are usually located by sonar. The divers are outfitted for mapping each site; they make notes and drawings of important features and the photographers record those. Sites that require ongoing management are also mapped and artifacts measured and sketched.

The most historic wreck in Burrard Inlet is SS *Beaver*, the first steamship on the North Pacific coast, which hit the rocks at Prospect Point on July 26, 1888. She sat there for four years while souvenir hunters took memorabilia. Finally breaking up in 1892, her remains are scattered on the floor of First Narrows. The boiler was raised for public exhibition in the early 1900s and is now in the Vancouver Maritime Museum. Early sports divers removed many artifacts but large sections of the hull survive.

A Lonsdale Quay wreck is suspected to be the remains of the *Canada*, which worked on Burrard Inlet as *Spratt's Ark* in the late 1800s. Not far to the west, at the mouth of MacKay Creek, the remains of one of the most powerful tugboats on the Pacific coast, *Superior Straits*, has rested on the bottom—27.5 metres down—since about 1971.

Bedwell Bay had been used for many years as a storage area for hulks or decommissioned military ships. The UASBC has studied four sunken remains there, one of them considered a "mystery wreck" because in 2001 her name had not yet been identified.[8]

The UASBC has worked over the years to educate the public to protect wrecks. For 25 years or so it has been considered very poor form for divers to remove artifacts, and "wreck looting" has generally ceased. The BC Heritage Conservation Amendment Act of 1994 outlaws removal of artifacts from shipwrecks or cargoes that have been sunk for more than two years, unless a written permit has been obtained from the government.[9]

Fire

Since the first buildings were constructed on the inlet fire has played a devastating role, starting with the 1874 blaze at Moodyville and the Vancouver conflagration in 1886. The combination of marine fuels, industrial material and wooden docks and pilings around the port causes constant concern about its fire potential. Since the 1970s several fires have taken their toll, but three stand out.

It was business as usual on the four fuel barges moored in Coal Harbour on the afternoon of Friday, January 4, 1974. John Campbell, manager of the *Home Oil Barge*, was assisting two boaters to fill the tanks of their white pleasure craft. Norman Robinson, a sales agent on the *Esso Barge* about 90 metres south, was cleaning up his small kitchen in preparation for a shift change.

Explosion and fire on Home Oil's barge in Coal Harbour on January 4, 1974, with police boat in foreground. *MBMW, photograper unknown*

At 2:23 p.m. flames shot out of the small boat tied to the *Home Oil Barge*, spreading to the barge itself. Black smoke spiralled hundreds of metres into the air, followed by a tremendous explosion that shook downtown office windows. In seconds the barge was engulfed in flames. The intense heat blistered paint and broke windows on the neighbouring barges. When Robinson ran outside he discovered debris spread across the water and on his deck, including a plank blasted from the *Home Oil Barge* with bumper tires still attached. Exploding oil drums littered the water. The burning 30-year-old wooden barge had a capacity of 295,490 litres of fuel, including diesel and stove oil. Explosions continued as more materials ignited.

The Lyttle Brothers tug the *Lawrence L.*, under the command of Captain Howie Keast and relief skipper Ken Arnison, immediately left her dock at the south end of Philip Avenue in North Vancouver and sped toward the fire, meeting *Fireboat 2* in Coal Harbour. Both trained their hoses on the flames, but the heat was intense. Attaching a line to the hulk was crucial as it began to float toward the *Esso Barge*, but the tug could get near only with a fog-mist nozzle spraying ahead and the fireboat's hoses concentrated on it. A thick nylon tow line thrown from the tug burned instantly. With the heat so high that they could hardly breathe, tug crewmen Raymond Smart and Ron Lowe attached a steel line from the *Lawrence L.*'s stern while Captain Keast held the tug almost directly against the side of the burning barge.

By this time several more tugs had gathered. Captain Dan Williams, skipper of the *Seaspan Venture*, saw that the barge was still attached to its pilings; he rammed his craft into the burning hulk and ripped out the mooring chains. He said later:

> There was nothing but a mass of flames and explosions. Oil barrels were popping all over the place and the house on the barge was afire. I was kind of hot and my face and my two crew members' faces got pretty black.[10]

Captain Keast, who had worked on tugs since he was 16, faced an unexpected complication:

> The fire boat came too close to us and her monitor [large nozzle] hit our floodlights on the mast's yardarm, and they fell to the deck. An alarm bell went off in our wheelhouse, indicating a fire in the engine room. The engineer rushed below and pulled a switch to isolate the short circuit. Our radio was cut off, so I couldn't receive any orders over the air for about 20 minutes while we were towing the barge. The harbour master, other tugs and fire boat couldn't reach us to give directions. So we did what we thought was best. Eventually radio power was restored.[11]

Within 15 minutes of the blast the barge was being towed out into the inlet, with water constantly directed onto the flames. The strong pressure from her own nozzles prevented the fireboat from remaining in position; the crews of small tugs had to lash their vessels to the sides of the barge to keep it in place. Other tugs helped the firefighters, who had run out of foam, by pumping thousands of litres of water onto the fire. To add to the crisis, because of Vancouver regulations the fireboat had to leave the scene at the centre of the inlet. As explosions continued, there was a very real threat that one of them might destroy the escorting vessels.

Finally the *Lawrence L.* beached the barge at Fullerton flats at the foot of Pemberton Avenue in North Vancouver, just east of Seaspan International. The tug dropped the tow line and the *Phyllis L.* and *Valerie L.* moved in to push the barge onto the beach. There were a few minutes of panic when a line hanging from the barge became entangled in the *Phyllis L.*'s propeller, but with some manoeuvring the crew slipped it out. Tugs, some with their rubber bumpers smoking from the heat, placed log booms around the hulk to prevent it from floating away. At 7:00 p.m. it was still exploding. The crew of the *Clean Seas Protector*, available in case of water contamination, remained nearby all night, watching for oil leaks.

The following day, National Harbours Board police retrieved two bodies from the water near Mosquito Creek on the North Shore; a third body was found later. John Campbell of Home Oil died with the two boaters he had been helping, Clifford Dawley and Edgar Attaed. Identification was made through dental records. Although cigarette smoking on the barge was suspected as the fire's cause, police did not rule out the possibility of illegal activities on the barge.

On October 1, 1974, the Royal Canadian Humane Association awarded bronze medals for bravery to Captains Keast and Arnison and mechanics Raymond Smart and Ron Lowe, all of the *Lawrence L.* In 1975 each also was awarded the Star of Courage by the government of Canada in recognition of their bravery.[12]

A group of workers was attempting to put out a small conveyor belt fire on Friday, October 3, 1975, on the top floor of the Burrard Terminals Ltd. building on the North Vancouver shore. Electrician Barney Chapman left them to get some oil from an outside shed to lubricate what they assumed was a piece of equipment that had seized up and was overheating. Chapman told his story later that day:

> There was a sharp explosion that must have shaken loose a lot of [grain] dust, and then came the big one—a great roar that went right through the building. I saw one man just outside who'd had his clothes ripped right off. Then others came staggering out of the building and even though I knew them all I couldn't recognize some of them because of the dirt and burns.[13]

A fire at Burrard Terminals Ltd. in North Vancouver roars hundreds of metres into the air on October 3, 1975. *NVMA 8512*

The fire that followed the explosion roared hundreds of metres into the air, blackening the sky with smoke. Tugs raced to tow the 14,000-tonne Russian freighter *Anton Chekhov* away from the loading dock on the west side of the terminal. Wooden power poles on the opposite side of the railway tracks ignited, and only water from firefighters' hoses prevented bushes and trees on the roadside embankment from burning.

The 122-metre-high "workhouse" complex had been built in 1928 and contained weighing and cleaning equipment used for grain before it was funnelled to the dock for loading. As fire consumed the structure, the upper section of its tower collapsed inward with a roar. The giant grain storage elevators to the west were connected to the workhouse by high conveyor belts and the flames began to spread along them, threatening to ignite the grain in the elevators.

Fire trucks from North Vancouver city and district raced to the waterfront, and Vancouver sent its boat and its Firebird high-platform unit, which could shoot water onto the conveyor belts. The fire blazed for two hours, but was prevented from spreading to the elevators.

One man was killed and 16 were injured. Lions Gate Hospital put its disaster plan into effect to deal with the influx of casualties and their families.

The government put an investigating team in place to determine the cause of the devastation. BC deputy fire marshal K.H. Collier noted the team suggested that fine particles of organic matter such as grain dust, suspended in the air, are extremely volatile and once ignited could cause an explosion.[14]

The channel leading out of False Creek, past the Esso fuel barge and the Canadian Coast Guard station, was a busy spot for weekend boaters heading into English Bay and beyond on Sunday, July 7, 1991. Howard Wong, his wife Cynthia and their 18-year-old daughter Vicki were looking forward to spending a day on their four-metre outboard pleasure boat. A few minutes after Howard started his motor at about 11:00 a.m., flames shot up. All three Wongs jumped overboard.

A small False Creek ferry was passing as the accident happened. The operator, Trevor Shaw, radioed the Coast Guard but couldn't go near, fearing for the safety of his 12 passengers. He recounted:

As soon as the boat touched the pilings, the flames shot up two to three times as high as the dock. I couldn't believe how fast it spread.[15]

The burning boat drifted in the current, up to the Coast Guard wharf, and immediately the creosote-soaked pilings erupted in a sheet of flame. A boater dragged Cynthia out of the water and a police craft rescued Vicki, but Howard drifted under the Coast Guard pier. With flames only a few centimetres above his head, he was able to grab a rope thrown by a passing boater who pulled him away and took him aboard.

Thick, black, oily smoke could be seen in the sky all over the Lower Mainland, and small explosions from fuel drums and oxygen tanks punctuated the roar as 15 fire vehicles arrived at the four-alarm blaze. The fire-fighters' first concern was to prevent the flames from spreading to the *Esso Marine Barge* and its 60,000 litres of fuel, only metres away and directly under the Burrard Bridge.

The smoke closed the Burrard and Granville Bridges, Granville Island and the Vancouver Aquatic Centre. Marine traffic was barred from False Creek. The fire destroyed the Coast Guard offices and helipad, two Coast Guard boats and seven vehicles owned by Coast Guard personnel and the RCMP. The Coast Guard moved to temporary offices at nearby Burrard Civic Marina[16] until their quarters were rebuilt at the old site, today part of the Kitsilano Search and Rescue Station.

Lighthouses

The yearly increases in the number of ships entering and leaving the port have made the lighthouses on the inlet more and more essential, but an article in The *Province* on October 29, 1968, marked the end of an era:

> A step taken by West Vancouver municipal council Monday night will contribute to the demolition of a beacon that has helped guide ships safely through First Narrows for 60 years. Council agreed to reserve 10 square feet of land, 600 feet northeast of the present beacon near the mouth of the Capilano River, for the Department of Transport. This means the DoT with a guaranteed new beacon site, can go ahead with plans to tear down the old [First Narrows] lighthouse . . . George Whitehurst [who worked in the signal station on the Lions Gate Bridge] said the lighthouse is also used for fog horns which are controlled by radio signal on the bridge and are tested every morning at 7 a.m.
>
> "You should hear the people in the high-rise apartments complain when she booms through the place," he chuckled. "We can't help it, but one guy even threatened to shoot us off the bridge."[17]

With dredging at First Narrows, the shoal on which the lighthouse stood was removed and a new beacon installed with almost the same bearing, so that the location was familiar to experienced ships' captains entering and leaving the port.

Electricity finally came to Point Atkinson Lighthouse the year Ernie Dawe retired as lightkeeper, in 1961. The old oil lamp was retired with him and a motor installed to run timers controlling the lights, radio frequencies and foghorn. Gordon Odlum, the new lightkeeper, had to climb the tower only twice a day to open and close the curtains at dusk and dawn.

The old fog alarm installed in 1912, powered by internal combustion engines and air compressors with diaphones, had long been a familiar sound to many North Shore and Vancouver residents; the voice of "Old Wahoo" was compared to an elephant with a cold. Electronic equipment replaced it in 1974 and the federal government's plan to automate its lighthouses moved a step ahead.

One insidious aspect of the light did not change, however. Because modern alloys were not available to manufacture ball bearings that could be used as its base when it was constructed, the light floated in a mercury bath. The use of mercury continued even after alloys were created and even though the danger of mercury poisoning through spills or evaporation was well documented. Gerry Watson and Donald Graham took over as lightkeepers in 1980 and each stood 12-hour watches seven days a week; Donald Graham kept a three-year record of the increasing mercury level in his blood and urine samples and finally refused to work with the system. The government replaced the mercury bath with a modern system in 1987, although some lighthouses continued to operate with the old format.

The panorama in 2000: Brockton Point light, Stanley Park, SeaBus on left, tug with barge at centre, Second Narrows Bridge in background. *MP*

Donald Graham, the former lightkeeper at Point Atkinson, on the dock below the automated light in 1997. The area is now a national historic site. *DA*

Night falls on Burrard Inlet. *MP*

In September 1994, 120 years after its construction, Point Atkinson Lighthouse and the point of land on which it stands became a National Historic Site. Less than two years later, the federal government kept a vow to automate the system in what it called a cost-cutting move. The Coast Guard estimated that savings from automating 18 Canadian lighthouses on the Atlantic and Pacific coasts would be $1.8 million per year. Critics suggested the costs would be much higher without lightkeepers on-site to report people in difficulty and aid in rescues. However, May 31, 1996 was the last day that dedicated keepers of the Point Atkinson light supervised the safety of mariners.[18]

Because of strong opposition to the removal of all lightkeepers, the federal government agreed to keep staff at some lights across the country. Burrard Inlet lighthouses were not among them.

As afternoon fades into evening, red beacons appear atop harbourside cranes. Rows of dazzling white lights illuminate Centennial Pier; other, yellowish bulbs follow the shore. The flashing beacon at Brockton Point becomes more evident as the water turns black, and shimmering lines of reflection appear, like wavering pathways leading to lights on the far shore.

A wheelhouse door opens on one of the Cates tugs moored at its North Vancouver wharf. A mariner approaches a set of pilings and tosses remnants of his dinner into the air. A Canada goose on top of a post reaches to catch the tidbits, then settles more comfortably on her eggs. White gulls shriek overhead, some diving into the water to retrieve their share of the goose's picnic.

The sky is lighter to the west and the shapes of moored tankers stand out as black silhouettes, dotted by white lights, against the sky. Stars appear.

A constant, unidentifiable hum pervades the stillness. The sound deepens as a SeaBus approaches the dock, a bright white light flashing on its mast. Suddenly the ferry's two harsh spotlights illuminate the terminal, shattering the mystical atmosphere.

One, two, then three Cates tugs move quietly from their berths, red and green running lights marking their courses out into the harbour. All three take up positions in a long line and wait to assist a ship heading for its berth.

The Nine O'Clock Gun booms its exclamation point to day's end.

NOTES

Throughout the text, Native stories and place names related by August Jack Khahtsahlano are drawn from his interviews with Major J.S. Matthews, as recounted in Matthews' book *Conversations with Khahtsahlano, 1932–1954*. August Jack was the grandson of Squamish Chief Khahtsahlanogh, from whom the Vancouver area of Kitsilano takes its name. All references to and translations of Squamish Native place names, and the anecdotes in Chapter 1, are from this book.

Major Matthews was the City of Vancouver's first archivist. He interviewed many early settlers and aboriginal people in the Vancouver area, documenting their stories in his five-volume book *Early Vancouver*. I have drawn on Matthews' interviews with, or written material from, these people.

Abbreviations:

BCA-British Columbia Archives
CVA-City of Vancouver Archives
NAC-National Archives of Canada

Introduction

1. I thank Jim Roddick, Geological Survey of Canada, for his help with this section.
2. Arthur S. Charlton, "The Belcarra Park Site," p. 57.
3. Charlton, p. 51.
4. Roy L. Carlson, ed., "Salvage '71," p. 138.
5. Alan D. McMillan, "The Original Inhabitants of the Port Moody-Coquitlam Area," Port Moody Historical Society, Occasional Paper No. 1, 1982, p. 4.
6. McMillan, p. 24.
7. Hilary Stewart, *Stone, Bone, Antler & Shell*, p. 62.
8. Stewart, p. 58.
9. E. Pauline Johnson-Tekahionwake, *Legends of Vancouver*.
10. Shelley A. Lugg, *Belcarra Regional Park: Archaeology, History, Interpretation—A Resource Book*, pp. 16–23.

Chapter 1: Early Exploration: 1791–92

1. These events are detailed in Warren Cook, *Flood Tide of Empire: Spain and the Pacific Northwest, 1543–1819*, Yale University Press, 1973.

2. Some evidence may exist that Captain Vancouver was not the first Englishman to name a coastal location on the Strait of Georgia. Samuel Bawlf, a British Columbia businessman with a lifelong interest in marine history and exploration, recently spent five years studying ancient maps and Elizabethan marine records at the British Library in London. His findings suggest that Sir Francis Drake's charts, showing that he went only as far north as 48 degrees latitude, were probably falsified on Queen Elizabeth I's orders. Drake believed he had found the Northwest Passage and England wanted to keep this discovery secret from King Philip of Spain. Bawlf has recorded his findings in a 300-page research document, "Secret Voyage to British Columbia," (*Vancouver Sun*, August 5, 2000, pp. B1–B6).

   The *Pelican*, later renamed the *Golden Hinde*, a 30.5-metre, three-masted gunboat carrying Drake and his crew, nosed out from Plymouth harbour into the English Channel on December 13, 1577. It was leaving on an extensive voyage of discovery that would reach around the world and enter uncharted seas. It could be that Drake was on a secret mission under Elizabeth's orders to locate a western entrance to the Northwest Passage without alerting the Spanish.

   Bawlf's research suggests Drake sailed to the Pacific, then as far north as southeast Alaska. In June and July of 1579 he could have followed the Inside Passage down the present British Columbia coast to an inland sea, the Strait of Georgia, where he may have pulled ashore on the east coast of Vancouver Island and named it Nova Albion, an ancient name for Britain. Continuing south he supposedly recorded a large, double-channelled river, which Bawlf feels was the Fraser. Just north of this waterway, the two landmarks Drake named Point of Sardines and Point St. Michaels Bawlf suggests were Point Atkinson and Point Grey.

   If the findings are correct, Drake and his crew would have been the first Europeans to visit British Columbia and view Burrard Inlet, 200 years earlier than previously accepted historical accounts.

3. Captain George Vancouver, *A Voyage of Discovery, 1791–1795*, June 13, 1792.

4. W.K. Lamb, ed., *Vancouver Discovers Vancouver*, an excerpt from the rough logs of Peter Puget, Burnaby: Vancouver Conference on Exploration and Discovery, Simon Fraser University, 1992, p. 13.
5. Tomas Bartroli, *Genesis of Vancouver City*, Vancouver: published by the author, 1997, p. 73.
6. A.G. Bradley, *Canada in the Twentieth Century*, p. 383.
7. This old song was known in western Europe under different names. Tomas Bartroli suggests it had the tune of "For He's a Jolly Good Fellow."
8. Bartroli, p. 100.
9. Historians have attempted to ascertain whether the name "Sasamat" referred to Indian Arm only or to the whole of Burrard Inlet. Bartroli concludes that "... the Alcala Galiano expedition understood, rightly or wrongly, that Sasamat was the name for the whole of Burrard Inlet." (p. 166). On the other hand, August Jack Khatsahlano, born at False Creek in 1877, said his people had no particular name for Burrard Inlet. (*Conversations with Khahtsahlano*, p. 59.)
10. For most details in the preceding sections I have used Henry R. Wagner's history *Spanish Explorations in the Strait of Juan de Fuca*, which includes translated copies of Eliza's and Galiano's logs. Major Matthews enlarged on Narvaez's possible route through Burrard Inlet in *The Vancouver Historical Journal* no. 4, January 1961. Captain Vancouver's log provided details regarding his explorations, as did Peter Puget's log.
11. Major J.S. Matthews, *Conversations with Khahtsahlano*, pp. 196–197.
12. Cole Harris, *The Resettlement of British Columbia*, Vancouver: UBC Press, 1997, p. 14.

Chapter 2: The First Commercial Enterprises: 1850–70

1. Alan Morley, *Vancouver, From Milltown to Metropolis*, p. 16.
2. W. Colquhoun Grant, "Description of Vancouver Island by its first Colonist," p. 314.
3. Captain George Richards' correspondence to Governor James Douglas, June 14, 1859.
4. Richards' correspondence to Rear Admiral Baynes, June 24, 1859.
5. Walter Moberly, *The Rocks and Rivers of British Columbia*, p. 31.

6. Moberly's correspondence to Magistrate Spalding, August 13, 1859.

7. Noel Robinson and the Old Man Himself, *Blazing the Trail Through the Rockies, The Story of Walter Moberly 1832–1915*, p. 24.

8. George Dietz and S.P. Moody's correspondence to the colonial secretary, November 24, 1864.

9. Peter N. Moogk, *Vancouver Defended*, p. 22.

10. For the logging and sawmill history in this chapter I have relied mainly on three references: James Morton's *The Enterprising Mr. Moody, the Bumptious Captain Stamp*, Derek Pethick's *Men of British Columbia* and F.W. Howay's article "Early Shipping in Burrard Inlet."

11. F.W. Howay, "Early Shipping in Burrard Inlet", pp. 5 and 6.

12. S.P. Moody & Company correspondence to Governor Frederick Seymour, February 16, 1865.

13. J.B. Launders' correspondence to the colonial secretary, June 3, 1865.

14. CVA, Simson, add. MSS 27, 565-G-6 file 9.

15. Charles Warren Cates, "The Development of Tugs on the BC Coast."

16. Major Matthews' records, add. MSS 54, vol. 1–13, file 01802, conversation with W.A. Grafton, May 4, 1939, CVA.

17. F.M. Chaldecott, *Jericho and Golf in the Early Days in Vancouver, 1892–1905*, pp. 5–6.

18. W. Wymond Walkem, *Stories of Early British Columbia*, p. 92.

19. F.W. Howay in "Early Shipping in Burrard Inlet" recorded the number of shipments from the inlet between 1864 and 1869, as reported in newspapers of the time: "1864, 1 vessel; 1865, 6; 1866, 5; 1867, 15; 1868, 33; 1869, 45."

20. Alan Morley, *Vancouver, From Milltown to Metropolis*, pp. 20–23.

21. West Vancouver Historical Society, "John 'Navvy Jack' Thomas," p. 2.

22. Norman R. Hacking, "British Columbia Steamboat Days, 1870–1883," p. 101.

23. *British Columbian*, August 12, 1865, p. 2.

24. West Vancouver Historical Society, "John 'Navvy Jack' Thomas," pp. 2–3.

25. Raymond Hull and Olga Ruskin, *Gastown's Gassy Jack*.

26. Thomas A. Lascelles, OMI, *Mission on the Inlet*, pp. 14 and 15.

Chapter 3: The Foundations for Maturity: 1870–90

1. The early history of Point Atkinson Lighthouse was recounted by Donald Graham in *Keepers of the Light*, pp. 64–67.
2. Muriel Crakanthorp, correspondence to Major J.S. Matthews, November 25, 1935, CVA.
3. West Vancouver Historical Society, "John 'Navvy Jack' Thomas."
4. Walter M. Draycott, *Recollections of a Pioneer's Early Days in Lynn Valley*, pp. 7–10.
5. Lynn Stonier-Newman, *Policing a Pioneer Province*, Madeira Park: Harbour Publishing, 1991, pp. 71 and 72.
6. *British Columbia Colonial Correspondence*, 1874.
7. Wayne Suttles, ed., *Handbook of North American Indians*, vol. 7, Washington: Smithsonian Institution, 1990, p. 160.
8. Robert Edgar Cail, *Land, Man and the Law*, Vancouver: University of British Columbia, 1974, p. 209.
9. CVA, *Mechanics Institute Minutes*, loc. 547-0-2, file 7.
10. John Warren Bell, "BC Memories," p. 50.
11. Bell, pp. 58 and 59.
12. *British Columbia Sessional Papers*, School Report, 1874–5, p. 95.
13. "Ramble on the Mainland," *Victoria Daily Colonist*, April 18, 1876.
14. George Green, *Early Electric Light on This Coast*, p. 10.
15. *Province*, February 27, 1943.
16. *British Columbia Directory*, 1891, p. 69.
17. Rev. William Stott, *The Early Story of North Vancouver*, p. 13.
18. Major J.S. Matthews, *Early Vancouver*, vol. 1, p. 268.
19. Matthews, vol. 2, p. 248.
20. Matthews, vol. 1, pp. 304–5.
21. *Victoria Daily Colonist*, August 29, 1884.
22. Matthews, vol. 2, p. 247A.
23. F.M. Chaldecott, *Jericho and Golf in the Early Days in Vancouver, 1892–1905*, p. 3.
24. Matthews, vol. 1, p. 191.
25. Matthews, vol. 5, p. 245.
26. Tom Koppel, *The Untold Story of Hawaiian Pioneers in British Columbia and the Pacific Northwest*, Vancouver: Whitecap Books, 1995, pp. 29, 91, 94 and 96.
27. "Burrard Inlet in the Seventies," *Province*, March 20, 1943.

28. CVA, Simson, add. MSS 170.

29. *British Columbia Sessional Papers, 1874–75*, School Report, p. 95.

30. Robert A.J. McDonald, *Making Vancouver, 1863–1913*, p. 44.

31. Eric Nicol, *Vancouver*, p. 163.

32. Matthews, *Early Vancouver*, vol. 1, p. 197.

33. C. MacDonald et al., *Between Forest and Sea*, pp. 22–25.

34. David Oppenheimer, Mayor, *The Mineral Resources of British Columbia*.

35. Edward Roper, *By Track and Trail*.

36. Newton H. Chittenden, *Travels in British Columbia, 1882*, p. 67.

37. *Port Moody Gazette*, vol. 1, no. 2 (December 22, 1883).

38. *Port Moody Gazette*, vol. 1, no. 16 (March 29, 1884).

39. D.M. Norton, *Early History of Port Moody*, p. 74.

40. *Port Moody Gazette*, vol. 1, no. 2 (December 22, 1883), p. 7.

41. Pierre Berton, *The Last Spike*, Toronto: McClelland & Stewart, 1971, p. 304.

42. These stories were included in Matthews' *Early Vancouver*, vol. 1.

43. Matthews, vol. 2, pp. 219–220.

44. Matthews, vol. 1, pp. 282–283.

45. Robert K. Burkinshaw, "False Creek," p. 17.

46. *The Semi-Weekly World*, October 22, 1897, p. 3.

47. Correspondence from Vancouver City Council to Dominion Government, May 17, 1886.

48. John Arthur Carver, *The Vancouver Rowing Club*, pp. 15–19, 24 and 31.

49. C. MacDonald et al., *Between Forest and Sea*, p. 27.

50. Norman R. Hacking, "British Columbia Steamboat Days, 1870–1883," p. 72.

51. Ruth Greene Bailey, "*Senator*, The Congenial Moodyville Ferry " Vancouver: *Harbour and Shipping*, August 1966, pp. 584–585.

52. Correspondence from Post Office Inspector's Office, Victoria to Postmaster General, Ottawa, August 24, 1886, NAC, file 1886–511.

53. *Vancouver News*, July 27, 1886.

54. Derek Pethick, *SS Beaver*, pp. 39–105.

55. *Vancouver News*, July 27, 1886.

Chapter 4: Growth and Development: 1890–1910

1. Donald Graham, *Keepers of the Light*, pp. 66–70.
2. Correspondence from J. Gaudin, Agent, to Colonel Anderson, Chief Engineer, Department of Marine and Fisheries, Ottawa, March 20, 1901, NAC, Burnaby Office.
3. Correspondence from Gaudin to Deputy Minister, Marine and Fisheries Department, Ottawa, March 21, 1899, NAC, Burnaby Office.
4. *Vancouver Harbour Aids*, accession 1802–2029, vols. 1 and 2, box 4, NAC, Burnaby Office.
5. Ken Drushka, *Against Wind and Weather*, Vancouver: Douglas & McIntyre, 1981, p. 209.
6. *Vancouver Daily News Advertiser*, August, 1897.
7. For this segment I have relied on Gerald A. Rushton's book *Whistle up the Inlet: The Union Steamship Story*.
8. *Vancouver Daily News Advertiser*, April 29, 1891, p. 1.
9. George Musk, *Canadian Pacific*, p. 213.
10. Fred Rogers, *Shipwrecks of British Columbia*, Vancouver: Douglas & McIntyre, 1980, pp. 226–27.
11. Rogers, pp. 230–31.
12. Norman R. Hacking, *Annals of the Royal Vancouver Yacht Club*, pp. 3 and 4.
13. *Vancouver World*, March 27, 1909, pp. 1 and 33.
14. *Province*, June 1, 1909, p. 1.
15. For much of the information in this section I have used Ruth B. Roberts' unpublished manuscript "The Ludgate Affair," Vancouver: March, 1976.
16. Howland Hoadley, "Vancouver's Playground," Vancouver: *Westward Ho!*, May 1908, pp. 12–18.
17. Major J.S. Matthews, *Early Vancouver*, vol. 4, pp. 228–30.
18. G.R.G. Conway, "Report on the Coquitlam-Buntzen Hydro-Electric Development."
19. *Vancouver World*, August 17, 1912, p. 5.
20. Matthews, *Early Vancouver*, vol. 1, p. 12.
21. Matthews, vol. 1, p. 87.
22. F.M. Chaldecott, *Jericho and Golf in the Early Days of Vancouver, 1892–1905*.
23. Robert K. Burkinshaw, "False Creek," pp. 22 and 25.
24. Daniel Francis, ed., *Encyclopedia of British Columbia*, p. 210.

25. *Province*, December 15, 1922, p. 10.

26. *Province*, August 11, 1900, p. 4.

27. Matthews, "The Nine O'Clock Gun," *Vancouver*, CVA, drawing with margin notations, photograph file StPk P198.

28. These images were derived from stories told by pioneering longshoremen in *Man Along the Shore!*, Vancouver: ILWU Local 500 Pensioners, 1975, pp. 10–18.

29. Ronald Kenvyn, "Vancouver's Harbour and Shipping," Vancouver: *British Columbia Magazine*, June 1911, pp. 474–76.

30. Anonymous, "Picturesque Vancouver, The Beachcombers," Vancouver: *British Columbia Magazine*, March 1911, p. 206.

31. Pixie McGeachie, *Burnaby, A Proud Century*, p. 32.

32. Matthews, *Early Vancouver*, vol. 4, p. 325.

33. West Vancouver Museum and Archives, file F35.

34. Gillian Roberts, *Burrard Inlet Pilotage*, pp. 19–25.

Chapter 5: A World Port: 1910–35

1. "Annual Report of the Harbour Commissioners of Vancouver for the year 1920."

2. "A Plan for the City of Vancouver," Vancouver City Council, 1928, p. 158.

3. J.A. Roddick and J. Luternauer, "GSC Teacher's Field-Trip Guide to the Geology of the Vancouver Area," p. 4.

4. Captain Kettle, Vancouver: *Harbour and Shipping*, vol. 3 (July 1921), p. 854.

5. Kettle, *Harbour and Shipping*, vol. 5 (June 1923), p. 303.

6. James H. Hamilton, *Western Shores*, pp. 159–66.

7. Details of H.H. Stevens' contributions to the port development are from several sources: Robert K. Burkinshaw, "False Creek"; Chuck Davis, ed., *The Greater Vancouver Book*, Surrey: Linkman Press, 1997, p. 838; Daniel Francis, ed., *Encyclopedia of British Columbia*, p. 433.

8. David Ricardo Williams, *Mayor Gerry*, Vancouver: Douglas & McIntyre, 1986.

9. L. Stevens, "Rise of the Port of Vancouver, British Columbia," pp. 65–67.

10. I am indebted to Alvin Sholund, a former Ioco employee, for his assistance with this section.

11. Robert Dollar, *Memoirs of Robert Dollar*, vol. 2, San Francisco: W.S. Van Cott, 1921, p. 13.

12. Dollar, 1921.

13. Robert D. Turner, *The Pacific Princesses*, pp. 121–25.

14. Sean Rossiter, "Vancouver International Airport," *The Greater Vancouver Book*, Surrey: Linkman Press, 1997, p. 468.

15. "V.H.C. Fish Dock is busy Spot," Vancouver: *Harbour and Shipping*, May 19, 1932, p. 146.

16. *"Man Along the Shore!"*, Vancouver: ILWU Local 500 Pensioners, 1975, pp. 34–90.

17. Francis, ed., *Encyclopedia of British Columbia*, p. 426.

18. Norman R. Hacking, *History of the Port of Vancouver*, c. 1976, pages unnumbered.

19. James H. Hamilton, *Western Shores*, pp. 149–52.

20. Peter N. Moogk, *Vancouver Defended*, pp. 51 and 52.

21. W. Kaye Lamb, "Building Submarines for Russia in Burrard Inlet," pp. 3–26.

22. Robie L. Reid, "The Inside Story of the Komagata Maru," pp. 7–21.

23. Reid, p. 22.

24. Hugh J.M. Johnston, *The Voyage of the Komagata Maru*, Vancouver: UBC Press, 1989, p. 128.

25. Swan, Joe, *"A Century of Service": the Vancouver Police, 1886–1986*, Vancouver: Vancouver Police Historical Society and Centennial Museum, 1986, pp. 31 and 69.

26. Betty O'Keefe and Ian Macdonald, *The Final Voyage of the Princess Sophia*, pp. 48 and 94–95.

27. "Brave skipper was hero of Rum Row," Vancouver: *Province*, March 10, 1999, p. C5.

28. Personal interview in 2000 with Donat McMahon, born in Vancouver in 1908.

29. Michael Sone, ed., *Pioneer Tales of Burnaby*.

30. Beryl Gray, "Older than Vancouver," Vancouver: *The Sunday Province*, November 25, 1928.

31. Point Atkinson Lighthouse Log Books, CVA, add. MSS 37, files 3 and 4, Canada Point Atkinson Lighthouse.

32. *Vancouver Harbour Aids*, accession 1988–89/205, vols. 1 and 2, box 4, NAC.

33. Dorothy Mawdsley Harrop interview, "Grace Darling of the Narrows,"

West Vancouver: West Vancouver Historical Association, November 1989.

34. *Vancouver Harbour Aids*, NAC.

35. Kathleen M. Woodward-Reynolds, *A History of the City and District of North Vancouver*, pp. 99–105.

36. *The Second Narrows Bridge*, pamphlet, 1925, pp. 5–17.

37. "Burrard Dry Dock History," vol. 2, produced by J.S. Marshall and Company Ltd., unpublished manuscript, c. 1978.

38. Burkinshaw, "False Creek," pp. 35–43.

39. June Cameron, *Destination Cortez Island*, Surrey: Heritage House, 1999, p. 15.

40. Major J.S. Matthews, *Early Vancouver*, vol. 1, p. 18.

41. Christopher Weicht, *Jericho Beach and the West Coast Flying Boat Stations*, pp. 9–29.

42. Personal interview with Les Rimes, West Vancouver, July 1998.

43. Graeme Wynne and Timothy Oke, eds., *Vancouver and Its Region*, pp. 281–82.

44. James W. Morton, *Capilano, The Story of a River*, pp. 51, 52 and 124.

45. "Tunnel Under Lions Gate Ready," Vancouver: *Province*, June 4, 1933.

46. British Columbia Geographical Names Office, Victoria.

47. Geo. S.B. Perry, "Between the Bridges," Vancouver: *The Express Empire Day Prosperity Edition*, May 24, 1912, p. 49.

48. *BC Saturday Sunset*, June 15, 1912, p. 9.

49. I am indebted to William G. Robinson, past president of the Royal Philatelic Society of Canada, for his expert advice on the history of floating post offices in Canada. So much has been written about the Burrard Inlet Travelling Post Office having been the first—in Canada, the British Empire, and even the world—that I had difficulty locating ironclad proof that the myth was untrue. Mr. Robinson cited ships and their routes from his own research and also as printed in *The Catalogue of Canadian Railway Cancellations and Related Transportaton Postmarks* by Lewis M. Ludlow, self-published in 1982 and updated.

50. Patricia Eaton, "The post office that sailed up Burrard Inlet," Vancouver: *The Magazine*, September 11, 1983, p. 5.

51. Matthews, *Early Vancouver*, vol. 4, p. 230.

52. Burkinshaw, "False Creek," pp. 32–35.
53. Wm. D. Hudson, "Proposed Spanish Banks Harbour Project," Vancouver: "A Plan for the City of Vancouver British Columbia," 1928, pp. 296–97.
54. CVA, Archibald, add. MSS 256, vol. 57, file 7, newspaper clipping.
55. R.H. Parkinson, "The Improvement of Vancouver Harbour," pp. 784–88.

Chapter 6: The War and Beyond: 1935–60

1. Peter N. Moogk, *Vancouver Defended*, p. 63.
2. *Vancouver World*, May 2, 1912.
3. For many details in this segment I have relied on Lilia D'Acres' and Donald Luxton's book, *Lions Gate*.
4. Personal interview with Eileen Scott, West Vancouver, March 1998.
5. Moogk, *Vancouver Defended*, pp. 61–63, 99 and 111–12.
6. Christopher Weicht, *Jericho Beach and the West Coast Flying Boat Stations*, pp. 39, 40, 44, 54, 186 and 190.
7. Barbara Winters, *HMCS Discovery*, c. 1996, chap. 2 and 4, pages unnumbered.
8. For this segment I have used information from George Edwards' book *Waterfront to Warfront*, and G.W. Taylor's *Shipyards of British Columbia*.
9. Chuck Davis, ed., *The Greater Vancouver Book*, Surrey: Linkman Press, 1997, p. 566.
10. Robert K. Burkinshaw, "False Creek," pp. 45–51.
11. Doreen Armitage, *Around the Sound*, Madeira Park: Harbour Publishing, 1997, pp. 208–9.
12. *Vancouver Harbour Aids*, accession 1988–89/205, vols. 1 and 2, box 4, NAC, Burnaby.
13. Personal interview with Aiden Butterfield, West Vancouver, March 2000.
14. *Vancouver Sun*, September 10, 1946.
15. "Fire Boat 'Orion' Placed in Commission," Vancouver: *Harbour and Shipping*, January 1932, p. 32, West Vancouver: Progress Publishing.
16. James Delgado, "History of Vancouver Fireboats—Part 2," *Harbour and Shipping*, January 1998, pp. 13–15.

17. "Finest Harbor Protector Here," *Province*, April 6, 1951.

18. Personal interview with Captain Cyril Andrews, West Vancouver, March 2000.

19. S.C. Heal, *The Maple Leaf Afloat*, pp. 129–30.

20. Gerald A. Rushton, *Whistle up the Inlet*, pp. 173–74.

21. James Delgado, *Creating the Vancouver Maritime Museum Forty Years Ago*, West Vancouver: Progress Publishing Co. Ltd., *Harbour and Shipping*, November 1999, pp. 20–22.

22. Personal interview with Harvey Burt, North Vancouver, March 15, 2000.

23. Tom Henry, *The Good Company*, Madeira Park: Harbour Publishing, 1994, pp. 115–19 and 132–36.

24. Rushton, *Whistle up the Inlet*, pp. 195–7.

25. Personal interview with Aiden Butterfield, West Vancouver, March 2000.

26. C. MacDonald et al., *Between Forest and Sea*, p. 64.

27. David Willock, "Store That Floats," Vancouver: *Weekend Magazine*, vol. 4 no. 42, 1954, pp. 25 and 26.

28. Debbie Smith, *Second Narrows Bridge Information Manual*, Burnaby: Regional Highways Engineer, c. 1979, pp. 30 and 35.

29. *Province*, October 15, 1947, p. 8.

30. Norman R. Hacking, *History of The Port of Vancouver*, c. 1976, pages unnumbered.

31. Extract from the "Annual Report of the National Harbours Board for 1958," CVA, Vancouver Harbour Commission, p. 92.

Chapter 7: Expansion, Reclamation and Protection: 1960–2000

1. Interview with John F. Wood, West Vancouver: West Vancouver Museum and Archives, Oral History Transcript, January 28, 1982, pp. 7 and 8.

2. Mike Steele, *Vancouver's Famous Stanley Park*, p. 21.

3. These images of the Burnaby squatters are taken from stories in *Pioneer Tales of Burnaby*, Michael Sone, ed.

4. Correspondence with Trudi Tuomi, April 2001.

5. Personal interview with Harvey Burt, North Vancouver, March 15, 2000.

6. Sheryl Salloum, *Malcolm Lowry: Vancouver Days*, Madeira Park: Harbour Publishing, 1987.

7. *Burrard Upgrade Project*, pamphlet, BC Hydro, Spring 1999.

8. *Versatile Pacific Shipyard Inc.*, Fonds 27, North Vancouver Museum and Archives, 1994.

9. Personal interview with Gary Penway, Planner, City of North Vancouver, February 2001.

10. Personal interview with Malcolm McLaren, North Vancouver, March 31, 2000.

11. Rosemary Eng, "Shipyard pioneer bids boats farewell," Vancouver: *Vancouver Sun*, January 11, 1988.

12. Personal interviews with Bob McKenzie and Margaret Jorgenson, May 2000.

13. Robert K. Burkinshaw, "False Creek," pp. 54–59.

14. Catherine Gourley, *Island in the Creek*, pp. 63, 66, 67 and 73.

15. Chuck Davis, ed., *The Greater Vancouver Book*, Surrey: Linkman Press, 1997, p. 568.

16. *Vancouver History*, vol. 18, 18:16–32 (August 1979).

17. Documentary Reprints, Kitsilano Indian Reserve, *Vancouver History*, vol. 18, pp. 16–32 (August 1979).

18. Deana Lancaster, "$92.5M payday for Squamish," North Vancouver: *North Shore News*, June 11, 2000, p. 1.

19. James Spears and Gary Hunter, "11 die in AirWest Coal Harbor Crash," Vancouver: *Province*, September 5, 1978, p. 1.

20. Al Arnason, "Texaco 'twixt Shot and Shell," Vancouver: *Province*, May 14, 1974, p. 1.

21. "Court Passes Sentence Tuesday in Wigwam Case," Vancouver: *Province*, October 27, 1962.

22. Personal interview with Rose Casano, North Vancouver, September 12, 2000.

23. "Legendary Wigwam Inn launches plush new era on Indian Arm," Vancouver: *Province*, September 12, 1980.

24. C. MacDonald et al, *Between Forest and Sea*, p. 120.

25. Personal interview with Zellah Leyland, North Vancouver, August 1998.

26. Personal interview with Harvey Burt, North Vancouver, March 15, 2000.

27. Foundation of Canada Engineering Corporation Ltd., "Preliminary

Study Indian Arm Causeway Vancouver Harbour British Columbia,"
July 15, 1967, pp. 3–5.

28. For this segment I have relied on a paper prepared by the Head of
the Inlet Park Development Committee, City of Port Moody, May
1986, and a personal interview in June 2000 with Ron Reichelt,
Acting Director of Leisure Services and Operations for the City of
Port Moody.

29. Patricia Mason, *The History of the Conservation Area at Maplewood
Flats*, West Vancouver: Minerva Publishing, 1995.

30. This environmental intervention information was taken from publications provided by the Burrard Inlet Environmental Action
Program, Burnaby.

31. Peter Hurme, ed., *Port of Vancouver International Handbook
1999–2000*, Seattle: Marine Digest, undated.

32. " 'Sceptre Fraser' Begins Vancouver Harbour Reclamation Project,"
West Vancouver: Progress Publishing Co. Ltd., *Harbour & Shipping*,
August 1966, p. 570.

Chapter 8: The Port of Vancouver

1. I derived a great deal of the port information from the *Port of
Vancouver International Handbook, 1999–2000*, Seattle: Marine
Digest.

2. James Delgado, *History of Vancouver Fireboats—Part 3*, *Harbour
and Shipping*, February 1998), pp. 15–17, West Vancouver: Progress
Publishing.

3. Telephone interview with Michael Cormier, Harbour Master's Office,
Port of Vancouver, June 6, 2000.

4. Personal interview with Ray Goode, president of BC Coast Pilots
Ltd., October 2, 2000; and information from the video *To Master's
Orders and Pilot's Advice*, BC Coast Pilots Ltd., 1996.

5. Personal interview with Ted Severud, Regional MCTS Program
Specialist, Marine Communications and Traffic Services, Fisheries
and Oceans Canada, Coast Guard, January 2001.

6. *Vancouver Sun*, November 6, 1971, p. 35.

7. *Marine Digest*, Seattle, April 9, 1988, p. 19.

8. David Leigh Stone, *Vancouver's Undersea Heritage*.

9. Personal interview with David Stone, Executive Director, Underwater
Archaeological Society, May 2000.

10. *Vancouver Sun*, January 5, 1974, p. 1.

11. Personal interview with Captain Howie Keast, May 11, 2001.

12. Fred Rogers, *More Shipwrecks of British Columbia*, p. 29.

13. Tony Eberts, "Grain inferno injures 16," *Province*, October 4, 1975, p. 5.

14. Eberts, "Grain inferno injures 16."

15. Dawn Hanna and Harold Munro, "Coast guard back in business after fire razes Kitsilano base," *Vancouver Sun*, July 8, 1991, p. A1.

16. Hanna and Munro, "Coast guard back in business after fire razes Kitsilano base."

17. "Knell for Beacon," *Province*, October 29, 1968, p. 34.

18. Doreen Armitage, *Around the Sound*, Madeira Park: Harbour Publishing, 1997, pp. 209–10.

SELECTED
BIBLIOGRAPHY

Abbreviations:
BCA-British Columbia Archives
CVA-City of Vancouver Archives
NAC-National Archives of Canada

Armitage, Doreen. *Around the Sound: A History of Howe Sound–Whistler*. Madeira Park: Harbour Publishing, 1997.

Armstrong, Dr. John E. *Vancouver Geology*. Vancouver: Geological Association of Canada, 1990.

Bartroli, Tomas. *Genesis of Vancouver City*. Vancouver: Published by the author, 1997.

Bell, John Warren. "BC Memories." Vancouver: unpublished manuscript, 1948. CVA.

Berton, Pierre. *The Last Spike*. Toronto: McClelland & Stewart, 1971.

Bradley, A.G. *Canada in the Twentieth Century*. London: Archibald Constable, 1905.

British Columbia Colonial Correspondence. BCA.

British Columbia Directory. Victoria: 1891–. CVA.

British Columbia Sessional Papers, 1874–5. BCA.

Burkinshaw, Robert K. "False Creek: History, Images, and Research Sources." Vancouver: Occasional Paper No. 2, 1984. CVA.

Cannings, Sydney, and Richard Cannings. *Geology of British Columbia, a Journey through Time*. Vancouver: Greystone Books, 1999.

Carlson, Roy L., ed. "Salvage '71." Burnaby: Simon Fraser University, 1972.

Carver, John Arthur. *The Vancouver Rowing Club*. Vancouver: Aubrey F. Roberts, 1980.

Cates, Charles Warren. "The Development of Tugs on the BC Coast." Vancouver: address to the Society of Naval Architects and Marine Engineers, BC Area, Pacific Northwest Section, 1958. CVA.

Chaldecott, F.M. *Jericho and Golf in the Early Days in Vancouver, 1892–1905*. Vancouver: pamphlet, personal publication, c. 1935. CVA.

Charlton, Arthur S. "The Belcarra Park Site." Burnaby: Simon Fraser University, 1980.

Chittenden, Newton H. *Travels in British Columbia, 1882*. Vancouver: Gordon Soules Book Publishers, 1984.

Conway, G.R.G. "Report on the Coquitlam-Buntzen Hydro-Electric Development, British Columbia." Ottawa: Dominion Water Power Branch, 1915.

D'Acres, Lilia, and Donald Luxton. *Lions Gate*. Burnaby: Talonbooks, 1999.

Dietz, George, and S.P. Moody. Correspondence to the Colonial Secretary, 1864. BCA.

Draycott, Walter M. *Recollections of a Pioneer's Early Days in Lynn Valley*. North Vancouver: *North Shore Times*, 1978.

Duncan, Nora M. "The Heroine of Moodyville: An epic of Burrard Inlet." Poem, 1936.

Edwards, George N. *Waterfront to Warfront*. Personal publication, 1995.

Fisher, Robin. *Vancouver's Voyage Charting the Northwest Coast 1791–1795*. Vancouver: Douglas & McIntyre, 1992.

Francis, Daniel, ed. *Encyclopedia of British Columbia*. Madeira Park: Harbour Publishing, 2000.

Graham, Donald. *Keepers of the Light*. Madeira Park: Harbour Publishing, 1985.

Grant, W. Colquhoun. "Description of Vancouver Island by its first Colonist." London: *The Journal of the Royal Geographical Society*, vol. 27, 1857.

Green, George. "Early Electric Light on This Coast." Victoria: Museum Notes, second series 1:8, March 1950.

Gourley, Catherine. *Island in the Creek*. Madeira Park: Harbour Publishing, 1988.

Hacking, Norman R. "British Columbia Steamboat Days, 1870–1883." Victoria: *The British Columbia Quarterly*, April 1947. BCA.

_____. *Annals of the Royal Vancouver Yacht Club*. Vancouver: Evergreen Press, 1965.

_____. *History of the Port of Vancouver*. c. 1976.

Hamilton, James H. *Western Shores*. Vancouver: Progress Publishing, 1932.

Heal, S.C. *The Maple Leaf Afloat*. Vancouver: Cordillera Publishing, 1992.

Howay, F.W. "Early Shipping in Burrard Inlet 1863–1870." Vancouver: *British Columbia Historical Quarterly*, vol. 1, no. 2 (April 1937).

Hull, Raymond, and Olga Ruskin. *Gastown's Gassy Jack: the life and times of John Deighton of England, California and Early British Columbia*. Vancouver: Gordon Soules *Economic Research, c. 1971*.

Hurme, Peter, ed. *Port of Vancouver International Handbook 1999–2000*. Seattle: Marine Digest, undated.

International Longshoremen's and Warehousemen's Union. *Man Along the Shore!*. Vancouver: Local 500 Pensioners, 1975.

Johnson, E. Pauline. *Legends of Vancouver*. Kingston: Quarry Press, 1991.

Lamb, W. Kaye. "Building Submarines for Russia in Burrard Inlet." Vancouver: University of British Columbia, *BC Studies*, no. 71 (Autumn 1986).

Lascelles, Thomas A., OMI. *Mission on the Inlet*. Vancouver: Order of the Oblates of Mary Immaculate, St. Paul's Province, 1984.

Launders, J.B. Correspondence to the colonial secretary, 1865. CVA.

Lugg, Shelley A. *Belcarra Regional Park: Archaeology, History Interpretation— A Resource Book*. Vancouver: GVRD Parks, 1985.

MacDonald, C.D., Drake, D., Doerksen, J., and Cotton M. *Between Forest and Sea, Memories of Belcarra*. Belcarra: The Belcarra Historical Group, 1998.

Matson, R.G., and Gary Coupland. *The Prehistory of the Northwest Coast*. San Diego: Academic Press, 1995.

Matthews, Major J.S. Add. MSS 54. CVA.

_____. *Conversations with Khahtsahlano*. Vancouver: 1955. CVA.

_____. *Early Vancouver*, vols. 1 to 5. Vancouver: CVA.

_____. *The Vancouver Historical Journal*, no. 4 (January 1961).

McDonald, Robert A.J. *Making Vancouver, 1863–1913*. Vancouver: UBC Press, 1996.

McGeachie, Pixie. *Burnaby, A Proud Century*. Vancouver: Opus Productions, 1991.

McLaren, Patrick. "Sediment Transport in Vancouver Harbour: Implications to the Fate of Contaminated Sediments and/or Dredged Material Disposal." Vancouver: Burrard Inlet Environmental Action Program, January 1994.

McMillan, Alan D. *Native Peoples and Cultures of Canada*. Vancouver: Douglas & McIntyre, 1988.

Meany, Edmond S. *Vancouver's Discovery of Puget Sound*. Portland: Binfords & Mort, 1957.

"Mechanic's Institute Minutes, Burrard Inlet, 1868–1864." North Vancouver: unpublished manuscript. Vancouver Archives, loc. 547-0-2 file 7.

Moberly, Walter. *The Rocks and Rivers of British Columbia*. London: Blacklock, 1885.

_____. Correspondence to Magistrate Spalding, 1859. BCA.

Moody, S.P. & Company. Correspondence to Governor Frederick Seymour, 1865. BCA.

Moogk, Peter N. *Vancouver Defended*. Surrey: Antonson Publishing, 1978.

Morley, Alan. *Vancouver, From Milltown to Metropolis*. Vancouver: Mitchell Press, 1961.

Morton, James. *The Enterprising Mr. Moody, the Bumptious Captain Stamp*. North Vancouver: J.J. Douglas, 1977.

_____. *Capilano, The Story of a River*. Toronto: McClelland & Stewart, 1970.

Musk, George. *Canadian Pacific*. London: David and Charles, 1981.

Nicol, Eric. *Vancouver*. Toronto: Doubleday Canada, 1970.

Norton, D.M. *Early History of Port Moody*. Surrey: Hancock House, 1987.

O'Keefe, Betty, and Ian Macdonald. *The Final Voyage of the Princess Sophia*. Surrey: Heritage House, 1998.

Oppenheimer, D., Mayor. *The Mineral Resources of British Columbia*. Vancouver: News-Advertiser Printers and Bookbinders, 1889.

Parkinson, R.H. *The Improvement of Vancouver Harbour*. Vancouver: *British Columbia Magazine*, vol. 8, no. 10 (October 1912).

Pethick, Derek. *SS Beaver: The Ship that saved the West*. Vancouver: Mitchell Press, 1970.

_____. *Men of British Columbia*. Saanichton: Hancock House, 1975.

_____. *Vancouver, the pioneer years, 1774–1886*. Langley: Sunfire Publications, 1984.

Puget, Peter. "A Log of the proceedings of *HMS Discovery*, January 1791 to January 14, 1793." London: Public Records Office.

Reid, Robie L. *The Inside Story of the Komagata Maru*. Vancouver: *British Columbia Historical Quarterly*, January 1941.

Richards, Captain George. Correspondence to Governor James Douglas, 1859. BCA.
_____. Correspondence to Rear Admiral Baynes, 1959. BCA.

Roberts, Gillian. *Burrard Inlet Pilotage*. Vancouver: *Vancouver History*, November 1979.

Robinson, Noel and the Old Man Himself. *Blazing the Trail Through the Rockies, The Story of Walter Moberly 1832–1915*. Vancouver: News-Advertiser Printers and Bookbinders, c. 1915.

Roddick, J.A., and L. Luternauer. "GSC Teacher's Field-Trip Guide to the Geology of the Vancouver Area," Vancouver: Geological Survey of Canada, 1994, Open File 3021.

Rogers, Fred. *More Shipwrecks of British Columbia*. Vancouver: Douglas & McIntyre, 1992.

Roper, Edward. *By Track and Trail, a Journey through Canada*. London: W.H. Allen, 1891.

Rushton, Gerald A. *Whistle up the Inlet, The Union Steamship Story*. Vancouver: Douglas & McIntyre, 1974.

Sone, Michael, ed. *Pioneer Tales of Burnaby*. Burnaby: Corporation of the District of Burnaby, 1987.

Steele, Mike. *Vancouver's Famous Stanley Park*. Surrey: Heritage House, 1993.

Stevens, L. "Rise of the Port of Vancouver, British Columbia." Worcester: Clark University, *Economic Geography*, vol. 12, no. 1 (January 1936).

Stewart, Hilary. *Stone, Bone, Antler & Shell*. Vancouver: Douglas & McIntyre, 1996.

Stone, David Leigh. *Vancouver's Undersea Heritage*. Vancouver: Underwater Archaeological Society of British Columbia, 1994.

Stott, Rev. William. *The Early Story of North Vancouver*. Victoria: Museum Notes, second series, 1:8 (March 1950).

Taylor, G.W. *Shipyards of British Columbia*. Victoria: Morriss Publishing, 1986.

Turner, Robert D. *The Pacific Princesses*. Victoria: Sono Nis Press, 1977.

Vancouver, George. *A Voyage of Discovery, 1791–1795*, vol. 3. London: Robinson and Edwards, 1798.

Wagner, Henry R. *Spanish Explorations in the Strait of Juan de Fuca*. California: Fine Arts Press, 1933.

Walkem, W. Wymond, MD. *Stories of Early British Columbia*. Vancouver: News-Advertiser Printers and Bookbinders, 1914.

Weicht, Christopher. *Jericho Beach and the West Coast Flying Boat Stations*. Chemainus: MCW Enterprises, 1997.

West Vancouver Historical Society. "John 'Navvy Jack' Thomas," unpublished manuscript. West Vancouver: 1995.

Woodward-Reynolds, Kathleen M. "A History of the City and District of North Vancouver." Vancouver: University of British Columbia, unpublished manuscript, 1943.

Wynne, Graeme, and Timothy Oke, eds. *Vancouver and Its Region*. Vancouver: UBC Press, 1992.

INDEX